# ADVANCES IN QUANTITATIVE ANALYSIS OF FINANCE AND ACCOUNTING

*Volume 2* • 1993 (Part B)

## Editorial Board

# ADVANCES IN QUANTITATIVE ANALYSIS OF FINANCE AND ACCOUNTING

*Editor:* CHENG F. LEE
*Department of Finance*
*Rutgers University—New Brunswick*

VOLUME 2 • 1993 (Part B)

JAI PRESS INC.

*Greenwich, Connecticut* *London, England*

*55 Old Post Road No. 2*
*Greenwich, Connecticut 06830*

*JAI PRESS LTD.*
*The Courtyard*
*28 High Street*
*Hampton Hill*
*Middlesex TW12 1PD*
*England*



*ISBN: 1-55938-565-0 (Part B)*
*ISBN: 1-55938-431-X (Set)*

*Manufactured in the United States of America*

# CONTENTS

## PART A

# PART B: LIST OF CONTRIBUTORS


| | |
|---|---|
| *Said Elfakhani* | University of Saskatchewan |
| *David P. Franz* | San Francisco State University |
| *Hung-Gay Fung* | University of Baltimore |
| *Dilip K. Ghosh* | Suffolk University |
| *Seong C. Gweon* | Merrill, Lynch. Pierce, Fenner & Smith, Inc. |
| *T. Harikumar* | University of Alaska Fairbanks |
| *Jiunn C. Huang* | San Francisco State University |
| *Hoje Jo* | Santa Clara University |
| *P. Kadapakkam* | University of Houston |
| *Philip Karpik* | University of Illinois at Chicago |
| *Cheng F. Lee* | Rutgers University—New Brunswick |
| *Wayne Y. Lee* | Kent State University |
| *Richard D. MacMinn* | University of Texas at Austin |
| *Dileep R. Mehta* | Georgia State University |
| *Gordian A. Ndubizu* | Drexel University |
| *Edgar Norton* | Fairleigh Dickinson University |
| *Hun Y. Park* | University of Illinois at Urbana–Champaign |
| *Bruce C. Payne* | University of Southwestern Louisiana |
| *Ahmed Riahi-Belkaoui* | University of Illinois at Chicago |
| *Tai S. Shin* | Virginia Commonwealth University |
| *K. C. John Wei* | Indiana University |
| *Dirk Zwemer* | Santa Clara University |

# OPTIMAL FINANCIAL LEVERAGE AND MANAGERIAL PRODUCTIVITY

Hung-Gay Fung and Dileep R. Mehta

## ABSTRACT

Modigliani and Miller demonstrate that under frictionless financial markets the market value of the firm is irrelevant to its capital structure; hence, the investment and financing decisions remain separable. Given the asymmetric payoffs and conflicts of interest between lenders and the firm (stockholders and managers), lenders want to take actions to *prevent* default and bankruptcy of the firm. The resultant costs of debt are linked to loss of managerial productivity. These costs when incorporated in a value-maximizing model along with the tax incidence lead to the optimal capital structure. The ensuing interaction between investment and financing decisions is then analyzed in order to arrive at the simultaneous optimality of both investment and financing decisions. Because the solution procedure is iterative, an example is provided to illustrate this procedure. Within the value-maximizing framework of the model, stockholders are shown to determine the optimal capital structure. However, when an incentive package for managerial compensation is tied to management productivity, leverage will he determined by the managers. Because the corresponding optimal leverage will be smaller than in the former case, the value of the firm may be lower in this case due to a lower tax shield on interest charges. On

**Advances in Quantitative Analysis of Finance and Accounting,**
**Volume 2, Part B, pages 1–18.**

**ISBN: 1-55938-565-0**

the other hand, in the absence of such a tax shield advantage, stockholders and managers will have the same preference for the level of debt policy irrespective of whether an incentive package is related to the value of the firm or tied to the productivity of the manager.

## I. INTRODUCTION

Optimality of capital structure has been obtained in the finance literature by invoking the assumption of heterogeneous expectations (Stiglitz, 1972), bankruptcy costs in conjunction with corporate taxes (Kim, 1978; Scott, 1976), and agency costs (Jensen and Meckling, 1976). These efforts have not remained unassailed. Heterogeneous expectations requiring pessimistic views of landers on the firm violate the spirit of the perfect market notion.[1] Similarly, losses in the bankruptcy phenomenon due to fractional value realized upon liquidation of physical assets are linked with capital budgeting decisions and not capital structure decisions (Haugan and Senbet, 1978, 1988). Even when bankruptcy costs are relevant, their potential impact is akin to "the tail wagging the dog" (Miller, 1977). Further, casual observations suggest that this line of reasoning is suspect since firms utilize much less debt in their capital structure than that implied by bankruptcy cost. Finally, the agency theory rests on the premise of conflicting interests of owners and managers; however, when their interests are identical, the interior optimal capital structure solution will not be obtained (Fama, 1980).

Given the limited liability of the stockholder and the existence of liquidation costs, lenders are likely to suffer losses in the case of bankruptcy. Hence, even without invoking heterogeneity of expectations, lenders would seek "me-first-rule" protection for their interest through efforts to *prevent* bankruptcy.[2] Such efforts entail agency costs of debts, namely, productivity loss in the firm. This perspective is explored in this study to shed light on the optimal capital structure issue.

Many studies have tried to establish causal links between bankruptcy and optimal capital structure. Titman (1984) provides a possible theoretical link between liquidation and financial structure, thereby linking the substantial costs of potential sale loss associated with liquidation. Altman (1984) attempted to measure the indirect costs of bankruptcy, which include loss of managerial energies. He finds that these costs are significant. We argue here that these bankruptcy-related costs are important for optimal capital structure decisions and can be summarized as managerial productivity loss.

Interaction of investment and financing decisions can lead to an optimal capital structure (for a review, see Ravid, 1988). The objectives of this paper are to (1) investigate *whether* there is an alternative explanation for capital structure optimality by integrating the impact of agency cost of debt and corporate taxes in the same light as Altman (1984), and (2) determine the optimal capital structure by linking simultaneously the interactions among investment and financing decisions and establishing criticalness of the viewpoint of the relevant party—lenders, stockholders or management.

This paper is organized as follows. In Section I, arguments are developed to suggest that an increase in financial leverage can be of special concern to lenders who, in turn, would impose costs on the organization even *prior* to default and bankruptcy. These costs are transformed into output reduction or efficiency loss for the firm. In Section III, a theoretical model of the firm incorporating the cost of leverage is developed for optimal debt level determination, and interaction between investment and financing decisions is then studied. Initially managers' interests are assumed to coincide exactly with those of the stockholders. Later, stockholders are assumed to provide incentive packages to managers to ensure actions in their (the stockholders') interest. In the final sections, the issue of which party (stockholders or managers) determines the capital structure is discussed and the summary of results is provided.

## II. LEVERAGE AND MANAGERIAL PRODUCTIVITY

Although Modigliani and Miller (MM) show that there is no optimal capital structure, they admit that the capital structure optimality may exist because "there are limitations imposed by lenders, as well as many other dimensions (and kinds of costs) in real-world problems of financial strategy which are not fully comprehended within the framework of static equilibrium models" (1963, p. 422). MM also stated that "in many forms of borrowing agreements, creditors are able to stipulate terms which the current management may regard as infringing on its prerogatives or restricting its freedom to maneuver" (1958, pp. 292–293). This section explores implications of some restrictions imposed by lenders on the firm's productivity.

Let the production function of the firm be $f(K,M)$, where $K$ denotes physical capital (machinery and other tangible assets) and $M$ managerial input (various levels of human resources ranging from manual labor to top management skills). It is argued here that the managerial input $M$ is not optimally utilized for productive activities when leverage is utilized, that is, $M_L$, the derivative of $M$ with respect to leverage $L$, is negative. The threat of default and bankruptcy increases due to unavoidable business risk for the firm as financial leverage increases. Miller (1977, p. 263) argued that the cost of bankruptcy includes the diversion or loss of the time and energies of management from tasks of greater productivity or the reluctance of customers and suppliers to enter into long-term commitments. We argue here that these bankruptcy-related costs loom important to the firm's lenders far before the event of bankruptcy occurs.

In the frameworks of Scott and Kim, lenders play a passive role in the bankruptcy risk because they are always properly compensated through higher (risky) interest rates, and any loss in the value of the firm due to bankruptcy is borne by stockholders. In reality, lenders do not take a passive role because higher interest rates may induce the firm to choose riskier or inferior projects and as a result they may not obtain adequate compensation (Stiglitz and Weiss, 1981). In absence of bankruptcy cost, when default occurs, it creates inconvenience for the lenders, who then may not feel adequately compensated by higher interest charges. In any case, lenders are prone to take monitoring actions because "management, acting in the stockholders' interest, has incentives to design the firm's operating characteristics and financial structure in ways which benefit stockholders to the detriment of bondholders" (Smith and Warner, 1979, p. 118). Indeed, the agency principle put forward by Jensen and Mackling (1976) usually utilizes measures other than the interest rate increases as the control device. These measures include, for instance, stringent loan covenants calling for restrictions on operating policies as well as more detailed reports with greater frequency. Similarly, lenders may exercise their right to inspect any or all of the records and property to verify the authenticity of the furnished statements and actual physical condition of assets.[3] Both sets of measures are likely to require management time, interfere with management activities, or both.

Finally, lenders may demand active participation in the managerial decision making, often via representation on the board through "co-optation," as Pfeffer (1972) suggests. Because they want to protect their interest in the loan, they are unlikely to be rubber stamps in the board's decision process. If a greater debt financing in the firm is to induce a greater "participation" from a larger number of financial institutions on the board, managers will have to spend more time with them (Dooley, 1969; Pfeffer, 1972b).[4] The resultant friction or interference created by the outside directors is underscored in a study of 103 large manufacturing corporations by Vance (1964), who contends that, on average, inside boards of directors have performance superior to that of outside boards. Further, Vance shows that outside directors can adversely effect the productivity of the firm.[5]

These control measures reducing the productivity of the firm need not be instigated solely by lenders who are financial institutions. As the leverage increases, managers also face working capital constraint from the trade creditors. Several ways are used by trade creditors to safeguard their interest. First, they simply stop supplying goods for fear of bad debts; managers have to spend time either to convince them, or find new sources of supplies. Second, they may supply to the firm on a consignment basis, which may result in smaller than the usual profit margins. Finally, trade creditors may require filing of the Uniform Commercial Code (UCC) forms, and at the extreme may demand delivery only upon receipt of satisfactory security or cash before shipment. In brief, lenders' actions stemming from fear of default (or on the heel of defaults) are likely to reduce the productivity of the firm.

It is plausible that efficiency may increase when "excessive" leverage leads managers and other employees of the firm to experience a "crisis" perception. The validity of the above assertion rests on several premises which merit further scrutiny. *First*, the above contention requires existence of substantial "slack" or inefficiency in the firm before the crisis occurs. The magnitude of the slack is unlikely to be substantial because of the mutual monitoring within the firm and competition among firms (Alchian and Demsetz, 1972; Fama and Jensen, 1983; Marris, 1964). Further, in an efficient financial market, the takeover possibility also plays an important role in eliminating any inept or cautious management allowing substantial slack. As Williamson (1975) suggests, the development of conglomerate structure also acts as a capital-market restraint on the managerial slack and favors the least cost behavior as opposed to excessive discretionary behavior.[6]

*Second*, it may be argued that the creditors would assume control of the firm and thus increase managerial input to the firm. However, lenders face substantial risk in controlling the firm's affairs not only because of legal or regulatory ramifications (e.g., securities laws violation) but also due to lenders' lack of familiarity with the business (*American Banker*, 1984; Douglas-Hamilton, 1975). Even when creditors are not hampered by regulations or lack of specifically requisite ability, they may heed the warning that "whenever a creditor contemplates taking a hand in the management of a financially troubled debtor, it should think of its deeper pockets and keep its hands there" (Douglas-Hamilton, 1975, p. 364).

*Finally*, it may be argued that when faced with the crisis, managers will work harder to have the firm. However, the increase in efficiency can be only a transient phenomenon. The restriction imposed by lenders may steer the managers to focus on the short-term activities of the firm, and the loss in productivity or efficiency in the long run may offset the additional effort of the managers. Further, additional efforts on the part of the managers cannot be physiologically sustained over a long period of time. When the crisis approaches, the manager may work harder because of the overall rise of adrenalin above the baseline levels. However, excessive secretion of the adrenalin to encounter stress will lead to precursors of disease or diseases themselves, as diagnosed in the "stress syndrome."[7] When the organization gets conditioned to the crisis, it generally lapses into the previous pattern, thus reversing the short-term gains. In addition, as leverage increases, the managers are likely to get demoralized due to the frustration at the "wasted" efforts in the wake of the crisis. The consequent departure of capable employees who do not want to be associated with the imminent "failure" of the firm is also not unlikely. Clearly, the overall efficiency of the firm will be adversely affected under such conditions.

In light of the above discussion, it seems reasonable to assume that managerial input in the production function decreases with leverage level.

## III. THEORETICAL MODEL OF THE FIRM

### A. Identity of Stockholder–Manager Interests

The purpose of this section is to provide a theoretical analysis of productivity loss on the capital structure of the firm. In this model, managerial markets are assumed competitive. This assumption allows us to avoid the stockholder–manager conflict raised in the agency theory[8] and retain consistency with the inference that the manager acts in the best interests of the stockholders.

Let the value of the firm net of initial investment be maximized subject to the production constraint $f(k, M)$. The firm recruits $M^o$ number of management units from the competitive managerial market. If there is no financial leverage in the firm, the managerial efforts $M$ being actually utilized or employed should be equal to $M^o$. However, as the financial leverage increases, some of the managerial input will be diverted away from the productive activities, as argued in the preceding section. Thus, this leakage will lead to a negative relationship between managerial input $M$ and financial leverage as described in the previous section.

The model uses the framework of the capital asset pricing model (CAPM). The physical capital of the firm, $K$, is being depreciated at the rate $\tilde{d}$ (with stochastic value signified by ~). A part of the capital is financed via debt (with interest rate $\tilde{r}$) and it is equal to $LK$, where $L$ is the debt ratio. The managerial compensation rate $m$ on $M^o$ managerial input is determined exogenously in the managerial market; it is assumed deterministic for expository conveniences. The total revenue $\widetilde{TR}$ is defined as the product of the price and the output. The production function $f(K, M)$ is assumed to be smooth and second order differentiable.

The residual flows for the firm, $\tilde{Y}$, at the end of the period will be

$$\tilde{Y} = (1 - \tau)(\widetilde{TR} - mM^o) + K - (1 - \tau)\tilde{d}K + \tau\tilde{r}D,$$

where $\tau$ is the appropriate tax rate for the firm. The cash flow $Y$ is the aftertax value of the net output (net of management compensation as well as the loss in the value of depreciable assets and including the tax shield on interest charges).

The return relative for the firm can be obtained by dividing the aftertax cash flows $\tilde{Y}$ by the levered, certainty-equivalent value $V_1$. The CAPM suggests the following form:

$$E(\tilde{R}_i) = (1 + r_f) + \lambda \operatorname{cov}(\tilde{R}_i, \tilde{R}_m)$$

where $\tilde{R}_i$ is the return relative for the $i$th firm, $r_f$ the risk-free lending or borrowing rate, and $\tilde{R}_m$ the market return relative. $E$ denotes the expectation operator, cov(. , .) the covariance, and $\lambda$ the market price of risk.

After substituting $Y/V_1$ for $R_i$ in the CAPM form and simplifying, the value of the levered firm obtained is[9]

$$V_1 = \frac{(1-\tau)T(Q) - (1-\tau)mM^o - (1-\tau)d^*K + K + \tau r_f D}{1 + r_f},$$

where

$$T(Q) = E(\widetilde{TR}) - \lambda \text{cov}(\widetilde{TR}, \widetilde{R}_m);\ r_f = E(\widetilde{r}) - \lambda \text{cov}(\widetilde{r}, \widetilde{R}_m);$$

$$d^* = E(\widetilde{d}) - \lambda \text{cov}(\widetilde{d}, \widetilde{R}_m).$$

$T(Q)$ may be interpreted as the certainty-equivalent revenue with the output $Q$; $r_f$ and $d^*$ as the certainty-equivalent borrowing and depreciation rates, respectively.

The goal of the firm is assumed to maximize its value *net of initial investment* $K$, that is, $V_1$, or maximize

$$NVP = [(1-\tau)T(Q) - (1-\tau)mM^o - cK + \tau r_f LK]/(1 + r_f).$$

The value of $c$ is the rental cost $(d^* + r_f - \tau d^*)$ on the depreciable asset.

The optimization problem (maximization of $NPV$ [net present value]) in the Lagrangian format is

$$\underset{K, M^o, L, Q}{L^P} = \frac{(1-\tau)T(Q) - (1-\tau)mM^o - cK + \tau r_f LK}{(1 + r_f)} + u[f(K, M) - Q],$$

where $u$ is the shadow price. The first-order conditions are

$$\partial L^P/\partial u = f(K, M) - Q \qquad = 0 \qquad (1)$$

$$\partial L^P/\partial K = [-C + \tau L r_f]/r' + u f_K \qquad = 0 \qquad (2)$$

$$\partial L^P/\partial M^o = -(1-\tau)m/r' + u f_M M_o \qquad = 0 \qquad (3)$$

$$\partial L^P/\partial L = \tau K r_f/r' + u f_M M_L \qquad = 0 \qquad (4)$$

$$\partial L^P/\partial Q = (1-\tau)T_Q/r' - u \qquad = 0, \qquad (5)$$

where $r' = 1 + r_f$. In the above analysis, $T_Q$ is the marginal certainty-equivalent revenue and $M = M(M^o, L)$. $\partial M/\partial M^o = M_o$ is defined above.

To ensure that there is a maximum, the function $L^P$ is assumed to satisfy the second-order sufficient condition.[10] In theory, all decision variables $(K, M^o, L, Q)$ can be solved in terms of other exogenous variables via the implicit function theorem. The solution procedure yields the following propositions.

*Proposition 1:* Given the optimal $K^*$ and $M^{o*}$, an increase in leverage will lead to a decrease in the managerial productivity.

Productivity $p$ is defined here as the output per unit of factor input employed; thus the notion of average product is being utilized. Differentiating the average product of the managers, $p^M$, with respect to $L$, yields

$$\partial p^M/\partial L = \partial(Q/M^{o*})/\partial L$$

$$= (\partial Q/\partial L)/M^{o*}$$

$$= f_M M_L/M_{o*} < 0. \tag{6}$$

Inequality (6) occurs because $M^{o*}$ is positive by definition and $uf_M M_L$ is negative from Eq. (4), where $u$ is positive from Eq. (5). This declining managerial productivity with leverage results from the agency cost of debt discussed in the previous section. This result is consistent with the argument put forth in other studies that there is a loss of managerial energy due to leverage (Altman, 1984; Miller, 1977; among others).

*Proposition 2:* In equilibrium, the optimal debt level is reached when the interest tax shield is equal to the product of the after-tax revenue, elasticity of revenue with respect to output and elasticity of productivity with respect to leverage.

The above proposition can be proved by multiplying Eq. (4) by $L$ and combining Eqs. (5) and (6). Given that managerial productivity $p^M$ is defined by the ratio ($Q/M$), we have

$$\tau D r_f = (1 - \tau)T(Q) \cdot e_{T(Q)} \cdot e_{PL},$$

where

$$e_{T(Q)} = \frac{\partial T(Q)}{\partial Q} \cdot \frac{Q}{T(Q)}, \quad e_{PL} = \frac{-\partial P^M}{\partial L} \cdot L/p^M.$$

The above proposition shows that an optimal debt level is endogenously determined with production. Thus, financing and investment decisions cannot be made independent of each other.

*Proposition 3:* An increase in the management sensitivity to financial leverage leads to a decrease in the optimal leverage.

Let $M_L$ be expressed as $-bG(L, M^o)$, where $G$ is an increasing function of leverage and $b$ the leverage-sensitivity parameter for management. Differentiating the first-order conditions totally with respect to $b$ yields

$$H^P \left[ \frac{du}{db} \; \frac{dk}{db} \; \frac{dM^o}{db} \; \frac{dL}{db} \; \frac{dQ}{db} \right]' = [\mathrm{O} \;\; \mathrm{O} \;\; \mathrm{O} \;\; uf_M G \;\; \mathrm{O}]'.$$

By making use of the Cramer rule, we have

$$\frac{dL}{db} = uf_M\, G(L)\, |H^P_{44}| / |\, H^P < 0,$$ [11]

The above proposition implies that the more (less) sensitive the managerial input to the leverage, the lower (higher) the level of financial leverage.

Interactions between output and financing decisions are examined in the following dual optimization problem. The present value of cost is defined as

$$C/r' = [(1-\tau)mM^{o} + cK - \tau LKr_f]/r'. \tag{7}$$

Since the optimal level of output, $Q^*$, is of special interest, the dual is formulated in terms of $Q^*$. The appropriate Lagrangian for the constrained cost minimization problem is

$$\underset{\{K,\, M^{o},\, L\}}{L^D} = \{[(1-\tau)mM^{o} + cK - \tau LKr_f]/r' + v[Q^* - f(k, M)]\},$$

where $v$ is the shadow price of the dual problem. The appropriate first-order conditions are

$$\partial L^D/\partial v = Q^* - f(K, M) \qquad = 0 \tag{8}$$

$$\partial L^D/\partial K = [C - \tau Lr_f]/r' + vf_K \qquad = 0 \tag{9}$$

$$\partial L^D/\partial M^{o} = (1-\tau)m/r' - vf_M M_o \qquad = 0 \tag{10}$$

$$\partial L^D/\partial L = -\tau Kr_f/r' - vf_M M_L \qquad = 0 \tag{11}$$

The second-order sufficiency condition for $L^D$ to have a minimum is that all principal minors starting with 3×3 of matrix $H^D$ should be negative (see Appendix A).

*Proposition 4:* In a world of uncertainty and risk-averse investors, the optimality condition for production in the firm states that risk-adjusted aftertax marginal revenue equals the risk-adjusted aftertax marginal cost.

To prove the above proposition, it is necessary to find the present value of marginal cost. Differentiating Eq. (7) with respect to $Q^*$ yields

$$\frac{1}{r'}\frac{dC}{dQ^*} = \frac{(1-r)m}{r'}\frac{dM^{o}}{dQ^*} + \frac{(C-\tau Lr_f)}{r'}\frac{dK}{dQ^*} - \frac{\tau Kr_f}{r'}. \tag{12}$$

Evaluation of the derivatives on the right-hand side of Eq. (12) requires total differentiation of the first-order conditions (8)–(11) with respect to $Q^*$:

$$H^D\left[\frac{dv}{dQ^*}\ \ \frac{dK}{dQ^*}\ \ \frac{dM^{o}}{dQ^*}\ \ \frac{dL}{dQ^*}\right]' = [-1\ \ 0\ \ 0\ \ 0]'.$$

Combining the first-order conditions (9)–(11) and substituting the appropriate derivatives of Eq. (13) into (12), we get, upon simplification, $[dc/dQ^*]/r' = v$. A comparison of Eq. (3) with (10) shows that the shadow price $v$ (the present value of the marginal cost) is equal to $u$, which is also the present value of the aftertax marginal revenue from Eq. (5). Hence, the proposition is obtained.

*Proposition 5:* In equilibrium, when the managerial input function is $M = M^o - g(L)$, where $g(L)$ is an increasing function of $L$, the optimal financial leverage is an increasing function of output.

When an additive relationship between $M^o$ and $L$, that is, $M = M^o - g(L)$, exists, it allows us to simplify Eq. (13) and obtain

$$\frac{dL}{dQ^*} = \frac{\tau r_f v(f_K f_{MM} - f_{KM} f_M)}{|H^D|} > 0.$$

The denominator on the right side of the above equation is negative by the sufficient condition. Further, the usual assumption of diminishing returns of the production function leads to $f_{MM} < 0$ and the other quantities in the numerator are positive (the usual cross-marginal product is positive, i.e., $f_{KM} > 0$); hence, the numerator is negative. As a result, $dL/dQ^*$ is positive, or the optimal financial leverage is an increasing function of output.

The above result is similar to Hite's results (1977). Note, however, that had there been a *multiplicative* relationship between $M^o$ and $L$, we would have been unable to obtain the simplification of Eq. (13) and thus unable to show that the numerator will be negative or $dL/dQ^*$ positive. The additive relationship between $M^o$ and L (where $M$ is a negative function of $L$) implies that for a given level of financial leverage, an additional unit of managerial input will be *entirely* devoted to the production process. Under the multiplicative relationship, because such an additional unit of managerial input may not be so devoted, the relationship between financial leverage and output remains indeterminate. In brief, under the present scenario it is possible to derive the Hite result of positive relationship between output and leverage only under the specific assumption of additive relationship between $M$ and $L$.

If the firm size can be used as a proxy for the output, we should observe that larger firms have higher leverage, given the validity of proposition 5 or Hite's result. Casual observation does not confirm the above relationship. Thus, the relationship between $M^o$ and $L$ is likely to be multiplicative in the present analytical framework.

The above analysis suggests that reduction of managerial productivity due to leverage (proposition 1) leads to interactions among investment and financing decisions, and capital structure optimality results (proposition 2). The optimal level of leverage is dependent on the managerial sensitivity to financial leverage (proposition 3) and is an increasing function of the firm's output decision, especially when there is an additive relationship between managerial and financial leverage (proposition 5). The conventional marginal (cost and revenue) analysis is shown to be valid even if there are interactions between investment and financing decisions (proposition 4). Finally, the analysis so far assumes that the lenders feel adequately protected by control measures imposed on the firm and, hence, do not see any need for an absolute limit on leverage. In this case, stockholder–manager identity of interests suggests that their (rather than the lenders') attitude will prevail in determining the leverage.

## B. Incentive Package for Managers

In the following analysis, the notion of managerial incentive package $i$ is introduced in the model to motivate the managers to work harder. This is a natural extension because productivity of the managers plays an important role in determining the optimal leverage (proposition 2). Further, such a package may be offered by stockholders to ensure that their interests are protected; that is, they incur a form of agency cost. In the remainder of this section, a direct effect of the incentive package on the managerial input is assumed to be positive but with decreasing effectiveness, that is $M_i > 0$ and $M_{ii} < 0$ (the usual diminishing return assumption).

In essence, the firm is paying the price of the incentive package to the managers to increase their productivity, which in turn increases the value of the firm. The cost of the incentive package is $I(i)$, where $I_i > 0$ and $I_{ii} > 0$ (the usual increasing cost assumption). Following the same procedure as above and substituting the cash flows adjusted for the incentive package into the CAPM framework, we can obtain the value of firm, $V_i$. In order to derive the optimal conditions for production and financing decisions, the Lagrangian problem is formulated to maximize $NPV$ as

$$\underset{\{K,\, M^{o},\, L,\, i,\, Q\}}{LL^{P}} = [(1-\tau)T(Q) - (1-\tau)mM - cK + \tau LKr_f - I(i)]/r' + u[f(K, M) - Q]. \tag{14}$$

The first-order conditions can be easily derived from Eq. (14) by partially differenting it with respect to $K$, $M^{o}$, $L$, $i$, and $Q$. To ensure $LL^{P}$ to have a maximum, the sufficient condition of the existence of the bordered Hessian matrix $BH^{P}$ is also assumed.

*Proposition 6:* The more effective the compensation package in motivating the manager to work harder, the greater should be its utilization.

Without loss of generality, $M_i = ah(M^{o}, L, i)$ is assumed, where $a$ denotes the effectiveness of compensation on the management input and $h$ is positive.

Totally differentiating the first-order conditions of Eq. (14) yields

$$BH^{P}\begin{bmatrix} \dfrac{du}{da} & \dfrac{dk}{da} & \dfrac{dM^{o}}{da} & \dfrac{dL}{da} & \dfrac{di}{da} & \dfrac{dQ}{da} \end{bmatrix}' = [0 \;\; 0 \;\; 0 \;\; 0 \;\; -uf_{M}h \;\; 0]'. \tag{15}$$

From Eq. (15), via the Cramer rule, we get

$$\frac{di}{da} = -uf_{M}h \,|BH^{P}_{55}| / |BH^{P}| > 0.$$

Because of the sufficient condition, $|BH^P| < 0$; $|BH^P_{55}| > 0$ since it is co-factor of the fifth row and fifth column of $BH^P$; by definition, $u > 0$; and $f_M > 0$. Hence, the proposition is obtained.

*Proposition 7:* Changes in the slope of the management-incentive package response function does not affect the optimal leverage value, if the managerial input function is $M = M^o - g(L) + g(i)$ where $g(.)$ is an increasing function of (.).

In the presence of the above specification for $M$ and from Eq. (15), $dL/da$ can be easily shown to be zero.[12] This proposition implies that an optimal structure can be determined *independently* of the incentive package if the leverage and incentive package have an additively separable effect on the managerial input. Otherwise, an optimal debt level should be a function of the incentive plan.

To investigate the output and financing decisions, the dual optimization problem is formulated as

$$LL^D = \{[(1-\tau)mM^o + cK - \tau Dr_f + I(i)]/r' + u[Q^* - f(K, M)]\} \tag{16}$$

The first-order conditions can then be easily obtained from Eq. (16). The second-order condition for the bordered Hessian matrix $BH^D$ obtained from (16) is assumed to hold.

Proposition 8: In the incentive package model, leverage is an increasing function of output when the managerial input function is as specified in proposition 7, that is, $M = M^o - g(L) + g(i)$.

Totally differentiating the first-order conditions of Eq. (16) yields

$$BH^D \left[ \frac{dv}{dQ^*} \;\; \frac{dk}{dQ^*} \;\; \frac{dM^o}{dQ^*} \;\; \frac{dL}{dQ^*} \;\; \frac{di}{dQ^*} \right]' = [-1 \;\; 0 \;\; 0 \;\; 0 \;\; 0]'. \tag{17}$$

From Eq. (17), simplification gives

$$\frac{dL}{dQ^*} = \frac{\tau r_f}{r'} \cdot \frac{[v^2(f_{KM}f_M - f_k f_{MM} f_M)M_{ii} + v(f_K f_{MM} - f_{MK} f_M)I_{ii/r'}]}{|BH^D|}.$$

Given $M_{ii} < 0$ and $I_{ii} > 0$; thus $dL/dQ^* > 0$, which proves the above proposition.

This proposition suggests that when an incentive package is provided to management, an additive effect of the incentive is needed to show the increasing function property of leverage with output. Hence, Hite's result referred to earlier represents only a special case.

From the above analysis, we find that investment and financing decisions are not separable. This situation is due to the productivity loss, which gives rise to an optimal capital structure (proposition 2). In addition, this capital structure optimality depends on the incentive package, unless the effects of the incentive package and leverage are additive on the managerial input (proposition 7). The incentive package model also implies that the optimal leverage may not necessarily be an increasing function of the output, as suggested by Hite (1977), but will depend on the responsiveness of managers to the financial leverage (proposition 5) and the incentive package (proposition 8).

## IV. ILLUSTRATION

Given the complexity of Eqs. (1)–(5), it is difficult to solve them analytically. To obtain insights into the nature of the interdependency of investment and financing decisions, a numerical example is provided. The Cobb–Douglas production function with homogeneity of degree one was used: $Q = AK^{\alpha}M^{\beta}$. Two types of managerial input functions were used: (1) a multiplicative model $M = M^{o}(1 - e_1L^{e})$; and (2) an additive model $M = M^{o} - b(L)L^2$, where $b(L) = b_0 + b_1L$. The certainty-equivalent revenue function $T(Q)$ is assumed to be $a_1Q^2 - a_2Q^2$. For expository purposes, the value of the incentive package is assumed zero.[13]

The optimal values of capital and managerial input were derived for arbitrarily assigned initial values of $Q$ and $L$. After obtaining the marginal product of $K$ and $M$ from the production function, we computed the value of the firm $V_1$, $NPV$, and the cost of capital, $k$ (the ratio of the expected cash flows to $V_1$, minus one). Then, the above procedure was repeated to obtain the following results.

The relationship between $NPV$ and leverage is shown in Figure 1. A family of concave output curves shows the optimum optimorum of $NPV$ at about 1255.152, with the optimal leverage level at 0.275 for the additive model, and 1255.504 and 0.2456, respectively, for the multiplicative model. As the firm expands output, the discount rate $k$ increases for a given level of leverage. This result can be easily explained. Expansion of output implies that the operating cash flows become riskier; hence, the discount rate increases. However, an increase in output beyond the optimal level can reduce the net present value of the firm, as shown by the downward shift of the output curve at the 36.9 level for the additive model. In addition, it should be noted that the result shown in Figure 1 is consistent with proposition 5 (that the optimal leverage is an increasing function of output) only for the additive model. If the model is multiplicative, the leverage–output relationship is *not* an increasing function. Furthermore, it should be clear that the minimization of the discount rate does not necessarily lead to the maximization of the firm's value. Given the output decision, the financial policy can reduce the discount rate because of the interest tax shield effect, thus accepting the project which might be initially rejected at a lower level of leverage.

## IV. CONCLUDING REMARKS

Although we do not invoke bankruptcy cost in our analysis, tentative comparison is possible between the present model and those of Scott and Kim. Since the purpose of the control measures by lenders is to *prevent* default and a fortiori

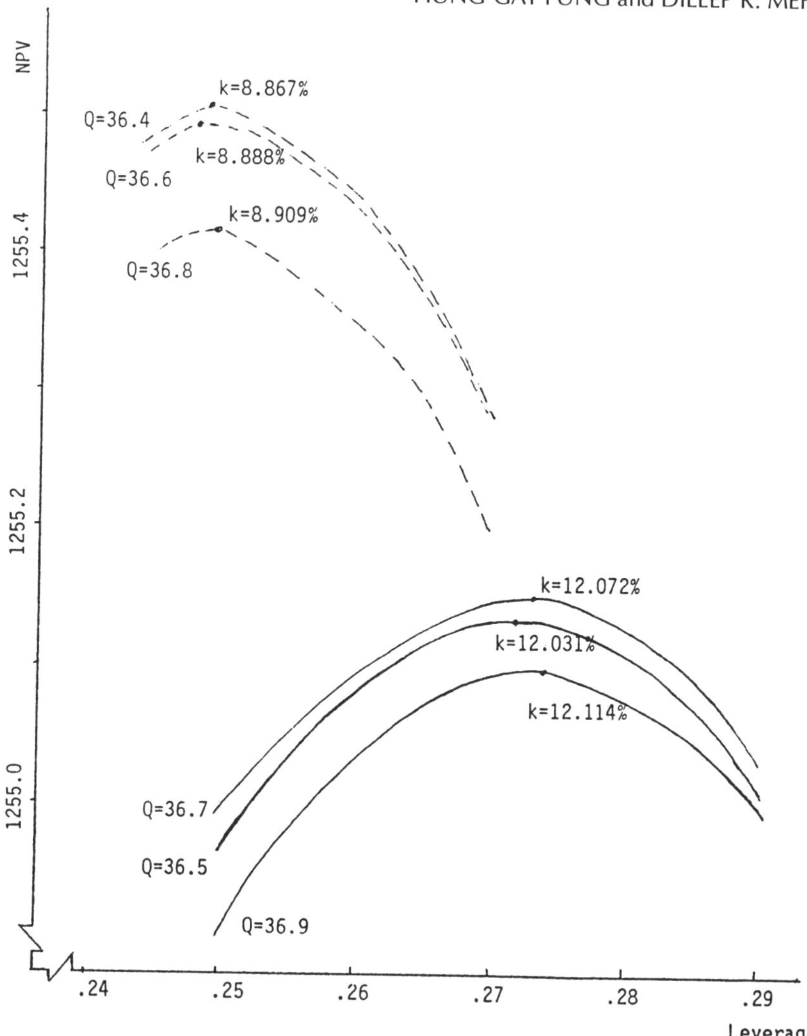


*Figure 1.* Relationship of Net Present Value (*NPV*) and Leverage with Different Levels of Output (*Q*) and the Corresponding Optimal Discount rate (*k*) for a multiplicative management leverage model (broken line) and an additive management-leverage model (solid line)

bankruptcy, the optimal level derived here should be lower than in the framework of Scott and Kim. However, the optimal $V_1$ obtained here is not unambiguously lower (or higher, for that matter) than that in their frameworks: if, among other things, the control measures do reduce the probability of bankruptcy, $V_1$ derived here may be higher than that for Scott and Kim, especially when the productivity loss is less than bankruptcy cost.

At the optimal leverage $L^*$ in our model, the productivity of the manager is still declining (proposition 1). Differentiating Eq. (6) yields $P^M{}_{LL} = [f_{mm}M^2{}_L + f_M M_{LL}]/M^{o*} < 0$. Hence, productivity of the manager is a concave function of leverage. At the optimal leverage, the productivity of the manager is lower than any leverage level smaller than $L^*$. If the stockholders try to tie the incentive structure of the firm to the *productivity* of the manager, managers will get higher compensation when the leverage is suboptimal. Hence, the capital structure level desired by the manager differs from the one when compensation is tied to the *value* of the firm. Indeed, the productivity-based incentive package will induce the classical "agency" syndromes of stockholder–manager conflict of interest when, ceteris paribus, the manager interest will prevail in determining leverage. On the other hand, in the case of a value-based incentive package, the role played by managers will be in interests consistent with those of the stockholders. Thus, an incentive package should be related to the value of the firm instead of following the conventional wisdom of linking the incentive package to the productivity of the managers.

Miller (1977) argues that an optimal capital structure does not exist at the firm level because the personal tax on the debt can exactly offset the interest tax shield in the corporation. If there is no interest tax shield advantage, the value of the firm will be independent of the financial leverage. However, when our model is cost in Miller's (or the original MM) framework, the output of the firm will start decreasing because the managerial time is lost as the firm utilizes leverage and the value of the firm decreases. If the stockholders want to maximize the value of the firm, the optimal leverage should be zero because the value of the firm is isomorphic to the productivity function of the manager. Further, use of an incentive package (whether it is tied to the value of the firm or to the productivity of the manager) in this case makes no difference to the value of the firm because both stockholders and managers prefer zero financial leverage. In other words, an optimal capital structure is determined and preferred simultaneously by the stockholders and managers.

In summary, a theoretical model in the value-maximizing framework developed to incorporate the agency costs of leverage yields the optimal capital structure by balancing the cost of input loss with the interest tax shield advantage. The optimal leverage was found a function of output, size of the firm, and incentive package. However, when an incentive package and leverage have additive effects in the managerial input, the optimal leverage will be determined independently of the incentive package. Because the solution for investment and financing decisions is iterative, a numerical example is provided to illustrate this procedure.

Stockholders are shown to determine the optimal capital structure after recognizing the cost and benefit of leverage. However, when an incentive package is tied to the productivity of the managers, an optimal leverage is determined by the managers. In addition, in the absence of interest tax shield advantage, stockholders and managers will have the same preference for the debt policy irrespective of whether an incentive package is tied to the value of the firm or productivity of the managers.

# APPENDIX A

$$H^P = \begin{bmatrix} 0 & f_K & f_M M_o & f_M M_L & -1 \\ f_K & uf_{KK} & uf_{KM} M_o & [\tau r_f / r' + uf_{KM} M_L] & 0 \\ f_M M_o & uf_{MK} & uf_{MM} M_o^2 + uf_M M_{oo} & uf_{MM} M_L + uf_M M_{oL} & 0 \\ f_M M_L & [\tau r_f / r' + uf_{KM} M_L] & uf_{MM} M_L M_o + uf_u M_{oL} & [uf_M (M_L)^2 + uf_M M_{LL}] & 0 \\ -1 & 0 & 0 & 0 & (1-\tau) T_{QQ}/r' \end{bmatrix}$$

$$H^D = \begin{bmatrix} 0 & -f_K & -f_M M_o & -f_M M_L \\ -f_K & -vf_{KK} & -vf_{KM} M_o & [-\tau r_f / r' - vf_{KM} M_L] \\ -f_M M_o & -vf_{MK} & vf_{MM} M^2{}_o - vf_M M_{oo} & [-vf_{MM} M_L - vf_M M_{Lo}] \\ -f_M M_L & [-\tau r_f / r' - vF_{MK} M_L] & -vf_{MM} M_L - vf_M M_{LO} & [-vf_{MM} (M_L)^2 - vf_M M_{Lo}] \end{bmatrix}$$

$BH^P$ and $BH^D$ can be derived similarly.


## ACKNOWLEDGMENTS

The authors would like to thank Cheng-Few Lee for helpful comments and suggestions.


## NOTES

1. Fama (1978) shows that homogeneous expectation is one of the critical assumptions in the perfect market notion.

2. Fama and Miller (1972) argue that lenders want to protect their interest in the firm by imposing "me-first-rules." These me-first-rules imply a set of actions or restrictions taken by the lenders on limiting the activities of the firm.

3. Institutional lenders usually make frequent inquiry with respect to the status of various assets and liabilities as well as activities of the firm such as inventories level, collections of accounts receivable, production activities, tax payments, and insurance.

4. Management literature on the interorganization interactions has been well documented by Pfeffer (1972a). Further, Pfeffer concludes that "board size and composition are not random or independent factors, but rather, rational organizational response to the conditions of the external environment" [1972b, p. 226).

5. Vance observes; "Boardroom structure does have some meaning for industrial productivity: when officer-directors assumed more responsible roles in managing and controlling the affairs of our companies, our industrial system's productivity surged; when, however, an increasing number of firms began to reject officer-directors, productivity slumped" (1983, p. 273).

6. Stigler (1976) also argues framework utilizing waste as a factor in its economic analysis is not useful in solving problems and explaining economic phenomena.

7. The evidence is documented by Reynolds (1976).

8. Fama (1980) demonstrates that if the managerial marginal product can be fully reflected in the market in the ex post sense, the issue of agency problem in the Jensen–Meckling framework can be solved.

9. Substituting $\tilde{Y}/V_1$ for the expected rate of return in the CAPM form yields

$$E(\tilde{Y}/V_1) = (1 + r_f) + \lambda \text{cov}(\tilde{Y}/V_1, \tilde{R}_m)$$

or

$$E[(1 - \tau)\tilde{TR} - (1 - \tau)mM^o + K - (1 - \tau)\tilde{d}K + \tau\tilde{d}K$$

$$= V_1(1 + r_f) + \lambda \text{cov}[(1 - \tau)\tilde{TR} - (1 - \tau)mM^o + K - (1 - \tau)dK + \tilde{\tau}rD, R_m]]$$

Or,

$$(1 - \tau)[E(\tilde{TR}) - \lambda \text{cov}(\tilde{TR}, \tilde{R}_m)] - (1 - \tau)mM^o + [E(\tau)\tilde{r}D - \lambda \text{cov}[(\tau)\tilde{r}D, \tilde{R}_m]]$$
$$= (1 + r_f)V_1.$$

Thus,

$$V_1 = [(1 - \tau)T(Q) - (1 - \tau)mM^o + K - (1 - \tau)d^*K + \tau r_f D]/(1 + r_f).$$

10. This sufficient condition suggests that the bordered Hessian matrix $H^P$, whose 3×3 determinant is positive and higher determinants alternate in signs.

11. Since $G$ is positive and $|H^P|$ is also positive from the sufficient condition, the sign of $dL/db$ depends on the sign of $|H^P{}_{44}|$. $|H^P{}_{44}|$ has the same sign as the principal minor formed by deletion of the fourth row of the matrix $H^P$. By the sufficient condition of the Hessian matrix, the principal minors alternate in sign. Hence, $|H^P{}_{44}|$ is negative. This is because the $H^P$ matrix after deleting the fourth row and fourth column should have the same sign as deleting the fifth row and fifth column, which is negative by the sufficient condition of the bordered Hessian matrix. Hence, the fifth variable can be reordered with the fourth variable without changing the property of the sufficient condition. For reference, see Kuska (1973).

12. If there is an interactive effect of leverage and incentive package, the sign of $dL/da$ is indeterminate. In fact, if $M_{Li}$ is 0, we also obtain proposition 7 without necessarily invoking additive function of $L$ and $i$. However in such a case, we have to assume no second derivative of $M$ for either $L$ or $i$.

13. The values of parameters used are $\tau = 0.5$, $m = 5.0$, $a_1 = 200.0$, $a_2 = 2.0$, $d^* = 0.09$, $\alpha = 0.4$, $\beta = 0.6$, $A = 0.05$, $r_f = 0.06$, $r = 0.07$, $b_o = 4$, $b_1 = 200$, $e_1 = 1.2$, and $e = 3.1$. The risk premiums for revenue and depreciation are $0.25Q^2$ and 0.1, respectively.

## REFERENCES

Alchian, A. A., and Demsetz, H. (1972). "Production, Information Costs and Economic Organization." *American Economic Review* (December): 777–795.

Altman, E. (1984). "A Further Empirical Investigation of the Bankruptcy Cost Question." *Journal of Finance* (September): 1067–1089.

*American Banker*, January 27, 1984.

American Bar Foundation. (1971). Commentaries on Model Debenture Indenture Provision of All Registered Issues, 1967.

Dooley, P. (1969). "The Interlocking Directorate." *American Economic Review* (June): 314–323.

Douglas-Hamilton, M. (1975). "Creditor Liabilities Resulting from Improper Debtor." *Business Lawyer* (November): 343–365.

Fama, E. (1980). "Agency Problems and the Theory of Firm." *Journal of Political Economy* (April): 288–307.

Fama, E. (1978). "The Effects of a Firm's Investment and Financing Decisions on the Welfare of Its Stockholders." *American Economic Review* (June): 272–284.

Fama, E., and Jensen M. (1983). "Separation of Ownership and Control." *Journal of Law and Economics* (June 1983): 301–325.

Fama, E., and Miller, M. (1972). *The Theory of Finance*. Dryden Press.

Haugen, R. A. and Senbet, L. W. (1978). "The Insignificance of Bankruptcy Costs to the Theory of Optimal Capital Structure." *Journal of Finance* (May): 383–393.

Haugen, R. A., and Senbet, L. W. (1988). "Bankruptcy and Agency Cost: Their Significance to the Theory of Optimal Capital Structure." *Journal of Financial and Quantitative Analysis* (March): 27–38.

Hite, G. L. (1977). "Leverage, Output Effects, and the M-M Theorems." *Journal of Financial Economics* (March): 177–202.

Hughes, K. (1982). *Corporate Response to Declining Rates of Growth*. Lexington Books.

Jensen, M. C., and Meckling, W. H. (1976). "Theory of the Firm: Managerial Behavior Agency Costs, and Ownership Structure." *Journal of Financial Economics* 305–360.

Kim, E. H. (1978). "A Mean-Variance Theory of Optimal Capital Structure and Corporate Debt Capacity." *Journal of Finance* (March): 45–63.

Kuska, E. A. (1973). *Maxima, Minima and Comparative Statics*. London: Weidenfeld and Nicolson.

Mace, M. (1971). *Directors: Myth and Reality.* Graduate School of Business Administration, Harvard University.

Marris, R. (1964). *The Economic Theory of "Managerial" Capitalism*. Free Press of Glencoe.

Miller, M. H. (1977). "Debt and Taxes." *Journal of Finance* (May).

Modigliani, F., and Miller, M. H. (1958). "The Cost of Capital, Corporation Finance and the Theory of Investment." *American Economic Review* (June): 261–297.

Modigliani, F., and Miller, M. H. (1963). "Corporate Income Taxes and Cost of Capital: A Correction." *American Economic Review* (June): 433–443.

Pfeffer, J. (1972a). "Interorganizational Influence and Managerial Attitudes." *Academy of Management Journal* (September): 317–330.

Pfeffer, J. (1972b). "Size and Composition of Corporate Boards of Directors: The Organization and Its Environment." *Administrative Science Quarterly* (June): 218–228.

Pfeffer, J. (1981). *Power in Organization*. Pitman Publishing.

Ravid, S. A. (1988). "On Interactions of Production and Financial Decisions." *Financial Management* (Autumn): 87–99.

Reynolds, V. (1976). *The Biology of Human Action*. W. H. Freeman.

Scott, J. H., Jr. (1976). "A Theory of Optimal Capital Structure." *Bell Journal of Economics* (Spring): 33–53.

Smith, C. W., and Warner, J. B. (1979). "On Financial Contracting." *Journal of Financial Economics* (June): 117–161.

Stiglitz, J. E. (1972). "Some Aspects of the Pure Theory of Corporate Finance: Bankruptcies and Take-overs." *Bell Journal of Economics and Management Science* (Autumn): 458–482.

Stiglitz, J. E., and Weiss, A. (1981). "Credit Rationing in Markets with Imperfect Information." *American Economic Review* 393–410.

Titman, S. (1984). "The Effects of Capital Structure on a Firm's Liquidation Decision." *Journal of Financial Economics* (March): 137–151.

Vance, S. (1964). *Boards of Directors: Structure and Performance*. Eugene: University of Oregon Press.

Vance, S. (1983). *Corporate Leadership: Boards, Directors and Strategy.* New York: McGraw Hill.

Williamson, O. E. (1963). "Managerial Discretion and Business Behavior." *American Economic Review* (December): 1032–1057.

Williamson, O. E. (1975). *Markets and Hierarchies: Analysis and Antitrust Implications*. Free Press.

Zinbarg, E. (1975). "The Private Placement Loan Agreement." *Financial Analysts Journal* (July–August): 33–36.

# A MULTIPLE DISCRIMINANT INVESTIGATION INTO THE FINANCIAL CHARACTERISTICS OF HIGH GROWTH FIRMS

Bruce C. Payne

## ABSTRACT

The phenomenon of growth, whether it be measured in sales, size, or the present value of invested dollars, has received a good deal of attention in financial and economic literature over the past three decades. Most previous studies have concentrated on factors that explain and influence growth within companies or address the question of whether there is an optimum growth rate. The purpose of this study is to establish a financial profile of firms characterized by extraordinarily high growth rates and to determine whether these firms differ significantly from firms selected at random. It is concerned with those variables that are indicators of the firms risk-return trade-off character. Significant differences were found between the two groups of firms and it is suggested that the financial variables unique to the growth firms in the study can be used to forecast growth. As in previous studies of this nature multiple discriminant

**Advances in Quantitative Analysis of Finance and Accounting,**
**Volume 2, Part B, pages 19–33.**

**ISBN: 1-55938-565-0**

analysis was used. The results were somewhat surprising in that growth firms were larger in size and possessed a lower level of unsystematic risk than firms selected at random. As was expected however, growth firms had higher price-earnings multiples and returns on total capital than the randomly selected firms.

## I. INTRODUCTION

The phenomenon of growth, whether it be measured in sales, size, or the present value of invested dollars, has received a good deal of attention in financial and economic literature over the past three decades (Basu, 1977; Goodman and Peavy, 1986; Melicher and Miedich, 1985, 1987; Shuman and Seeger, 1986). Most of the previous studies have concentrated on the factors that explain and influence growth within companies (Basu, 1977; Goodman and Peavy, 1986; Shuman and Seeger, 1986). There have been other studies that sought to answer the question of whether there is an optimum growth rate. For example, Nerlove (1968) and Stano (1976) found significant positive relationships between sales growth rates and stockholder returns. Meidich and Melicher (1985) extended their efforts and examined the relationship between sales growth rates and stockholder returns to determine whether optimal sales growth rates are identifiable. By examining a 450-firm sample covering the 1964–1978 period, they (1987) found a consistently positive relationship between sales growth rates and stockholder returns even at very low and very high growth rates. They also examined (1985) whether the growth-return relationship continues to hold in a risk-return market framework and concluded that the relationship does hold when the experimenter controls for systematic risk. In addition *Fortune* and *Business Week* annually rank the top five hundred fastest growing firms in the United States. The *Fortune* group encompasses both large and small companies as well as a wide range of industries and regions (Gannes, 1988). *Business Week* annually ranks the best companies according to results in earnings and sales growth over a three-year period (Stano, 1976). In a recent year-end double issue, the editors offered the opinion that the decade of the 1980s would be remembered as a period of "deals," companies about to the taken over, or "whispers," those rumored to be deal companies. They further suggest that the 1990s would be an era where growth would replace the aforesaid deals and whispers as the most attractive characteristic of a company (Lakonishok and Lev, 1987).

Despite a high degree of academic and professional interest in growth there have been no studies that sought to identify the financial characteristics of growth firms. The term *growth company* may be distinguished from that of *growth stock*. Growth companies have historically been defined in terms of extraordinary growth in sales and earnings. Solomon recognized a growth company as one that had the management ability and opportunities to invest in projects that yielded a greater return than the firm's required rate of return. Thus, the growth firm was defined in terms of causes rather than results (Solomon, 1963). The term *growth stocks*, on the other hand, simply refers to stocks that possess superior return capabilities when compared to other stocks in the market with similar risk characteristics. In this study the traditional definition is used: companies that have excelled in the past three years in sales and earnings growth. Growth is thus defined in terms of results rather than causes, a definition more consistent with the purpose of the study.

The purpose of this study is to identify the financial characteristics of companies characterized by high growth rates in sales. More specifically, the study is concerned with those variables that are indicators of the firm's risk-return trade-off character, and a measure of how that risk-return trade-off is perceived by professional analysts and investors at the margin. It is the action of this latter group in buying and selling that determines the value of firm. If the set of financial variables that describes growth firms is found to be unique, it is possible that the set could be used to identify those firms that may become growth firms. This information would have implications for investors, investment counselors, and managers. Thus the study also contains a test of the predictive power of the aforesaid set of variables.

## II. METHODOLOGY

The question to be resolved is one of classification or prediction and evaluation of the accuracy of that classification. More specifically, can firms be assigned on the basis of selected variables to one of two groups: (1) firms known to be high growth firms, or (2) firms selected at random? Multiple discriminant analysis (MDA) provides a procedure for assigning firms to predetermined groupings on the basis of variables or attributes whose values may depend on the group to which the firm actually belongs.

If the purpose of the study were simply to establish a financial profile of growth firms, simple ratios would be adequate. Part of the purpose, however, involves prediction. In a seminal paper on the use of MDA in finance, Altman (1968) showed that sets of ratios used in multivariate analysis were better descriptions of the companies and had more predictive power than individual ratios used in univariate tests.

The use of MDA in the social sciences for the purpose of prediction is well known. It is appropriate when the dependent variables are nominally or ordinally measured and the predictive variables are intervally measured. In addition to its use in the Altman study to predict corporate bankruptcy, MDA has been used to predict common stock quality ratings (White, 1975), the credit worthiness of used car loan applicants (Durand, 1941), financially distressed property-liability insurance firms (Treschmann and Pinches, 1973), and the failure of small businesses (Edminister, 1982). All the studies mentioned had one thing in common. The groups in which the firms are classified are nominally measured: good–bad, failing–nonfailing, likely to bankrupt–not likely to bankrupt, or in the case of stock quality ratings ordinally measured. This study, as in the studies referred to, employs nominally measured dependent variables and internally measured predictive variables. MDA is then appropriate for this study, and its use in finance is well established.

## III. SELECTION OF SAMPLE AND INDEPENDENT VARIABLES

The sample consists of two groups of fifty firms. The first was selected randomly from the aforementioned *Business Week* ranking. That is, firms that have excelled in the past three years in sales and earnings growth (Appendix A). The second group is a group of firms selected at random (Appendix B), but from the same industries as the first group. In addition to the two groups used in the analysis, it was necessary to select an additional one hundred firms to validate the test (Appendix C). This validation sample was chosen at random, but again from the same industries used for the first and second groups and with the same degree of concentration in each industry. Thus, the entire study involved two hundred firms positioned in twenty-three industries.

Previous studies on this subject have chosen explanatory variables by various methods and logical arguments. The group of explanatory variables chosen for analysis simply contains two well-known measures of risk, a measure of return, a multiple that indicates how the risk-return measures are viewed, and a variable that measures the size of the firm. The two measures of risk of the firm are the firm's beta coefficient, used as a measure of market or systematic risk, and the residual variance found in computing those betas used as a measure of company or unsystematic risk. The measure of return is return to total capital. The measure of return to total capital includes a return to creditors as well as owners, and recognizes that the value of the firm is affected by the cost of debt. A measure of return to equity could properly be used but it would ignore the cost of debt and the fact that assets are financed by debt as well as equity. In order for changes in risk and return variables to have any affect on the value of the firm, the changes must provoke some reaction from investors. To get an indication of that reaction, the analysis contains the price earnings multiple (*P/E* ratio). This multiple is established by the action of investors and their reaction to any change or perceived change in the firm's risk-return character. In addition, a variable to measure size is included because it is not clear from previous studies whether growth is in any way associated with size.

In summary, there were to be four areas of comparison: (1) return on investment, (2) risk, (3) how the risk-return trade-off characteristics are perceived by investors and investment counselors, and (4) size. The five variables chosen to measure the four above-mentioned areas are as follows:

- $X_1$ Price-earnings multiple. The price earnings multiple is used as an indicator of how all investors at the margin view the firm's risk-return character. In this study the source of all data was the Value Line Data Base II and Merrill Lynch's Risk Evaluation published in June 1989.
- $X_2$ Logarithm of sales. The logarithm of sales is used as a measure of the size of the company.

$X_3$ Return to total capital. The percentage return on total capital is used as a measure of return.

$X_4$ Market risk. Sharpe's beta is used as a measure of market or systematic risk.

$X_5$ Company risk. The residual variance from the regression equations used to determine the beta coefficients is used as the measure of company or unsystematic risk.

The final variable profile does not contain the most significant variables on a univariate basis. Moreover, the variables chosen may not be the best measures of those characteristics they purport to measure. The dilemma, however, is to choose that combination of variables that not only adequately measures the attributes, but that also has a relatively low degree of correlation with one another and is available in a usable form. This final variable profile is that desired combination, and the individual variables have been discussed extensively in financial literature.

## IV. TEST AND RESULTS

The discriminant function used was of the form

$$Z_j = V_1 Z_{1j} + V_2 X_{2j} + .... + V_n X_{nj}, \quad (1)$$

where $X_{ij}$ is the company's value for the $i$th independent variable, $V_i$ is the discriminant coefficient for the $i$th variable, $Z_j$ is the $j$th individual's discriminant score.

The function derived from the data in this study is

$$Z_j = 34.13135_{x1} + 0.01647_{x2} + 0.01700_{x3} + 0.15598_{x4} - 1.39450_{x5}. \quad (2)$$

Classification of firms is relatively simple. The values of the five variables for each firm are substituted into Eq. (2). Thus, each firm in both groups receives a $Z$ score. If a firm's $Z$ value is greater than a defined value, the firm is classified in group two (nongrowth firms). Since the two groups are heterogeneous, it is expected that all firms in the growth group will fall into one group and nongrowth firms will fall into the other. The variances of the two groups are statistically equal. Therefore, the value midway between the two groups means can be defined as the critical value. This is the value that minimizes overlap and the probability of misclassification. The mean $Z$ value for group one is 0.03813, the mean $Z$ value for group two is 0.02251, and the critical $Z$ value is 0.03032.

Interpretation of the results of discriminant analysis is usually accomplished by addressing four basic questions:

1. Is there a significant difference in the mean vectors of variables for the two groups of firms?
2. How well did the discriminant function perform?

3. How well did the independent variables perform?
4. Will this function discriminate as well on any random sample of firms as it did on the original sample?

The Mahalonobis $D^2$ statistic measures "a generalized distance between two groups, where each group is characterized by the same set of $n$ variables and the variance-covariance structure is the same for both groups" (Cooley and Lohnes, 1971, p. 32). The $D^2$ statistic when transformed to the more familiar $F$ statistic can be used to determine whether there is a significant difference between the two mean vectors. In this analysis,

$$F = 7.34\ c\ 5 \text{ and } 94 \text{ degrees of freedom is greater than } F_{0.05} = 2.33.$$

The null hypothesis that there is no significant difference between the financial profiles of growth firms and firms selected at random is therefore rejected, and the first conclusion of this study is that the two groups of firms have significantly different financial characteristics. The discriminant function thus has the power to separate the two groups. However, this does not mean that it will in fact separate them or that it can be used to predict which firms may become growth firms.

The ultimate value of a discriminant model for predicting growth depends on the results obtained from the model. That is, what percentage of firms were classified correctly and is that percentage significant? The percentage classified correctly measures how well the discriminant function performed and the predictive power of that function.

Of the fifty firms in the group of growth firms, forty were classified correctly, and ten were misclassified. Of the fifty firms chosen at random, thirty-nine were classified correctly and eleven were misclassified. Thus seventy-nine firms, or 79%, were classified correctly. The results are shown in Table 1.

To test for significance of the 79% classified correctly, a chi-square test is appropriate. In this case,

$$\text{chi}^2 = 33.63 \text{ is greater than } \text{chi}^2{}_{0.05} = 3.84\ c\ 1 \text{ d. f.}$$

The null hypothesis that the percentage classified correctly is not significantly different from what would be classified correctly by chance is therefore rejected, and the conclusion can be drawn that the discriminant function is not only capable of separating the two groups, but it did in fact separate them well.

*Table 1.* Classification Results

| | *Actual Results* | *Predicted Results* |
|---|---|---|
| Growth | 40 | 11 |
| Nongrowth | 10 | 39 |

*Table 2.* Relative Contribution of the Variables

| *Variable* | *Adjusted Coefficient* | *Rank* |
|---|---|---|
| Price earnings ratio | 5387.95 | 1 |
| Logarithm of sales | 0.000639 | 3 |
| Return to total capital | 0.000607 | 4 |
| Systematic risk | 0.023789 | 2 |
| Unsystematic risk | –0.549488 | 5 |

The predictive power of the model was further tested by counting the number of growth firms in the sample that were not listed as growth firms three years prior to being listed the first time, and were characterized by the same financial profile. Of the fifty growth firms listed in the sample, thirty-nine, or 78%, were not listed three years before, yet they had the same financial characteristics. Again, this is a significant percentage; the conclusion is thus forced that the model can be used for predicting growth.

The relative contribution of each variable to the total discriminating power of the function may be obtained by adjusting the discriminant coefficients for differences in the units of measure of the original variables. This adjustment is made arithmetically by multiplying the square root of the diagonal elements of the variance covariance matrix for each variable by the discriminant coefficient of that variable. The product of this multiplication gives the relative contribution of each variable to the total discriminating power or the function (Altman, 1968). The adjusted coefficients are shown in Table 2. An examination of Table 2 reveals that the price earnings ratio is the variable with the greatest contribution to the overall discriminating function, followed by systematic risk, the logarithm of sales, return to total capital, and unsystematic risk, respectively.

Before any general conclusions can be drawn, it must be determined whether the model can be expected to work for any group of randomly drawn firms. The possibility that the difference between the two groups is the result of sampling errors or search bias must be eliminated. This involves validating the model. The procedure used to validate the model is a modification of the split sample approach (Durand, 1941).

## V. VALIDATION OF THE MODEL

The model classified 79% of the sample firms correctly. That test is biased because the discriminant function was applied to the same two groups used to derive the discriminant coefficients. The validation procedure involved gathering information for one hundred new firms. The discriminant coefficients derived from the original sample were then multiplied by the values of the variables for the one hundred new firms. It was expected that the proportion of firms classified correctly in the validation sample would be less than that in the original sample due to the systematic bias associated with sampling errors. The fact that the validation test is expected to classify a smaller proportion correctly is not important. The major question is: Will the proportion classified correctly by the validation test differ significantly from the original test? In other words, the difference in the two proportions classified correctly by the two tests is due to bias. The objective is to see if this bias is significant. The values of the variables for the one hundred new firms were substituted into Eq. (2). This procedure resulted in the correct classification of seventy-three firms, or 79%. Since there are only two samples for analysis the binomial test is appropriate.

$$\frac{73 - 100\,(0.68)}{\sqrt{100\,(0.79)\,(0.21)}} = -1.47 \text{ is less than } t_{0.05} - 1.645.$$

Thus the null hypothesis that there is no significant difference in the proportion of firms classified correctly in the original test and the proportion classified correctly in the validation test cannot be rejected, and it can therefore be concluded that while there was some bias in the original analysis, it was not significant. The procedure will classify new firms as well as it did in the original analysis.

## VI. CONCLUSIONS

The purpose of this study was to clearly establish a financial profile for firms characterized by high rates of growth and to see if that profile could be used to predict which firms would become growth firms. More specifically, the financial profile would include measures of risk and return. In addition, there is a measure of how investors at the margin perceive the firms and a measure of size. Investors at the margin trade proxies for risk and return when making purchasing decisions that determine market value. These decisions are roughly reflected in the price-earnings ratio. The arithmetic signs for the adjusted coefficients in Table 2 are important. A positive sign indicates the greater a firm's value for that variable the more likely it will be a growth firm. On the other hand a negative sign for an adjusted coefficient means the greater a company's value for that variable the less likely it is a growth firm. Thus, according to Table 2 the greater the size of the firm, the greater the price earnings ratio, the greater the return to total capital and the greater the market risk, the more likely it is that the firm is a growth firm. Conversely, the greater the amount of unsystematic or company risk, the less likely the firm will be a growth firm. A major conclusion follows from the analysis. Current growth firms are larger in size, have higher price earnings multiples, have greater returns to total capital, and possess greater systematic risk than firms selected at random. In addition, it may be concluded that growth firms have less unsystematic risk than firms in general. On the basis of the analysis it is argued that this unique combination of characteristics can be used to predict growth in firms that have not yet achieved that characteristic.

There will be no attempt here to try to establish cause and effect relationships that will explain why growth firms have a unique financial profile. That would be beyond the scope of this study, but certainly it is a subject that deserves further research. In spite of this, however, a few comments and observations may be in order.

Three of the five results may have been expected, and two were mild surprises. Table 2 shows that the price earnings multiple was the most important variable distinguishing between growth firms and firms selected at random. The fact that growth firms have higher price earnings multiples may have been expected. Investors at the margin seem to value growth, and therefore it may be reasonable to expect that premiums would have been placed on their earnings. This finding is also consistent with the statement by the editors of *Business Week*, mentioned in the introduction, that in the decade of the 1990s growth would be the most attractive characteristic of the firm. It may also have been expected that systematic risk would be higher in growth firms since growth is highly correlated with returns, and the risk-return trade-off relationship indicates higher levels of systematic risk with higher returns. It was further expected that returns to total capital would be higher for growth firms than for firms selected at random. This is consistent with the previously mentioned findings of Nerlove (1968) and Stano (1976).

Unsystematic risk is said not to be relevant in valuing portfolios. Capital market theory assumes that markets are efficient and that if investors can diversify away unsystematic risk, they will in fact diversify away that risk. However, to the extent that markets are not perfect, unsystematic risk becomes important. Firms that are characterized by higher returns to total capital and high rates of growth may be expected to have higher levels of unsystematic risk. Thus it was surprising that unsystematic risk was lower in growth firms than it was in firms selected at random. If there was a genuine surprise from the analysis, it was that growth firms were larger than firms selected at random. One would expect that on a percentage basis smaller firms would have higher growth rates; that was not the case. The larger the firm the more likely it was to be a growth firm. There is nothing in the literature that seeks to explain why this may be true. The explanation for the causes of these relationships, as stated earlier, is beyond the scope of this study. A study is needed that will seek to explain why the characteristics of growth firms are as they are. Another potential area for productive research may seek to explain why growth firms become more or less attractive to investors over the years. In the late 1960s institutional investors were attracted to super-high-growth companies known as go-go firms. It was not uncommon for these firms to sell at sixty or seventy times earnings. After the oil-embargo-induced recession beginning in late 1973, the market value of go-go firms fell further and faster than firms in general. After the long recovery, they never regained their popularity with institutional investors. As mentioned earlier however, during the decade of the 1990s, growth is expected to be the most attractive characteristic of a company.

This study has resulted in a contribution toward constructing a profile of the financial characteristics of today's growth firms. The establishment of such a financial profile will aid investors in identifying firms that have a potential attraction for institutions and other investors interested in growth. Results of the study should also aid investors in identifying a synthesis of characteristics that have been attractive to them in the past.

## APPENDIX A: GROWTH FIRMS

1. Sigma Designs
2. Universal Medical Buildings
3. V Band
4. Tech Data
5. Intergraph
6. M D C Holdings
7. Cray Research
8. Battle Mountain Gold
9. Royalpar Industries
10. TCBY Enterprises
11. Preferred Health Care
12. Vanguard Tech International
13. Coated Sales
14. Sound Advice
15. Ohio Art
16. Traditional Industries
17. Interactive Technologies
18. Viatech
19. Mylan Laboratories
20. Inverson Technology
21. Buffets
22. Martin Lawrence Limited Editions
23. Spearhead Industries
24. Duquesne Systems
25. X-Rite
26. Swift Energy
27. American Home Shield
28. Macneal-Schwendler
29. Air Cargo Equipment
30. Dotronix

31. Dycom Industries
32. Crown Crafts
33. General Sciences
34. Bolar Pharmaceuticals
35. Rotech Medical
36. Expeditor International of Washington
37. McGrath Rentcorp
38. Careercom
39. Par Pharmaceuticals
40. Cherokee Group
41. State O Maine
42. Spartan Motors
43. Sbarro
44. Dynamic Research Corp
45. Lindal Cedar Homes
46. Escalade
47. Good Guys
48. St. Jude Medical
49. Diagnostic Products
50. Biocraft Laboratories

## APPENDIX B: CONTROL GROUP

1. AGS Computers
2. Ashton-Tate
3. Automatic Data Processing
4. Bolt Beranek
5. Computer Association
6. AST Research
7. Altos Computers
8. CCT Corporation
9. Adams-Millis
10. Crystal Brands
11. Agency Rent-A-Car
12. American Building Maintenance
13. Allen Group
14. Amrep Corporation
15. Arrow Electronics
16. Augat Inc.
17. Avantek Inc.
18. Avnet
19. Aydin

20. Bell Industries
21. Burndy Industries
22. Action Industries
23. Best Products
24. Heilig-Meyers Company
25. CML Group
26. Child World Inc.
27. Blount Inc.
28. American Standard
29. American Business Products
30. Belding Heminway
31. Alcan Aluminum
32. American Medical International
33. Basic American Medical
34. Beverly Enterprises
35. Charter Medical
36. Coleco Industries
37. American Home Products
38. Bristol-Meyers
39. Cetus Corporation
40. Forest Labs
41. Baker Hughes
42. Chubb Corporation
43. AAR Corporation
44. ADC Telecommunication Inc.
45. AMR Corporation
46. Block (H & R)
47. Foote, Cone, & Belding
48. Bob Evans Farms
49. Luby's Cafeteria
50. Flightsafety

## APPENDIX C: VALIDATION GROUP

1. Computer Science
2. Cullinet
3. General Motors
4. ISC Systems
5. Intelogic Trace
6. Lotus
7. Microsoft
8. National Data

51. Gordon Jewelry
52. Greenman Brothers
53. Ameron Inc.
54. Apogee Enterprises
55. Bairnco Corporation
56. Bird Inc.
57. Dennison Manufacturing
58. Diebold Inc.

9. Shared Medical Systems
10. Telecredit Inc.
11. Apollo Computer
12. Apple Computer
13. Applied Magnetics
14. C 3 Inc.
15. Commodore International
16. Compaq Computer
17. Farah Inc.
18. Garan
19. Hartmarx Corporation
20. Kellwood Company
21. Angelica Corporation
22. Banner Industries
23. Browning Ferris
24. Equifax Inc.
25. Champion Spark
26. Echlin
27. Deltona Corporation
28. Chicago Milwaukee
29. CTS Corporation
30. California Microwave
31. Canadian Marconi
32. Cubic Corporation
33. DBA Systems
34. Dynatech Corporation
35. Emerson Radio
36. General Instrument
37. Gould Inc.
38. Harris Corporation
39. Molex Inc.
40. Pittway Corporation
41. Regency Electronics
42. Rogers Corporation
43. Horn & Hardart Co.
44. Claires Stores Inc.
45. Clothestime Inc.
46. Crazy Eddie Inc.
47. Fabri-Centers
48. Fur Vault Inc.
49. General Host
50. General Nutrition
59. Guilford Mills
60. Fieldcrest Cannon
61. Battle Mountain Gold
62. Asarco Inc.
63. Community Psychiatry
64. Comprehensive Care
65. Hospital Corporation
66. Humana Inc.
67. Manor Care
68. Maxicare Health
69. National Medical Entpr.
70. Omnicare Inc.
71. Cross (A.T.) Company
72. Hasbro Inc.
73. Genentech
74. INC Pharmaceutical
75. Lilly (Eli) & Company
76. Marion Labs
77. Merck & Company
78. Mylan
79. Pfizer Inc.
80. Robins (A.H.) Company
81. Cameron Iron
82. Daniel Industries
83. Continental Corporation
84. Fireman's Fund
85. ARX Inc.
86. Adams Russell Elect.
87. Andrew Corporation
88. Burnup & Sims
89. Airborne Freight
90. Alaska Air
91. American Express
92. CUC International
93. Interpublic
94. Ogilvy Group
95. Jerriko Inc.
96. Church's Fried Chicken
97. Collins Foods
98. Dunkin Donuts
99. International Tech.
100. Kelly Services

# APPENDIX D: INDUSTRIES

| *Industries* | *Number of Growth Firms* |
|---|---|
| 1. Computers and peripherals | 3 |
| 2. Computer services | 5 |
| 3. Apparel | 2 |
| 4. Restaurants | 2 |
| 5. Industrial services | 3 |
| 6. Auto parts | 1 |
| 7. Real estate | 1 |
| 8. Electronics | 7 |
| 9. Retail-specialty line | 5 |
| 10. Building | 2 |
| 11. Office equipment and supplies | 1 |
| 12. Textiles | 1 |
| 13. Metals and mining | 1 |
| 14. Medical services | 4 |
| 15. Toys and school supplies | 1 |
| 16. Drug | 4 |
| 17. Oilfield services | 1 |
| 18. Insurance-property | 1 |
| 19. Aerospace | 1 |
| 20. Telecommunications equipment | 1 |
| 21. Air transport | 1 |
| 22. Financial services | 1 |
| 23. Advertising | 1 |

# REFERENCES

Altman, E. I. (1968) "Financial Ratios, Discriminant Analysis and the Prediction of Corporate Bankruptcy." *Journal of Finance* 23 (September): 589–609.

Basu, S. (1977). "The Investment Performance of Common Stocks in Relation to Their Price-Earnings Ratio: A Test of the Efficient Market Hypothesis." *Journal of Finance* (June): 663–682.

Brown, P., Kleidon, A. W., and Marsh, T. A. (1983). "New Evidence of the Nature of Size Related Anomalies in Stock Prices." *Journal of Financial Economics* (June): 33–35.

Cook, T., and Rozeff, M. (1984). "Size and Earnings/Price Ratio Anomalies: One Effect or Two?" *Journal of Financial and Quantitative Analysis* (December): 449–466.

Cooley, W. W., and Lohnes, P. R. (1971). *Multivariate Data Analysis*. New York: John Wiley & Sons.

Dixon, W. J., ed. (1971). *Biomedical Computer Programs*. Berkeley: University of California Press.

Durand, D. D. (1941). "Risk Elements In Consumer Installment Financing." *Studies In Consumer Installment Financing*. New York: National Bureau of Economic Research, pp. 105–142.

Edmister, R. O. (1982). "An Empirical Test of Financial Ratio Analysis for Small Business Failure Prediction." *Journal of Financial and Quantitative Analysis* 7 (March): 1477–1492.

Frank, R. E., Massey, W. F., and Morrison, D. T. (1965). "Bias in Multiple Discriminant Analysis." *Journal of Marketing Research* 11 (August): 227–130.

Gannes, S. (1988). "America's Fastest-Growing Companies." *Fortune* (May 23): 127–130.

Goodman, D. A., and Peavy, J. W., III. (1986). "The Interaction of the Firm Size and Price-Earnings Ratio on Portfolio Performance." *Financial Analyst Journal* (January–February): 9–12.

Laderman, J. M. (1989). "Coming Home To Growth Stocks." *Business Week* (December 25): 106–107.

Lakonishok, J., and Lev, B. (1987). "Stocks Splits and Stock Dividends: Why, Who, and When?" *Journal of Finance* 13, No. 4 (September): 913–1032.

Melicher, R. W., and Miedich, S. J. (1985). "Corporate Sales Growth Rates and Stockholder Returns: A Risk-Return Market Analysis." *Review of Business and Economic Research* (Spring): 34–44.

Melicher, R. W., and Miedich, S. J. (1987). "Corporate Sales Growth Rates and Stockholder Returns: A Reply." *Review of Business and Economic Research* (Fall): 50–57.

Miller, E. M. (1987). "Growth and Stockholder Returns: A Comment on Miedich and Melicher." *Review of Business and Economic Research* (Spring): 77–83.

Nerlove, M. (1968). "Factors Affecting Differences Among Rates of Return on Investments in Individual Common Stocks." *Review of Economics and Statistics* (August): 312–331.

Shuman, J. C., and Seeger, J. A. (1986). "The Theory and Practice of Strategic Management in Smaller Rapid Growth Firms." *American Journal of Small Business* (Summer): 7–18.

Solomon, E. (1963). *The Theory of Financial Management.* New York: Columbia University Press, pp. 55–68.

Stano, M. (1976). "Monopoly Power, Ownership Control, and Corporate Performance." *Bell Journal of Economics* (Autumn): 672–679.

Treschmann, J. S., and Pinches, G. E. (1973). "A Multivariate Model for Predicting Financially Distressed Property-Liability Insurers." *Journal of Risk and Insurance* 40 (September): 327–333.

Wallace, D., with Mason, T. (1988). "The Hot 100 Growth Companies." *Business Week* (May 23): 120–132.

White, R. E. (1975). "A Multivariate Analysis for Common Stock Quality Ratings." Paper presented to the 1975 meeting of the Financial Management Association, Kansas City, October.

# AN EQUILIBRIUM APT AND THE ROLE OF THE MARKET PORTFOLIO

Cheng F. Lee, Hun Y. Park, and K. C. John Wei

## ABSTRACT

This paper develops an equilibrium APT which is an exact pricing model without any approximation or the condition of a well-diversified market portfolio in a given factor structure. This equilibrium APT is compared with the Ross–Connor APTs and the CAPMs. Of particular interest is that the market portfolio plays an important role explicitly in this equilibrium APT, which is consistent with Shanken. Our equilibrium APT is, coincidentally, in the same spirit of the third alternative asset pricing relation proposed by Shanken and is consistent with Wei, McElroy and Burmeister, and others.

## I. INTRODUCTION

As an alternative to the capital asset pricing model (CAPM), the arbitrage pricing theory (APT) has been proposed by Ross (1976, 1977) and extended by Huberman (1982), Grinblatt and Titman (1983), Chamberlain and Rothschild (1983), Connor (1984), and others.[1] One of the reasons that the APT is generally accepted as a plausible alternative to the CAPM is that the market portfolio does not play a special

**Advances in Quantitative Analysis of Finance and Accounting,**
**Volume 2, Part B, pages 35–43.**

**ISBN: 1-55938-565-0**

role in the APT whereas the identification of the true market portfolio is critical for testing the validity of the CAPM (see Roll, 1977). However, in his two recent articles, Shanken (1982, 1985) questioned the testability of Ross's APT. Shanken (1985, p. 1191) argues that "the APT restriction is an approximation, one which prices 'most' assets well but permits arbitrarily large deviations from exact pricing for a finite set of assets. Thus, it is difficult to conceive of any (finite) empirical procedure that could be used to refute the actual conclusion of the APT. In this sense, the theory is untestable in principle."

Recently, Connor (1984) has derived an exact pricing relation relying on the principles of a competitive equilibrium rather than arbitrage arguments. A crucial condition in Connor's "competitive APT" is that the idiosyncratic risks of assets, defined relative to a given factor structure, are completely diversified away in the market portfolio. Chen and Ingersoll (1983) reached a similar condition. In other words, if the market portfolio is not completely diversified, the Ross APT is not an exact pricing relation but only an approximate one.

This paper develops an exact pricing model (which will be referred to as "equilibrium APT") without any approximation (unlike Ross APT) or the assumption of perfect diversification in the market portfolio (unlike Connor APT). Shanken (1985, p. 1189) argues: "The equilibrium (CAPM) paradigm emphasizes the role of covariance between asset returns and an endogenous preference-based aggregate, while the arbitrage (APT) paradigm focuses on the covariance between asset returns and factors in the return generating process. The emerging equilibrium factor paradigm encompasses each of these relations as well as a third-covariance between the factors and the equilibrium aggregate."

Coincidentally, our equilibrium APT is in the same spirit of the third alternative asset pricing relation proposed by Shanken (1985) and consistent with the unified asset pricing theory (UAPT) of Wei (1988). The equilibrium APT is compared with the Ross–Connor APT and the CAPMs. Of particular interest is that the Ross–Connor model is shown to be a special case of the equilibrium APT only when risk-averse investors are assumed to hold perfectly diversified portfolios of many assets or when the market portfolio is well diversified in a factor model. It is also shown that the equilibrium APT becomes equivalent to intertemporal asset pricing models if the factor realizations play the role of state variables. More important, the market portfolio is shown to play an important role explicitly in the equilibrium APT.[2]

Dybvig and Ross (1985a) have analyzed the security market line deviations caused by a choice of an inefficient market portfolio. This paper shows the deviation of the APT caused by the inefficient market portfolio defined in a factor economy. Section II derives the equilibrium APT and shows that the market portfolio is one of the priced factors in a given factor structure. We also compare the equilibrium APT with the Connor APT. Section III compares the Ross APT and the CAPMs with the equilibrium APT. Section IV contains a brief conclusion.

## II. THE EQUILIBRIUM APT IN A FINITE-ASSETS MARKET

We assume that the capital markets are perfectly competitive and frictionless. Individuals are assumed to believe homogeneously that random returns on the underlying assets are generated by an approximate $K$-factor structure of Chamberlain and Rothschild (1983):

$$\tilde{R}_{it} = E_i + b_{i1}\tilde{f}_{it} + \ldots + b_{iK}\tilde{f}_{Kt} + \tilde{e}_{it}, \tag{1}$$

where

$\tilde{R}_{it}$ = the random return on security $i$ during the period $t$,
$E_i$ = the expected return on security $i$,
$b_{ij}$ = the factor loading of security $i$ on factor $j$,
$\tilde{f}_{jt}$ = the factor score on the systematic factor $j$ during the period $t$, and
$\tilde{e}_{it}$ = the random error term.

The factor scores have mean zero and are assumed to be mutually independent and independent of random error terms. The random error terms are assumed to have mean zero. Here, we do not assume that the error terms are mutually independent. We also assume that all investors are risk averse and expected utility maximizers. Given the $K$-factor return generating process for n risky assets as shown in Eq. (1), the return on any portfolio for investor $p$ with a composition of $X^p$ with $(X^p)'l = 1$ can be given by[3]

$$\tilde{R}^p = (X^p)'E + (X^p)'B\tilde{f} + (X^p)'\tilde{e}, \tag{2}$$

where $B$ is a $n \times k$ matrix of $b_{ij}$. Further, we assume that portfolio cash flows for the investor $p$ are generated at the end of the period. Following Losq and Chateau (1982), we also assume that in addition to financial assets, there exist $G$ consumption goods (or commodities) whose future spot prices $\tilde{P}_g$ ($g = 1, \ldots, G$) fluctuate stochastically. More specifically, suppose that each commodity future spot price is fully explained by the $K$ factors defined in Eq. (1), and each investor has the same expectation about this relationship.[4] That is,

$$\tilde{p}_{gt} = P_g(\tilde{f}_{1t},\ldots,\tilde{f}_{kt}),\ g = 1, \ldots, G.$$

Given these stochastic information sets, investor $p$ is to find the set of asset weights, $X^p$, to maximize the expected value of his multiargument utility function over the single-period investment horizon subject to his budget constraint:

$$\max E\{U^p[\tilde{W}^p, P(\tilde{f}), c^p]\}$$

$$\{X^p\}$$

$$s.t.\ W + c = W_T \text{ and } X'1 = 1,$$

where $U^p(\cdot)$ = investor $p$'s indirect utility function, assumed twice continuously differentiable,

$$P(\tilde{f}) \equiv [P_1(\tilde{f}), \ldots, P_g(\tilde{f})] = \text{the row vector of commodity prices,}$$

$$W_T = \text{total initial wealth for investor } p\text{, and}$$

$$c = \text{investor } p\text{'s current period consumption.}$$

Assume that the $K$ factors follow a two-parameter distribution. Then the above objective function can be rewritten as

$$\max_{\{X^p\}} U^p\{E(\tilde{W}^p, \text{var}(\tilde{W}^p), \text{cov}(\tilde{W}^p, \tilde{f}), c^p\}$$

$$s.t. \;\; W + c = W_T \text{ and } X'1 = 1, \tag{3}$$

We will drop the superscript $p$ throughout this paper, except where required for clarity. Then, $\tilde{W}$ $E(\tilde{W})$, var($\tilde{W}$), and cov($\tilde{W}, \tilde{f}$) can be defined by

$$\tilde{W} = W(1 + \tilde{R}^p) = W(1 + X'E + X'B\tilde{f} + X'\tilde{e})$$

$$E(\tilde{W}) = W(1 + E(\tilde{R}^p) = W(1 + X'E)$$

$$\text{var}(\tilde{W} = (W)^2\text{var}(\tilde{R}^p) = (W)^2(X'VX)$$

$$= (W)^2[X'(BDB' + \Omega)X]$$

$$\text{cov}(\tilde{W}, \tilde{f}) = WX'BD$$

where

$\Omega$ = $n{\times}n$ covariance matrix of $\tilde{e}$.

$D$ = $k{\times}k$ diagonal variance-covariance matrix of returns on common factors, $\tilde{f}$,

$V$ = $n{\times}n$ covariance matrix of $\tilde{R}$ and equal to $BDB'{+}\Omega$,

$X$ = $n{\times}1$ vector of assets weights held by the investor, and

$W$ = the wealth allocated to all assets for the investor.

We can solve the individual's constrained optimization by forming the Lagrangian function $L$, from Eq. (3) as follows:

$$L = U\{E(\tilde{W}), \text{var}(\tilde{W}), \text{cov}(\tilde{W}, \tilde{f}), c\} + q_1(W_T - W - c) + q_2(X'1 - 1), \tag{4}$$

where $q_1$ and $q_2$ are Lagrangian multipliers. Taking partial derivatives with respect to $X$ and $c$, and equaling them to zero, we have

$$WU_1E + 2W^2U_2\,(BDB' + \Omega)X + WBDU_f - q_21 = 0 \tag{5}$$

$$\partial EU/\partial c - q_1 = 0. \tag{6}$$

In Eq. (5), $U_1 = \partial U/\partial E(W)$, $U_2 = \partial U/\partial \mathrm{var}(\tilde{W})$, and $U_f = \partial U/\partial \mathrm{cov}(\tilde{W}, \tilde{f})$. The Lagrangian multiplier $q_1$ in Eq. (4) is defined as the rate of change of the maximum value of $U$ in Eq. (3) with respect to a small increase in the invested wealth $W$, that is, $q_1 = \partial U/\partial W$. Inserting this definition into Eq. (6), we get $\partial U/\partial c = \partial U/\partial W$. This is the envelope condition to equate the marginal utility of current consumption to the indirect marginal utility of wealth for future consumption.[5]

Assuming that the expected return on the zero-beta portfolio with weights of $X^0$, or the risk-free asset (if it exists), is $E_0$, Eq. (5) premultiplied by $(X^{0\prime})$ and setting $(X^0)'B = 0'$, $(X^0)'\Omega = O'$, and Eq. $(X^{0\prime}l = 1$, we obtain $q_2 = WU_1E_0$. Substituting this result back into Eq. (5) and rearranging, we have

$$T^p(E - E_0 1) = (BDB' + \Omega)X^p W^p - BDHP_{f'}\ , \tag{7}$$

where $T^p = -U_1^p/2U_2^p$, a measure of absolute risk tolerance, and $H_f^p = U_f^p/2U_2^p$. Summing up Eq. (7) for all investors in the market and rearranging, we have

$$\begin{aligned} E - E_0 1 &= (BDB' + \Omega)X^m M/T^m - BDH_f^m/T^m \\ &= VX^m R^m - BDH_f^m R^m/M \\ &= \sigma_{am} R^m - BDH_f^m R^m/M, \end{aligned} \tag{8}$$

where $\sigma_{am}$ is $n \times 1$ covariance vector between individual securities and the market portfolio, $X^m$ is the weight of the market portfolio, $M$ is the total market value of all assets, $T^m = \Sigma T^p$, $R^m = M/T^m$, and $H_f^m = \Sigma H_f^p$. Here, we consider $T^m$ and $R^m$ as the market absolute risk tolerance and the market relative risk aversion, respectively.

The portfolio, whose return is perfectly correlated with common factor $j$, with weights vector $X^j$, has the following properties:[6] (1) $(X^j)'B$, a row vector, which has zero elements, except for the $j$th column, which is unity; and (2) $(X^j)'E = E^j$. We call these portfolios the fundamental portfolios (or fundamental funds). Then, premultiplying Eq. (8) by the market portfolio, $(X^m)'$ and $(X^j)'$, we have

$$\begin{bmatrix} E^m - E_0 \\ E^f - E_0 1 \end{bmatrix} = \begin{bmatrix} \sigma_m^2, \sigma_{m1}, \ldots, \sigma_{mk} \\ \sigma_{1m}, \sigma_1^2, \ldots, 0 \\ \cdot, \cdot, \cdot, \ldots, \cdot \\ \cdot, \cdot, \cdot, \ldots, \cdot \\ \sigma_{km}, 0, \ldots, \sigma_k^2 \end{bmatrix} = \begin{bmatrix} R^m \\ -R^m h_1^m/M \\ \cdot \\ \cdot \\ -R^m h_k^m/M \end{bmatrix} \tag{9}$$

$$= \Sigma \begin{bmatrix} R^m \\ -H^m R^m/M \end{bmatrix},$$

where $E^f = [E^1, \ldots, E^k]'$; $E^m$ is the expected return on the market portfolio; $\sigma_j^2(\sigma_m^2)$ is the variance of the return on factor $j$ (the market portfolio); $\sigma_{mj}$ is the covariance between the market portfolio and factor $j$; and $h_j^m$ is the $j$th row of $H_f^m$.

Let us denote $\lambda_j(\lambda_m)$ for the risk premium for factor $j$ (the market portfolio). Then Eq. (9) can be written as

$$\lambda_j = E^j - E_0 = [\sigma_{jm} - \sigma_j^2 h_j^m/M]R^m, \ j = 1, \ldots, k \tag{10a}$$

$$\lambda_m = E^m - E_0 = [\sigma_m^2 - \sum_{j=1}^{k} \sigma_{mj} h_j^m/M]R^m. \tag{10b}$$

Equations (10a) and (10b) show that the risk premium for the common factor (market portfolio) is a function of the market relative risk aversion, the variance of the common factor (market portfolio), the covariance between the market portfolio and the common factor, and the market perception, $h_j^m$.

Substituting Eq. (9) into Eq. (8), we arrive at the equilibrium APT as follows:

$$E - E_0 1 = (\sigma_{am}, BD)\sum^{-1} \begin{bmatrix} E^m - E_0 \\ E^f - E_0 l \end{bmatrix}$$

$$= \beta_{a,mf} \begin{bmatrix} E^m - E_0 \\ E^f - E_0 1 \end{bmatrix} \tag{11a}$$

or

$$E_f - E_0 = \beta_{im}(E^m - E_0) + \beta_{i1}(E^1 - E_0) + \ldots + \beta_{ik}(Ek - E_0)$$

$$= \beta_{im}\lambda_m + \beta_{i1}\lambda_1 + \ldots + \beta_{ik}\lambda_k, \tag{11b}$$

where $\beta_{a,mf}$ is an $n\times(k+1)$ matrix of multiple regression betas for all assets on the market portfolio and on the assets perfectly correlated with the changes of the common factors.

Equation (11) is consistent with the UAPT of Wei and similar to the Connor APT. However, it is important to note that when the Connor condition (well-diversified market portfolio) is not imposed, the market portfolio factor enters the pricing relation explicitly as one of the priced factors. As a result, in order to obtain an exact pricing model in a factor economy, either the market portfolio should be well diversified or it should enter the pricing equation explicitly. Since the market portfolio is, in general, correlated with the common factors, $\beta_{a,mf} \neq (\beta_a^m, B)$, where $\beta_a^m$ is the beta coefficient in the CAPM. If and only if the market portfolio is independent of all common factors, the equality relationship holds.

# III. COMPARISON OF THE ROSS APT AND CAPMS WITH THE EQUILIBRIUM APT

This section shows that the Ross APT can be easily derived from the equilibrium APT by imposing the assumption that the portfolio held by an agent is perfectly diversified, that is, $(X^p)'\tilde{e} = 0$, which is unlikely in the finite-assets market. If $X'\tilde{e} = 0$, then the variance of wealth can be written as $\text{var}(\tilde{W}) = (W)^2\text{var}(\tilde{R}_p) = (W)^2 X'BDB'X$. Under this special situation, following the procedures in Section II, the equations corresponding to (7), (10a) and (11) can be written as follows:

$$T^p(E - E_0 1) = BDB'X^pW^p - BDH_f^p \tag{12}$$

$$\lambda_j - E^j - E_0 = (b_{jm} - h_j^m/M)\sigma_m^2 R^m, \tag{13}$$

$$E^i - E_0 = b_{i1}(E^1 - E_0) + \ldots + b_{ik}(E^k - E^{\text{o}})$$

$$= b_{i1}\lambda_1 + \ldots + b_{ik}\lambda_k. \tag{14}$$

It can be seen that Eq. (14) is exactly the Ross APT. However, the condition of the perfect diversification was imposed.

Note that the equilibrium APT of Eq. (11) is compatible with Long's CAPM, Merton's intertemporal CAPM, and Wei's UAPT. It is well known that the multi-period decision can be reduced to a single period decision with a derived utility function which is state dependent. Thus, the equilibrium APT of Eq. (11) can be interpreted as equivalent to the intertemporal asset pricing model if the factor realizations play the role of the state variables. Note also that Eq. (11) will reduce to the traditional CAPM if an investor's utility is only a function of the mean and variance of his or her end-of-period wealth. In this sense, the equilibrium APT is a hybrid form of the Ross APT and the CAPMs. Of particular interest is that the Ross APT is a special case of the equilibrium APT only when risk-averse investors are assumed to hold perfectly diversified portfolios.

Comparing Eq. (14) with Eq. (11), it is apparent that the market portfolio does not play any role explicitly in Eq. (14) but it does in Eq. (11). We can also derive Eq. (14) from Eq. (11) by imposing the Connor constraint. If the market portfolio is a well-diversified portfolio in the $k$-factor structure, then $E_m - E_0 = b_{m1}\lambda_1 + \ldots + b_{mk}\lambda_k$. Substituting this relationship into Eq. (11b), we can obtain Eq. (14). Thus, whether the market portfolio enters the asset pricing equation depends upon whether the market portfolio is well diversified in the finite-factor economy.

Recently, Dybvig and Ross (1985a) have analyzed security market line (SML) deviations caused by a choice of an inefficient market portfolio. In this paper, we have shown the APT deviations caused by the inefficient market portfolio defined in a factor structure.

# IV. CONCLUSION

This paper has developed the equilibrium APT which is an exact pricing model without any approximation or the assumption of perfect diversification in the market portfolio. The equilibrium APT is compared with the Ross–Connor APTs and the CAPMs. Of particular interest is that the Ross–Connor APT is a special case of the equilibrium APT only when investors are assumed to hold perfectly diversified portfolios or when the market portfolio is well diversified in a factor model. It is also shown that the equilibrium APT becomes equivalent to intertemporal asset pricing models if the factor realizations play the role of state variables. More important, the market portfolio plays an important role explicitly in the equilibrium APT. Thus, the APT appears to be subject to somewhat the same empirical problems as the CAPM, as pointed out by Shanken (1982, 1985). The equilibrium APT in this paper is, coincidentally, in the same spirit of the third alternative asset-pricing relation proposed by Shanken (1985) and is consistent with the model of Wei (1988) and McElroy and Burmeister (1988).

# NOTES

1. See Dybvig and Ross (1985b) for a support of the APT and a complete bibliography of articles on the APT. See also Shanken (1982, 1985) for a criticism of the APT.
2. Even though the market portfolio plays a crucial role in both our equilibrium APT and Connor's (1984) competitive APT, the purposes of the market portfolio are completely different from each other. The market portfolio in our model replaces the approximation of the Ross APT as a systematic factor common to all securities. On the other hand, the market portfolio in Connor's model is used to test the condition on which the idiosyncratic risk is completely diversified away. As Shanken (1985) points out, "The requirement that the market portfolio be well-diversified, with respect to a given set of factors, should be considered a joint hypothesis in a test of the Connor model."
3. For simplicity, we assume here for a moment that a risk-free asset does not exist. It is easy to generalize from the result in the absence of a risk-free asset to the case that a risk-free asset exists simply assuming that the weight of the portfolio includes the risk-free asset.
4. This argument has been supported by the recent empirical work by Chen, Roll, and Ross (1984). They found that factor scores are functions of state economic variables.
5. This is similar to the result derived from the intertemporal CAPM of Merton (1973).
6. Breeden (1979) has shown that it is not required to have a perfect correlation between the return on fund $j$ and the change in the state variable $j$. It is sufficient to derive the model with the maximum correlation between the return on fund $j$ and the change in state variable $j$.

# REFERENCES

Breeden, D. (1979). "An Intertemporal Asset Pricing Model with Stochastic Consumption and Investment Opportunities." *Journal of Financial Economics* (September): 265–296.

Chamberlain, G., and Rothschild, M. (1983). "Arbitrage, Factor Structure, and the Mean-Variance Analysis on Large Asset Markets." *Econometrica* (September): 1281–1304.

Chen, N. F., and Ingersoll, J. (1983). "Exact Pricing in Linear Factor Models with Finitely Many Assets: A Note." *Journal of Finance* (June): 985–988.

Chen, N. F., Roll, R., and Ross, S. A. (1984). "Economic Forces and the Stock Market: Testing the APT and Alternative Asset Pricing Theories." Mimeo.

Connor, G. (1984). "A Unified Beta Pricing Theory." *Journal of Economic Theory* (October): 13–31.

Dybvig, P., and Ross, S. (1985a). "The Analytics of Performance Measurement Using a Security Market Line." *Journal of Finance* (June): 401–416.

Dybvig, P., and Ross, S. (1985b). "Yes, the APT is Testable." *Journal of Finance* (September): 1173–1188.

Grinblatt, M., and Titman, S. (1983). "Factor Pricing in a Finite Economy." *Journal of Financial Economics* 12: 497–507.

Huberman, G. (1982). "A Simple Approach to Arbitrage Pricing Theory." *Journal of Economic Theory* (October): 183–191.

Losq, E., and J. Chateau. (1982). "A Generalization of the CAPM Based on a Property of the Covariant Operator." *Journal of Financial and Quantitative Analysis* (December): 783–797.

McElroy, M. and Burmeister, E. (1988). "Arbitrage Pricing Theory as a Restricted Nonlinear Multivariate Regression Model." *Journal of Business and Economic Statistics* (January): 29–42.

Merton, R. (1973). "An Intertemporal Capital Asset Pricing Model." *Econometrica* (September): 867–887.

Roll, R. (1977). "A Critique of the Asset Pricing Theory's Tests." *Journal of Financial Economics* (May): 129–176.

Ross, S. (1976). "The Arbitrage Theory of Capital Asset Pricing." *Journal of Economic Theory* (December): 341–360.

Ross, S. (1977). "Return, Risk, and Arbitrage." In *Risk and Return in Finance*, Vol. 1, edited by I. Friend and J. Bicksler. Cambridge, MA.

Shanken, J. (1982). "The Arbitrage Pricing Theory: Is It Testable?" *Journal of Finance* (December): 1129–1140.

Shanken, J. (1985). "Multi-Beta CAPM or Equilibrium-APT?: A Reply." *Journal of Finance* (September): 1189–1196.

Wei, R. (1988). "An Asset Pricing Theory Unifying the CAPM and APT." *Journal of Finance* (September): 881–892.

# THE ASYMMETRIC INFORMATION HYPOTHESIS AND DIVIDEND POLICY:

## A MICROSTUDY OF DIVIDEND SIGNALS

Said Elfakhani

## ABSTRACT

This research proposes a comprehensive new methodology to test multiattribute multisignals to explain prevailing dividend policies. The dividend signal has two dimensions: its quality as related to both the content (capital investment, capital structure and/or agency) and direction (favorable or unfavorable) of inside information and its strength as related to the magnitude of the dividend change (positive or negative). In this context, market reaction to dividend signals is tested around the dividend announcement. The results show that dividend changes must be evaluated in connection with the number and content of balance sheet changes made prior to the dividend announcement, and that the more uncertainty is resolved, the more useful is the dividend signal. The market reaction relies more on the information content and direction as well as the clarity of the signal than on the sign (positive or negative) of the dividend change.

Advances in Quantitative Analysis of Finance and Accounting,
Volume 2, Part B, pages 45–76.

ISBN: 1-55938-565-0

# I. INTRODUCTION

The theory of finance posits that the value of a firm is a function of its expected future cash flow. The market increases the value of a firm only if its expected rate of return (rather than its dividend yield) is greater than what is required by the market, given the same risk and with other things being equal. Following this reasoning, Modigliani and Miller (1961) conclude that dividend payouts should not theoretically change the aggregate riskiness of the firm, or increase its perceived value.

However, empirical evidence by Lintner (1956), Fama and Babiak (1968), and Black (1976) shows that firms in the United States behave as if they have certain target levels of dividend payouts that they are reluctant to change. They also suggest that U.S. corporations raise their dividend payouts only when they are sure that they can maintain them over the long term. Furthermore, practitioners argue that many large financial institutions and some investors, such as retired people, would rather receive dividend income, despite its tax disadvantage, than be forced to create their own dividends or receive capital gains. Thus, we have a conflict between theory and practice.

Given this behavior, what factors influence the firm's decision to pay, or not to pay, any dividends? Why are there such differences in dividend levels between similar firms? And more important, why are dissipative dividends welcomed by investors and how do they perceive changes in dividend policies?

This research investigates the effect of dividend announcements by exploring the interrelation between balance sheet signals and dividend signals using a new testing methodology. This procedure treats specific changes in the balance sheet and dividend payout as part of a signaling process of multiple stages with the intent of reducing the uncertainty regarding the firm. The importance of the dividend announcement increases with the successful reduction of uncertainty and the consistency of the signaling process; hence, this would be a case of the finest signal quality.

The modern finance literature focuses on the information content of dividend announcements. One implication of this hypothesis is that new information is transmitted to the market through dividend signals and that these signals reduce uncertainty regarding the firm's activities. This hypothesis is favorably substantiated in numerous studies, such as those of Pettit (1972, 1976), Charest (1978), and Asquith and Mullins (1983), and more recently Wansley and Lane (1987), Healy and Palepu (1988), and Wansley et al. (1991); although weak opposing evidence is reported by Watts (1978).

The approach to signaling theory used in this study is developed by Ross (1977), Bhattacharya (1979, 1980), Riley (1979), Hakansson (1982), Myers and Majluf (1984), John and Williams (1985), Miller and Rock (1985), and Makhija and Thompson (1986) for one signal and one attribute (investment), and Asquith and Mullins (1986), John and Kalay (1982, 1985), Ambarish, John, and Williams

(AJW) (1987), and Ofer and Thakor (1987) for one private attribute (investment) and multiple signals (two or less).

This theory contends that dividend changes signal valuable inside information related to the firm's future profitability which is not known to the market. In order to employ a dividend signal, firms may have to operate suboptimally by forgoing some positive net present value (NPV) projects and instituting a higher level of "residual" dividends (Miller and Rock, 1985).

Ambarish, John, and Williams (1987) further argue that when the asymmetric information condition results from the assets in place, a higher valued firm will forego positive NPV investments. If the source of the asymmetry is investment opportunities, a higher valued firm will use both dividend and investment signals by paying positive dividends and undertaking negative NPV projects, a decision that has less marginal cost for a high valued firm than a lower valued firm. Investment signals can, however, be replaced by net new equity signals. This complex, dynamic environment may require more than the two signals (investment and dividend) and extended periods to assimilate all nondissipative information that has been released.

The modern signaling theory is, however, limited because it postulates that asymmetric cash flow information reflects only one attribute (investment). The effects of other pertinent attributes, such as financing decisions and agency problems, on future profitability are not accounted for in dividend signaling equilibrium models (e.g., AJW). Furthermore, the theory restricts the number of signals that can be used by management; for instance, AJW (1987) assume that debt is zero, which implicitly denies the use of a financing decision as a signaling device. In other studies, the superiority of the dividend signal is questioned; for example, Miller and Rock (1985) argue that the role of the dividend signal is to help prediction of current earnings, which in turn signal future earnings. In contrast, Ofer and Siegel (1987) provide evidence that earnings forecasts that incorporate information contained in an unexpected change in dividend are more accurate predictors of the firm's expected performance than that made before the dividend change.

To summarize, the precise way in which the market uses the announced dividend policy of the firm is still an open theoretical question. The manner in which dividend announcements provide new and relevant information for the market is a subject that is ripe for expanded investigation.

In this paper, the effect of the interaction between earnings and dividend announcements as observed by Kane, Lee, and Marcus (1984) and Miller and Rock (1985) and AJW's (1987) signaling frameworks are integrated to produce an improved version of the current dividend signaling theory in which dividend change can be part of a signaling process (or multisignals sequence) that includes balance sheet and earnings signals followed by dividend signals. In this context, a dividend announcement can be seen as a "carrier" of new information pertaining to future profitability *and/or* an "interpreter" of *unclear* information that is embodied in other signals released as part of earnings announcements. The distinguishing contribution of this paper, however, is the methodology used to test multiattributes, multisignals. The dividend signal can exhibit only one of several possible levels of clarity and strength that may be associated with one or more firm-specific information attributes. In particular, the analysis focuses on two dimensions of the dividend signal: (1) its quality as related to the clarification it provides as to the future uncertainty of the firm and direction (favorable or unfavorable) of the inside information to be signaled; and (2) its strength as related to the magnitude of the dividend change. Although these dimensions may seem interrelated, a strong dividend change (increase or decrease) is necessary to demonstrate the extent (more or less) of clarification conveyed in the dividend announcement but it is not sufficient, since other signals in the financial statements along with the dividend signal determine the signaling quality.

Results show that the market response to dividend announcements depends on both the content (capital investment, capital structure, and agency) and direction of the information that is released by the firm and supported by an appropriate change in dividend payout, rather than solely on the sign (positive or negative) of the change. The signal should be consistent with the other signals provided in the earnings announcement, though.

An expansion of the signaling theory and a new methodology to test it are proposed in Section I, in which dividend signals are part of a multiple-signal process carrying one or more attributes. In Section II, hypotheses are formed to implement the methodology and data sources are described. The results and interpretations of the tests are found in Section III, with Section IV providing conclusions.

## II. THE SIGNALING THEORY: A PROPOSED TESTING METHODOLOGY

The signaling hypothesis assumes that managers possess inside information about investment opportunities (i.e., one attribute) that relates to better prediction of future cash flows (and therefore profitability), which is not known to the public.

One way to deliver this private information is by releasing various corporate news and financial statements. However, investors do not always trust the speeches and declarations of the firm's management so they may discount them and instead use financial statements "signals" to assess the firm's activities as indicated by the changes in the sources and uses of funds when compared to those of prior periods. Each of these changes may be considered a signal. For example, a significant drop in cash holdings may signal a liquidity problem, while a significant increase in investment may signal a positive NPV project. An equity for debt swap or debt for equity swap unaccompanied by notable changes in cash and investment may result in potential change in future cash flows that must be reflected in the stock valuation. In this context, the current signaling hypotheses reflect only capital investment information and fail to capture the possible effect of cash flows caused by changes in capital structure and other corporate decisions.

However, the interpretation of these signals as related to ex-post information is not always satisfactory and sometimes cannot clear up all the confusion or uncertainty about the firm's expected future success or intentions. In other words, uncertainty regarding the firm's value may be significantly reduced by balance sheet signals, and therefore a dividend change may not add new information. Alternatively, uncertainty may remain high; in this case management may use ex-ante dividend changes solely to continue the process of conveying relevant information to the public and therefore reducing uncertainty or may use other signals such as net new issues with or without a dividend change (AJW, 1987). The choice of the signaling process to be implemented requires valid economic sense and rigid cost-benefit analysis; hence the signal must be efficient and "clear." Conditions under which dividend signals would be superior (or inferior) to all other alternative nondissipative or dissipative signaling devices such as earnings announcements, stock repurchases, stock issues, bond redemptions, bond issues, equity-debt swaps, stock splits, stock dividends, spin-offs, divestures, and other possible signals have not been studied. This paper is no exception in the theoretical or modeling sense; however, it offers an opportunity to reexamine dividend announcements in relation to earnings and balance sheet announcements for possible ease of future modeling.

The following assumptions are made in order to test the proposed expansion of signaling theory:

1. There is an information asymmetry between managers and investors. Managers know more than the market and can anticipate the market reaction to dividend decisions (Stackelberg game).
2. Firm's attributes are directly related to changes in the balance sheet. Insiders use these changes to signal valuable asymmetric information to common stockholders.
3. Outsiders observe the changes in financial statements but cannot always fully infer all inside information.
4. The firm is owned by a homogeneous clientele of investors. Each clientele represents a consensus group with homogeneous expectations.
5. The market is efficient in the semistrong form; however, high uncertainty about the true value of the firm, perceived equally by all investors, may take a long time to be cleared. In this case a dividend as the sole signal may or may not serve to clarify this ambiguity.
6. No events or factors (endogenous or exogenous) other than earnings and dividend announcements have any discernible effect on security prices during the announcement period.
7. Any changes in the firm's balance sheet between an earnings announcement and a dividend announcement are zero.[1]

8. Stock returns are independent and stationary over time with finite variance. Hence, portfolio returns, given a large sample, have a log-normal distribution.

## A. The Model

Near cash ($C$) is defined as cash, marketable securities, accounts receivable, and any other current assets except inventory. Investment ($I$) is defined as all net fixed assets plus inventory. Debt ($B$) is defined as short- and long-term liabilities, including preferred stocks. Finally, common stocks (par) and paid-in-capital are combined into one common stock account ($CS$), while retained earnings ($RE$) is handled separately.

At any date $q$, absolute changes in uses of funds would reflect equal absolute changes in sources of funds, and therefore,

$$\Delta C_q + \Delta I_q = \Delta B_q + \Delta CS_q + \Delta RE_q, \tag{1}$$

where $\Delta(\ )_q =$ is the change in ( ) from date $q - 1$ to $q$.

During each quarter $q$ of the firm's operation, the following scenario normally takes place:

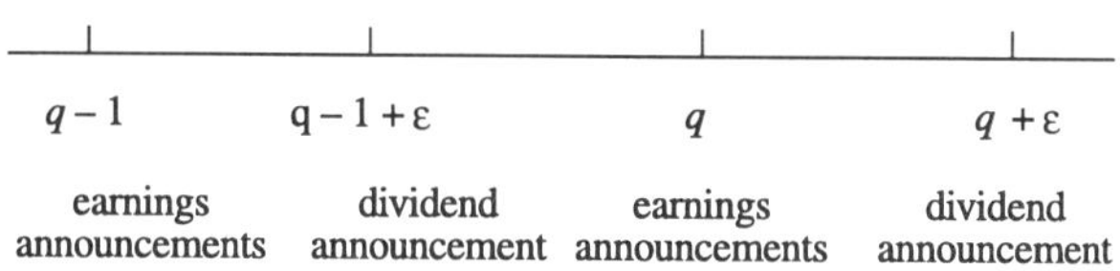


where $q = 1, \ldots, T$; $\varepsilon =$ a few days into the quarter during which management first announces its quarterly financial statements and decides on the dividend to be paid. The financial statements reflect the changes (positive or negative) in the firm's activities from quarter to quarter, and these changes are known to the market upon the release of the new balance sheet for quarter $q$. The new dividends are then announced at $q + \varepsilon$.[2]

The conjecture is that, in some cases, dividend announcements can eliminate ex-post confusion or confirm ex-post understanding; hence, dividends are treated as "interpreters" or "translators" with no signaling pertaining to future activities. On other occasions, dividend announcements "signal" information about future activities including, but not limited to, the sign and magnitude of future cash flows. Thus, the market reacts to their announcements in this framework. This is consistent with the notion of dividend announcements reflecting information on "assets in place" as argued by Myers and Majluf (1984) and AJW (1987).

In this context, the value of the firm $V_j(g)$ as assessed by managers or insiders is a function of ($g$) which is the set of information items revealed through changes in the sources and uses of funds. Each of these items can be considered as an ex-post attribute signal. Thus, in this model, $j$ is a multivariate private information attribute(s) reflecting the information set contained in $g$.

$$V_j(g) = a_j + b_jK(g) + c_jL(g), \tag{2}$$

where

$V_j(g)$ = market value of the firm at the dividend announcement day as predicted by insiders (CEOs and the members of the board of directors) after the release of earnings and financial statements,

$a_j$ = market value of the firm before the dividend announcement. Assuming asymmetric information, this value reflects a subset of the valuation for assets and liabilities currently in place and opportunities that have been identified,

$K(g)$ = present value of expected incremental cash flows from existing assets and liabilities, known only to insiders,

$L(g)$ = present value of expected incremental cash flows from investment opportunities and other activities such as changes in capital structure and agency costs, known only to insiders.

In other words, the value of the firm as estimated by insiders differs from that observed by outsiders by two additional incremental values; one pertains to existing assets and liabilities which may be evaluated differently by managers and outsiders (i.e., $K(g) \neq 0$ and $L(g) = 0$), and the other relates to future plans which are not anticipated by marginal investors (i.e., $K(g) = 0$ and $L(g) \neq 0$). Both values, however, can be fully or partially transmitted to the market through dividend signals. Few examples may make things clearer. A firm that has undertaken a new project financed solely with debt sent a positive capital budgeting signal. This signal, however, is mixed with an increase in debt ratio and possibly more restrictive bond indentures and an increase in risk. The first signal ($\Delta I > 0$) (i.e., reflecting capital budgeting attribute) had already been captured when the investment decision was made; the effect of the capital structure signal (i.e., the higher debt ratio) is still to be clarified. If the partial increase in leverage risk is overridden by more future cash savings as a result of financing the project with debt rather than equity, an immediate cash advance in the form of a dividend increase would provide a convincing argument and thus reduce or eliminate any confusion about the firm's assets and financing policy in place.[3] In this capacity, the dividend acts as an interpreter of ex-post events. A firm that accumulates cash financed with new equity or debt that is not invested yet and follows that by increased dividends may "signal" some new information to the market about future investments. In this case, the market tries to analyze balance sheet signals along with the dividend signal in terms of the expected (possibly true) market value compared to the market value observed before the signal was released.[4] Dividend announcement can also signal a conflict between shareholders and bondholders (agency problem). For instance, increased dividends financed with debt when there is no foreseen investment opportunity may serve as a means of transferring some wealth from unprotected debtholders to shareholders.[5] This action can result in a depressed bond price. A dividend can also be used to reduce the effect of equity dilution, as argued by John and Williams (1985). Thus, this model expands the concept of signaling from one attribute (investment opportunities), as is shown by AJW (1987) or others, to include two additional attributes, financing decision and agency problem, each or any combination of which may influence market assessment of the firm's future cash flows and therefore its value.

It must be noted that by design the intercept $a_j$ is set as a constant positive known ex-post by the market. Management, to certain extent, has control over the process of revealing the true values of $K(g)$, $L(g)$, $b_j$, and $c_j$. This control may be exercised through dividend payout and the quality of the signaling process.

The more undervalued the firm is perceived by insiders [i.e., the larger $K(g)$ and/or $L(g)$ is], the greater the incentive for a change in dividend policy. This is directly related to the strength and direction (favorable or unfavorable) of the dividend change. It is argued that the deeper the undervaluation of the firm, the larger the magnitude (strength) of the dividend change. The direction of the change (positive or negative) must, however, be consistent with prior changes in the sources and uses of funds. Under certain conditions, no change in dividend payouts may result in market disappointment, which is expressed in a continuing or worsening undervaluation. Of course, a negative incremental value will force $V_j(g)$ below $a_j$ [Eq. (2)].

The parameters $b_j$ and $c_j$ are known only after the dividend announcement and should take any value between zero and one (although they may occasionally take negative values). In theory, the more the dividend signal reveals about the true value of $K(g)$ and/or $L(g)$, the closer the value of $b_j$ and/or $c_j$ to one. This process is directly connected to the quality of the signal. In other words, a "clearer" signal reveals up to the full incremental value to outsiders.

One feature of Eq. (2) is that it distinguishes between dividend decisions as "interpreters" of current asymmetric information (i.e., $c_j$ equals zero) or as "carriers" of new information about future actions (i.e., $b_j$ is zero). Negative $b_j$ or $c_j$ when $K(g)$ or $L(g)$ is positive reflects the market disappointment at the quality of the dividend signal. Positive $b_j$ and $c_j$ involves a more complex signaling quality and interpretation.

## B. Quality of Dividend Signals

Since the asymmetric information to be signaled by dividend changes can include several diverse attributes with corroborating direction or possibly conflicting effect on stock price, the interpretation of balance sheet signals (i.e., perception of the true firm value) may not always be clear. If balance sheet signals provide a high degree of information clarity (and therefore a high degree of certainty) about the firm's attributes, then a consensus firm value is equally perceived by all investors; hence these signals are of the finest quality. In this case, dividend announcement confirms this certainty and may *or* may not result in additional market reassessment. On the other hand, balance sheet signals may send positive and negative news at the same time, the net effect of which is still not known prior to the dividend announcement. In this case a dividend may play significant role in resolving uncertainty. If it significantly reduces uncertainty, the dividend signal is of great value and therefore of finest quality. If it fails to do so or if the dividend signal is not efficient (i.e., it is economically unjustifiable), it might take other signals unrelated to financial statement and/or more time to net out the information effects and to fully capture them in the market price. In other words, resolving uncertainty can be achieved right after the earnings announcements, can wait until the dividend announcement, or can use other signaling devices. This results in several levels of balance sheet-dividend signaling quality.

The quality of the signaling process is defined by (1) its clarity as to resolving uncertainty with respect to the firm's attributes and direction (favorable or unfavorable) of these attributes and (2) the speed by which the market makes inferences from the released multiple signals. This concept of clarity as related to the quality of the signalling process is depicted as follows.

| earnings announcements | dividend announcement | |
|---|---|---|
| *Uncertainty* | *Uncertainty* | *Dividend Signal Quality* |
| Low | Low | Neutral |
| High | Low | Clear |
| High | High | Unclear |

Thus dividend signal quality is defined three ways: neutral, clear, and unclear.

*Neutral signal.* A signal is neutral when there is one attribute inferring one value before and after the dividend announcement. Upon the release of an earnings announcement and therefore balance sheet signals, there is little uncertainty and hence investors know precisely how to interpret a later announced positive or negative change in dividends as a signal of the firm's expectations about the future. After the dividend announcement, reassured investors will react according to their understanding of the revealed attribute and correctly value the firm through the share price.

*Clear signal.* A signal is clear when, prior to the dividend announcement, there is little certainty about the firm's state. This occurs when there are at least two attributes contained in earnings announcement with conflicting directions (favorable and unfavorable), but after the dividend announcement it becomes clear as to which direction (favorable *or* unfavorable) can be inferred from those attributes. Managers use the dividend change to signal a clear indication of the valuableness of the information released.

*Unclear signal.* A signal is unclear if the high uncertainty and the conflicting attribute news before *and* after the dividend announcement are partially resolved or not resolved. This is not to say that one dividend signal has zero value, but it would not have the same value as a higher quality signal. Since various investors have and react to different beliefs, we observe only the result of their net trade.

The conjecture is that management would try to send only a neutral or clear signal and that no attempt will be made to maintain high uncertainty. An unclear signal is likely dictated by complicated changes in the investment and financing decisions prior to the dividend announcement. It is also argued that the market reaction to an unclear signal should be slower because it will take more time to release scarce new information and to be captured in the market price. Prior to the dividend announcement, the market cannot tell which of the two interactions will prevail ex-ante but can still speculate. Illustrative examples of different quality signals and how are they formulated are presented.

| *Changes in Balance Sheet [Eq. (1)]* | *Changes in Dividends* | *Assigned Quality* |
|---|---|---|
| $\Delta C > 0, \Delta I > 0, \Delta B > 0, \Delta CS = 0, \Delta RE = 0$ | $\Delta D > 0$ | Neutral |
| $\Delta C > 0, \Delta I = 0, \Delta B > 0, \Delta CS < 0, \Delta RE = 0$ | $\Delta D > 0$ | Clear |
| $\Delta C > 0, \Delta I = 0, \Delta B > 0, \Delta CS < 0, \Delta RE > 0$ | $\Delta D = 0$ | Unclear |

The first combination implies that the firm has undertaken a new project financed by debt; hence, this is capital budgeting information. At the same time, the firm experienced an increase in liquidity ($C$). A stable dividend policy may not influence the clarity of the situation and therefore the dividend signal is treated as "neutral." In this case, most or all of the market adjustment will take place right after the earnings announcement. However, an increase in the dividend would reinforce this positive interpretation. In the latter case the "neutral" signal would be perceived "favorably" by the market. The second entry presents a case of a debt for equity swap unaccompanied by new investment. The effect of this change is not certain and its interpretation can be a capital restructuring decision *or* a transfer of wealth. The latter is confirmed by a dividend increase. Thus, this signal is labeled "clear." A similar debt for equity swap, but with a positive change in ($RE$) and no change in dividends, is presented in the last entry. The market classifies this case as "unclear" because it can be associated with any of the three different scenarios: possible future investment (i.e., $L(g) > 0$) supported by an accumulation of cash (positive or negative signal); a possible transfer of wealth to shareholders (agency problem), or a possible refinancing decision (could be either a positive or negative signal). The lack of a change in dividend payout eliminates the agency motivation (wealth transfer) behind the change in capital structure, resulting in a mixed attribute (investment financing), the net result of which is not yet known.

The process of classifying signaling quality may seem subjective since conflicting views among various informed analysts may result in different quality classifications. In this research, this is perfectly permissible because this situation is similar to other cases where financial analysts' forecasts of earnings per share can vary significantly. The conjecture is that the market will average all of these into one particular quality classification.

Consequently, the three levels of signal quality are ranked from finest to lowest, a clear signal being the highest quality and a neutral signal being the lowest quality. The conjecture, however, is that the market will react least to the neutral signal since no or little new information is provided and since there is little uncertainty. The greater the increase in the knowledge of the firm's activities resulting from the dividend signal, the more valuable it is to the market, and the more market reaction should be observed following the signal.

## C. Further Insights into the Model

The relationship between Eqs. (1) and (2) can be further clarified. The inside information signaled by a dividend change has at least three components: (1) the *attribute* (investment, financing, and/or agency), (2) the *direction* (favorable, unfavorable), and (3) the *strength* (strong, weak).

The attribute conveyed to the market by the balance sheet-dividend signal can include management's belief on up to three attributes. The number of attributes ($j$) signaled increases directly with the increase in nonzero changes in Eq. (1). However, each type of attribute can require more than one change in the five balance sheet variates. A new investment financed by a debt issue requires changes to two variates, $\Delta I$ and $\Delta B$.

The release of information attributes in Eq. (1) conditioned by the level of clarity may be fully or partially captured in $a_j$ [Eq. (2)]. In the partial case, management uses a dividend change to "translate" or "signal" the true value of $K(g)$ and/or $L(g)$. This can cause the market to react in a positive or negative manner depending on whether the direction of the news is favorable or unfavorable or whether the dividend change is in the correct direction. A favorable response would be reflected in $V_j(g) > a_j$.

The third component, strength (i.e., strong or weak) pertains to the market reaction to the dividend change, its sign (+,0,–), and its magnitude.[6] This in turn depends on the magnitude of $K(g)$ and/or $L(g)$ and the quality of the signal.

## III. TEST DESIGN AND DATA SOURCES

Following the suggested work in which signaling is expected to operate, three hypotheses are formed to interpret the relationship between dividend announcements and market reaction after consideration of the quality and the sign of the dividend change. In particular, the hypotheses are as follows.

*Hypothesis 1*

Dividend announcements do not convey new and valuable information beyond that provided by other management announcements.

This hypothesis tests whether dividend announcements, as distinguished from earnings and other statements releases by the firm, can influence the market evaluation of price. This result holds in general and regardless of the sign of the dividend change or its rejection of this hypothesis corroborates earlier evidence on the dividend information content effect.

*Hypothesis 2*

The dividend change sign (increase (+), decrease (–), stable (0)) does not affect the value of the dividend announcement.

Rejection of hypothesis 2 implies that the market reaction to the signal depends on the change in dividend payout.

*Hypothesis 3*

For each unique combination of changes in the firm's sources and uses of funds, dividend announcements do not convey any new and valuable information beyond that provided by other financial statement signals.

Rejection of this hypothesis for any particular substate suggests that a correct interpretation and a proper market reaction to any dividend announcement must incorporate all readily available information from early releases of the firm's financial statements. A dividend signal is valuable if it communicates significant new information above what was known to the market before the announcement. In this context, a dividend increase (decrease) does not necessarily imply good (bad) news unless it is consistent with prior financial statement signals. The data and statistics allowing for the testing of these hypotheses are described next.

### A. Design Description

The sampled data are first arranged so they describe all possible states of the firms' activities in one period (quarter) prior to the dividend announcement so that dividend changes can be categorized with respect to quality. The effect of a dividend change will be observed around the dividend announcement day of that period.

The strength of the signal is captured by the sign of the dividend change from one quarter to another quarter, which is initially classified as: increase, decrease, or stable. Omitted dividends are treated as decreases in dividends because boards of directors often announce that no dividend payments will be made for several quarters following their omission. Because these predictions are frequently known to the market, any negative effect to a dividend omission would have been *anticipated* well before the dividend announcement (Kalay and Lowenstein [1985]). The effect of *unanticipated* dividend omission, however, can be captured when examining the dividend decrease category. The sudden remission of a dividend payout policy is included under increases in dividends for sampling purposes. In this context, dividend changes are measured by the dollar change in dividend per share from one quarter to the next.[7]

Changes in the firms' activities from one quarter to another are measured by positive, negative, or zero dollar changes in cash, investment, debt, common stocks, and retained earnings. The changes in these five major items of the balance sheet allow for $3^5$ (i.e., 243) different states ($\theta$), where each state represents a unique combination of these changes (i.e., a unique ($g$) information set). For each state, three substates ($\theta_s$) also arise depending on whether the announced dividend change is positive, negative, or zero, delivering $j$ information attributes. Thus, there is a maximum of 729 distinct substates, which is a large number to analyze and interpret. However, the final number of states and substates is reduced by a number of infeasible states where unequal or opposite changes in assets and liabilities on the same balance sheet imply that sources and uses of funds are unequal.[8] Also, if there are fewer than five sample points in one substate, it is dropped since it provides little or no opportunity for empirical testing. There are 95 firm states and 147 substates which meet the conditions outlined above. Each substate is then labeled by signal quality, expected direction of news, type(s) of private information available prior to the dividend announcement, and type(s) of information filtered after the announcement.[9]

### B. Sampling Criteria and Data Sources

All firms on both the Compustat quarterly tapes and Center for Research in Security Prices at the University of Chicago (CRSP) tapes are filtered with respect to the following restrictive criteria:

1. Firms must use the same quarterly fiscal system.
2. Regulated firms are discarded because they have regulated constraints on earnings and dividend payments.
3. Firms that observed noisy events around the estimation period are discarded. Such events include major management changes, significant lawsuits, labor disputes, and so on. This filter allows close examination of dividend information effect.
4. Firms reporting negative earnings for two consecutive quarters are discarded for those two quarters. Firms with negative earnings in one quarter

and positive earnings in the adjacent quarters are included in the sample. Although it could be considered a selection bias, consecutive negative earnings are discarded because it is not expected that managers or the market would rely as much on dividends as an important device in the presence of a concern about their firm's survival.[10]

5. Nondividend distributions made near a dividend announcement disqualify the dividend events from the sample.
6. Firms which pay only semiannual or annual dividends are not included.
7. Cash dividends announced on the same day as stock dividends are included since noncash dividends are treated as nontaxable distributions and therefore should not disqualify the dividend event.
8. Cash dividends announced on the same day as stock splits are discarded. Also eliminated are the cases where stock splits fall within the dividend event period or the comparison period.
9. Nonregular extra, special, or year-end dividends are excluded because they are short-lived and therefore they do not carry any signaling value. Regular dividend announcements made on the same day as nonregular dividends are sampled.
10. Firms which undertake mergers or acquisitions during any period are discarded for the year in which it occurs because of the possible effect of these events on changes in their activities, earnings level, and dividend policy.
11. Firms which announce earnings after dividend announcements are not included because dividend signals will be less useful in interpreting ex-post changes in the firm's financial statements.[11]
12. Firms must have their earnings announcements made at least five trading days before dividend announcements but not earlier than twenty days. Ex-dividend days should occur at least five days after dividend announcement days. This condition is necessary in order to isolate the dividend announcement effect from any possible noise coming from earnings announcements.[12]
13. Less actively traded stocks are included if they are traded at least on the announcement day.[13]

Standard and Poor's quarterly Compustat tape data are the source for book values of quarterly cash balances, investment, leverage, common stocks (including paid-in-capital), retained earnings, earnings per share, and earnings announcement dates. Dividends per share, dividend announcement dates, ex-dividend days, and daily stock prices and returns are available on the CRSP tape. Dates of earnings and dividend announcements are from CRSP or from the *Annual Wall Street Journal Index*. Omitted dividend announcement dates are available only from the *Annual Wall Street Journal Index*, and omitted ex-dividend days are reported in the *Wall Street Journal*.[14]

The sampling period is from January 1, 1976, through December 31, 1985, i.e., a total of forty quarters. The total number of sampled firms is 478 and the total sampled events is 3,791.

## C. Tests Description

The now classical procedure for testing for the effects of announcement events is to investigate whether there are abnormal stock returns on or around the announcement date, as in Asquith and Mullins (1983). If abnormal returns are not observed, then the null hypothesis is not rejected. One accepted methodology for using daily data relies on the use of mean-adjusted returns. This method is shown by Brown and Warner (1985) to be as good as the market model in detecting abnormal daily returns. It requires only the assumption of the stationarity of the returns-generating process. Moreover, this method does not require a determination of the kind of risk (systematic or unsystematic) or a specification of the market portfolio as in the market model. However, this approach requires that the dividend announcement days not be clustered in calendar time; otherwise, it will lose its advantage over the market model. Given the fact that this research design includes large numbers of substates for each period, clustering is not a serious problem.

The mean-adjusted returns model assumes that the return-generating process for stock $i$ is stochastic of the form:

$$\tilde{R}_{i,t} = \hat{\mu}_i + \tilde{\varepsilon}_{i,t}\,, \tag{3}$$

where

$E(\tilde{\varepsilon}_{i,t}) =$ 0; and $\text{cov}(\tilde{\varepsilon}_{i,t}, \tilde{\varepsilon}_{i,t-1}) = 0$; $v_{i,t}$
$R_{i,t} =$ return on (firm) stock $i$ at day $t$; and
$\mu_i =$ unbiased estimate of the mean return of stock $i$ prior to the event period.

In this problem, each substate represents an event to be studied. The associated dividend announcements provide the event sample points, which depend in turn on both a number of different firms and times. For the purpose of testing, a period of ten trading days (days –4, . . , +5) is defined around each dividend announcement date: four days before the announcement day; the announcement day and the day after, and four days after the announcement day. A nonevent period is set at fifteen trading days in length ending at least ten days prior to the earnings announcement date in such a way as to be as free as possible of any other related announcement effects.[15] The abnormal returns are computed for event sample $k(e_{lk}(i,q))$ in substate $(\theta_s)$ at time $t$ in quarter $q$. The average abnormal returns $(\overline{AR}_{s,t})$ are calculated by forming an equally weighted portfolio of all individual abnormal returns for each event day $t$. This average is standardized using the portfolio standard deviation over the nonevent period.[16]

For each substate, event days are grouped into three subperiods ($n$) and one overall period. The first period includes preannouncement days, –4, . . . , –1. The second period includes both the announcement day 0 and day 1 because sometimes the dividend announcement is reported at the end of the announcement day so that there will be no market reaction until the next day. The third subgroup includes postannouncement days 2, . . . , 5. The overall period includes days –4 . . . , 0, . . . 5. It is now possible to form the cumulative average abnormal returns ($\overline{CAR}$) for each substate ($\theta_s$). To do so, define: $t = -4, \ldots, -1$, for $n = 1$; $t = 0,1$, for $n = 2$; $t = 2, \ldots, 5$, for $n = 3$; $t = -4, \ldots, 0, \ldots 5$ for $n = 4$; and

$$\overline{CAR}_{s,n} = \sum_{t=1}^{l_n} \overline{AR}_{sn,t} \,. \tag{4}$$

The hypothesis to be tested is defined for every subperiod and for the overall announcement period as

$$H_0\colon \overline{CAR}_{s,n} = 0$$

$$H_A\colon \overline{CAR}_{s,n} \neq 0.$$

To test this hypothesis, the following student $t$-statistic is used:

$$t^* = \overline{CAR}_{s,n}/\sqrt{l_n}\,\overline{\sigma}_s, \tag{5}$$

where $l_n$ is the number of days in subperiod $n$ and $\overline{\sigma}_s$ equals 1.

The purpose of dividing the substate period into three subperiods is to identify the timing of the response of the market to dividend signals before, on, or after the announcement. The results of testing the hypotheses are discussed next.

## IV. RESULTS AND INTERPRETATIONS

Table 1 displays substates and sampled points which are classified by signal quality, information attribute(s), and the direction of the dividend change. The table is divided into three horizontal panels, each representing one level of signal quality, and the different types of attribute information and dividend changes in each case have been identified within each level of signal quality. For example, the first row refers to substates in which firms made an "investment" decision by increasing their capital investment ($\Delta I > 0$). The second entry is an example of a "pure" financing decision, where sampled firms have adjusted their capital structure with no apparent changes in capital investments. Table 1 displays 26 substates in this class; 6 of them have experienced dividend increases, 17 have stable dividends, and 3 show dividend decreases. The numbers in parentheses represent the total number of sample points for each cell.

*Table 1.* Substates Classified on Signal Quality, Attribute, and Dividend Change Sign

| | | *Dividend Change Sign* | | | |
|---|---|---|---|---|---|
| *Signal Quality* | *Signal Attributes* | *Dividend Increase (+) State Sample-Pts.* | *Stable Dividend (0) State Sample-Pts.* | *Dividend Decreases (–) State Sample-Pts.* | *Total State Sample-Pts.* |
| Neutral | Investment | 6 (149) | 17 (1014) | 3 (44) | 26 (1207) |
| | Financing | 3 (18) | 5 (255) | 1 (5) | 9 (278) |
| | Agency | 6 (80) | 3 (171) | —— | 9 (251) |
| Clear | Investment | 1 (6) | 7 (362) | 2 (33) | 10 (401) |
| | Agency | 1 (6) | —— | —— | 1 (6) |
| | Investment-financing | —— | 5 (72) | —— | 5 (72) |
| | Investment-agency | 13 (252) | 9 (253) | 1 (7) | 23 (512) |
| Unclear | Investment | 1 (6) | 1 (8) | —— | 2 (14) |
| | Financing | —— | 1 (13) | —— | 1 (13) |
| | Investment-financing | —— | 15 (128) | —— | 15 (128) |
| | Investment-agency | 7 (54) | 17 (347) | 2 (15) | 26 (416) |
| | Financing-agency | 2 (35) | 2 (152) | 1 (11) | 5 (198) |
| | Investment-financing agency | 1 (8) | 12 (269) | 2 (18) | 15 (295) |
| Total | | 41 (614) | 94 (3044) | 12 (133) | 147 (3791) |

*Notes:* Numbers in parentheses represent sample points for that particular cell. The sample period is 1976–1985.

The table shows a total of 147 substates, which are distributed as follows: 44 substates with neutral signals, 39 clear substates, and 64 unclear substates with (1,736), (991), and (1,064) sample points, respectively. There are 41 substates with dividend increases, 94 with stable dividends, and 12 dividend decreasing substates that include (614), (3,044), and (133) sample points, respectively. It is notable from the table that about 80% of the sampled events have stable dividends (i.e., zero change) and are distributed over 64% of the substates. Of these events, almost half sent neutral signals that added little information to what was already known to the market, and about one-third represented strong ambiguous (unclear) cases where dividend changes could have little clarification value. Most of the remaining 20% of the sampled firms used dividend changes to send clear and unclear signals when they were urgently needed to reduce uncertainty due to the complexity of the firms' activities. This observation is consistent with prior literature which argues that firms

*Table 2.* Substates Classified on Signal Quality, Dividend Change Sign, and Number of Balance Sheet Variates Changing Simultaneously

| Signal Quality | Dividend Change | *Zero Variate* | | *One Variate* | | *Two Variate* | | *Three Variates* | | *Four Variates* | | *Five Variates* | | *Total* | |
|---|---|---|---|---|---|---|---|---|---|---|---|---|---|---|---|
| | | *State* | *(Sample)* | *State* | *(Sample)* | *State* | *(Sample)* | *State* | *(Sample)* | *State* | *(Sample)* | *State* | *(Sample)* | *State* | *(Sample)* |
| | Dividend increases | 1 | (11) | 5 | (112) | 6 | (97) | 2 | (21) | 1 | (6) | — | — | 15 | (247) |
| Neutral | Stable dividends | 1 | (113) | 8 | (598) | 11 | (590) | 4 | (118) | 1 | (21) | — | — | 25 | (1440) |
| | Dividend decreases | 1 | (9) | 1 | (20) | 2 | — | — | — | — | — | — | — | 4 | (49) |
| | Dividend increases | — | — | — | — | 2 | (40) | 5 | (106) | 6 | (73) | 2 | (45) | 15 | (264) |
| Clear | Stable dividends | — | — | — | — | 4 | (84) | 10 | (429) | 6 | (158) | 1 | (16) | 21 | (687) |
| | Dividend decreases | — | — | — | — | — | — | 2 | (33) | 1 | (7) | — | — | 3 | (40) |
| | Dividend increases | — | — | — | — | 3 | (30) | 3 | (34) | 3 | (29) | 2 | (10) | 11 | (103) |
| Unclear | Stable dividends | — | — | — | — | 8 | (180) | 13 | (283) | 18 | (309) | 9 | (145) | 48 | (917) |
| | Dividend decreases | — | — | — | — | — | — | 2 | (19) | 2 | (15) | 1 | (10) | 5 | (44) |
| Total | | 3 | (133) | 14 | (730) | 36 | (1041) | 41 | (1043) | 38 | (618) | 15 | (226) | 147 | (3791) |

*Notes:* Numbers in parentheses represent sample points for that particular cell. The sample period is 1976–1985.

do not change dividend payouts unless they can maintain the new levels and supports this author's conjecture that the market reacts to dividend announcements in terms of their signal quality, the type(s) of information, and relevant news content, as well as changes in dividend policy.

Table 2 demonstrates that the subjective criterion used to assign dividend signals to the various quality levels reveals an interesting observation. The majority (82%) of neutral substates do not involve changes to more than two of the five balance sheet variates ($\Delta C$, $\Delta I$, $\Delta B$, $\Delta CS$, $\Delta RE$) at the same time. In other words, fewer changes in the financial position are normally associated with the lower quality "neutral" signals. Clear signals, however, are clustered around two (15.4%), three (43.6%), and four (33.3%) changing variates; clear signals are never associated with less than two variate changes. A similar pattern, although skewed to the right, can be observed with unclear signals which are clustered around three (28.1%), four (35.9%), and five (18.8%) simultaneous variate changes. The relationship between the quality of the signal and the number of changing variates supports the idea that conditional ambiguity which is associated with a larger number of changes in the balance sheet from one quarter to another can be fully clarified by a higher quality signal (clear) or partially clarified by a lower quality signal (unclear).

Table 3 reports the results for hypotheses 1 and 2. Inspection of the table reveals that announcements of dividends in general contain significant information for the market. Hypothesis 1 is rejected at the 0.03 level. Using a significance level of 0.05, a positive change in dividends is significant. The minus change in dividends is significant only at the 0.12 level.[17]

*Table 3.* Car Results for Dividend Signal Hypotheses

| *Hypothesis* | *Preannouncement* (4 to –1) | *On Announcement* (0 to + 1) | *Postannouncement* ( + 2 to + 5) | *Total* (–4 to + 5) |
|---|---|---|---|---|
| Hypothesis 1 | –0.55 | 6.55** | 0.99 | 7.00* |
| | (0.40) | (0.07) | (0.33) | (0.03) |
| Hypothesis 2 | | | | |
| + | 1.82 | 12.35* | 2.63 | 16.80* |
| | (0.22) | (0.04) | (0.14) | (0.01) |
| 0 | –0.91 | 3.44 | 0.08 | 2.61 |
| | (0.34) | (0.15) | (0.48) | (0.22) |
| – | –0.18 | 2.38 | 1.74 | 3.93 |
| | (0.47) | (0.17) | (0.22) | (0.12) |

*Notes:* Conventional *t*-test methodology: CARs are cumulative of standardized portfolio average abnormal return for all three subevent periods and for the total event period and are in percent. Hypothesis 1 pertains to dividend announcements in general and hypothesis 2 relates to the sign of the change in dividends. Numbers in parentheses represent *p*-values. The sample period is 1976–1985.

*Significant at the 0.05 level.

**Significant at the 0.10 level.

*Table 4.* $\overline{CAR}$ Results for Dividend Neutral Signal Hypothesis

| *State of Balance Sheet Changes* | *Sample Points* | *Cumulative Abnormal Returns* *Before* | *On* | *After* | *Overall* |
|---|---|---|---|---|---|
| **A. Investment Attribute** | | | | | |
| $\Delta C>0, \Delta I>0, \Delta B>0, \Delta CS=0, \Delta RE>0, \Delta D>0$ | 6[4] | 3.35** | 2.09 | 0.45 | 5.89* |
| | | (0.10) | (0.19) | (0.42) | (0.05) |
| $\Delta C>0, \Delta I=0, \Delta B=0, \Delta CS>0, \Delta RE=0, \Delta D>0$ | 44[31] | 3.01 | 5.41** | 3.16 | 11.58* |
| | | (0.12) | (0.09) | (0.11) | (0.01) |
| $\Delta C=0, \Delta I>0, \Delta B>0, \Delta CS=0, \Delta RE>0, \Delta D=0$ | 6[2] | –0.07 | –2.41 | –6.23* | –8.70* |
| | | (0.49) | (0.17) | (0.03) | (0.02) |
| $\Delta C=0, \Delta I=0, \Delta B=0, \Delta CS>0, \Delta RE=0, \Delta D<0$ | 20[14] | 2.61 | –1.08 | 2.84** | 4.37** |
| | | (0.15) | (0.30) | (0.07) | (0.08) |
| $\Delta C=0, \Delta I=0, \Delta B=0, \Delta CS=0, \Delta RE=0, \Delta D=0$ | 113[62] | –1.47 | 2.73 | –5.67* | –4.41** |
| | | (0.26) | (0.15) | (0.04) | (0.10) |
| **B. Financing Attribute** | | | | | |
| $\Delta C<0, \Delta I=0, \Delta B<0, \Delta CS<0, \Delta RE=0, \Delta D>0$ | 6[6] | 7.56* | 1.32 | –0.29 | 8.58* |
| | | (0.02) | (0.26) | (0.45) | (0.01) |
| **C. Agency Attribute** | | | | | |
| $\Delta C>0, \Delta I=0, \Delta B>0, \Delta CS<0, \Delta RE=0, \Delta D>0$ | 8[8] | 5.61* | 12.07* | –1.40 | 16.28* |
| | | (0.04) | (0.04) | (0.27) | (0.01) |

*Notes:* Conventional t-test methodology: $\overline{CAR}$s are cumulative of standardized portfolio average abnormal returns for all three subevent periods and for the total event period and are in percent. Each portfolio represents one substate where each Δ refers to a change in one balance sheet item from one quarter to another and that a change can be positive (>0), negative (<0), or no change (=0). Sample points in each portfolio are reported with the numbers in brackets representing the events that had an overall CAR sign consistent with that of the substate portfolio. Numbers in parentheses represent *p*-values. The sample period is 1976–1985.
*Significant at the 0.05 level.
**Significant at the 0.10 level.

Tables 4–6 are related in the sense that they all test the third null hypothesis of dividend irrelevance for neutral, clear, and unclear signals, respectively. They report the cumulative standardized abnormal returns (CAR) for every statistically significant substate, over the period before the dividend announcement (days –4, . . . , -1), during the announcement days (0,1), after the announcement (days 2, . . . , 5), and the overall announcement period (days –4, . . . , +5).[18] The numbers in parentheses shown under CAR represent the significance levels for each period and each substate. The numbers in parentheses adjacent to the sample points represent observations that reflect a market reaction which is consistent with the sign of CAR. For easier reading, each table is organized into panels which present one class of information attribute (investment, financing, agency, or any combination) which is revealed to the market through a dividend change ($\Delta D > 0$, $\Delta D = 0$, $\Delta D < 0$). For example, panel A in Table 4 includes all the substates that involve an investment decision ($I$) followed by a dividend change. Since the same type of attribute remains after the announcement, the signal is labeled "neutral."

Tables 4–6 are uniquely important because they represent the first comprehensive attempt at the microlevel to analyze market reaction to dividend policies as related to balance sheet signals released prior to the dividend announcement. This process is conditioned on the signal quality, its content, and its direction. Although security analysts may differ on the ad hoc classification of the signal quality, it is argued that the majority of them will agree and that their agreement will reflect in the sell or buy positions around the dividend announcement. Moreover, one may, with minor error, anticipate a dividend change before it occurs given the state of the firm and assess the expected behavior of management in terms of the quality of the signal to be released in such circumstances. The combination in the ninth row of panel D in Table 6 is an example where a reduction in dividends can be good news if it is made to support an asset investment decision which is expected to improve future earnings (favorable news), while an unanticipated dividend increase that increases shareholders' wealth at the expense of bondholders can be bad news if it jeopardizes liquidity levels, thus possibly leading to lower stock price as shown in the first row of panel A in Table 6.

The following examples illustrate the subjective criteria of quality, direction, and information attribute classifications. The first entry in panel A of Table 4 shows increases in cash ($\Delta C > 0$), investment ($\Delta I > 0$), debt ($\Delta B > 0$), and retained earnings ($\Delta RE > 0$), and no change in equity ($\Delta CS = 0$); all of which were observed prior to the announcement. This combination implies that the firm in that substate has undertaken a new project financed by debt. At the same time, the firm experienced an increase in liquidity ($C$) and positive earnings ($RE$) ex-post. Thus, even before the dividend announcement, news is categorized as capital budgeting information. This is evident in the market reaction to the financial statement signals even prior to the dividend announcement, which is significant at 10%. An increase in dividends would only reinforce a positive interpretation as indicated by a moderate increase in market value on the announcement day and a cumulative increase in the overall event period (significant at 5%). The second combination displays an increase in cash ($\Delta C > 0$) and external equity ($\Delta S > 0$), and no change in investment, debt, or retained earnings. This can signal to the market that cash was accumulated for an investment decision which is about to be made. This brings a modest market reevaluation of the stock price (significant at 12%) that intensifies once an increase in dividends is declared, confirming market analysis in a strong CAR significant at the 9% level on the dividend announcement day and at the 1% level throughout the event period.

The first combination in panel B displays a significant reduction in the amount of cash used to redeem both debt and equity, which reduces the general level of capital but does not necessarily improve the debt-equity ratio. This action was followed by increased dividends for remaining shareholders, a reinforcing signal

*Table 5.* $\overline{\text{CAR}}$ Results for Dividend Clear Signal Hypothesis

| *State of Balance Sheet Changes* | *Sample Points* | *Cumulative Abnormal Returns* *Before* | *On* | *After* | *Overall* |
|---|---|---|---|---|---|
| **A. Investment Attribute** | | | | | |
| $\Delta C$=0, $\Delta I$>0, $\Delta B$>0, $\Delta CS$<0, $\Delta RE$=0, $\Delta D$=0 | 17[17] | 0.86 | 0.92 | 4.67* | 6.44* |
| | | (0.12) | (0.32) | (0.04) | (0.04) |
| $\Delta C$>0, $\Delta I$=0, $\Delta B$=0, $\Delta CS$>0, $\Delta RE$>0, $\Delta D$<0 | 11[3] | −0.20 | 3.41 | 4.04** | 7.25* |
| | | (0.47) | (0.13) | (0.07) | (0.03) |
| $\Delta C$>0, $\Delta I$=0, $\Delta B$>0, $\Delta CS$>0, $\Delta RE$=0, $\Delta D$<0 | 22[14] | −1.45 | 3.80 | 3.74** | 6.09* |
| | | (0.26) | (0.12) | (0.08) | (0.05) |
| **B. Investment-Financing Attributes** | | | | | |
| $\Delta C$>0, $\Delta I$=0, $\Delta B$>0, $\Delta CS$<0, $\Delta RE$>0, $\Delta D$=0 | 23[14] | 1.38 | 2.48 | 1.70 | 5.56* |
| | | (0.27) | (0.16) | (0.23) | (0.05) |
| $\Delta C$<0, $\Delta I$=0, $\Delta B$>0, $\Delta CS$<0, $\Delta RE$=0, $\Delta D$=0 | 8[5] | 2.03 | 1.81 | 2.42 | 6.25* |
| | | (0.47) | (0.21) | (0.13) | (0.04) |
| $\Delta C$>0, $\Delta I$=0, $\Delta B$>0, $\Delta CS$>0, $\Delta RE$>0, $\Delta D$>0 | 34[18] | 2.95 | 3.27 | −0.16 | 6.06* |
| | | (0.12) | (0.13) | (0.47) | (0.05) |
| $\Delta C$>0, $\Delta I$=0, $\Delta B$=0, $\Delta CS$>0, $\Delta RE$>0, $\Delta D$>0 | 33[21] | 4.59** | 5.03** | 7.22* | 16.83* |
| | | (0.06) | (0.09) | (0.02) | (0.01) |
| $\Delta C$>0, $\Delta I$=0, $\Delta B$=0, $\Delta CS$=0, $\Delta RE$>0, $\Delta D$>0 | 9[7] | −0.45 | 5.02** | 4.07** | 8.64* |
| | | (0.42) | (0.09) | (0.06) | (0.01) |
| $\Delta C$=0, $\Delta I$=0, $\Delta B$<0, $\Delta CS$>0, $\Delta RE$>0, $\Delta D$>0 | 12[8] | 0.82 | 2.67 | 3.31** | 6.81* |
| | | (0.36) | (0.16) | (0.10) | (0.03) |
| $\Delta C$>0, $\Delta I$=0, $\Delta B$>0, $\Delta CS$>0, $\Delta RE$=0, $\Delta D$>0 | 41[23] | −0.01 | 2.69 | 3.92** | 6.59* |
| | | (0.50) | (0.15) | (0.08) | (0.04) |
| **C. Investment-Agency Attributes** | | | | | |
| $\Delta C$=0, $\Delta I$>0, $\Delta B$=0, $\Delta CS$>0, $\Delta RE$>0, $\Delta D$>0 | 15[12] | 0.08 | 4.41** | 3.40** | 7.89* |
| | | (0.48) | (0.10) | (0.08) | (0.02) |
| $\Delta C$>0, $\Delta I$>0, $\Delta B$>0, $\Delta CS$<0, $\Delta RE$>0, $\Delta D$>0 | 5[4] | 3.54** | 0.89 | 1.17 | 5.61* |
| | | (0.07) | (0.32) | (0.30) | (0.04) |
| $\Delta C$<0, $\Delta I$>0, $\Delta B$>0, $\Delta CS$>0, $\Delta RE$=0, $\Delta D$>0 | 8[6] | 1.65 | 1.20 | 3.41** | 6.25* |
| | | (0.24) | (0.28) | (0.08) | (0.04) |
| $\Delta C$<0, $\Delta I$>0, $\Delta B$<0, $\Delta CS$>0, $\Delta RE$>0, $\Delta D$=0 | 16[10] | 2.21 | 1.92 | 2.99** | 7.12* |
| | | (0.15) | (0.20) | (0.10) | (0.02) |
| $\Delta C$>0, $\Delta I$=0, $\Delta B$>0, $\Delta CS$>0, $\Delta RE$>0, $\Delta D$=0 | 87[45] | 3.11 | 3.08 | −0.35 | 5.83* |
| | | (0.11) | (0.14) | (0.44) | (0.05) |
| $\Delta C$>0, $\Delta I$=0, $\Delta B$>0, $\Delta CS$>0, $\Delta RE$>0, $\Delta D$<0 | 7[5] | 0.39 | 3.51 | 1.02 | 4.92** |
| | | (0.43) | (0.13) | (0.32) | (0.06) |

*Notes:* See Table 4.

of an improved financing structure. This drew a strong positive market reaction (significant at 1%). With regard to agency attributes in panel C, the first row shows a debt for equity swap that causes an increase in cash and debt levels which is unaccompanied by a new investment. This event exemplifies a signal of wealth transfer (agency problem). This was confirmed by an increase in dividends (significant at 4%). The first substate of panel B (Table 5) displays a similar case but with a positive change in retained earnings and no change in dividend policy. The market classifies this signal as unclear because it can be associated with three different scenarios: possible future investment supported by an accumulation of cash, a possible transfer of wealth to shareholders, or a possible refinancing decision. The lack of change in dividend policy eliminates the agency motivation behind the change in capital structure, resulting in two mixed attributes, investment-financing, both of which draw a positive market reaction (significant at 5%). Thus, high uncertain situation becomes less uncertain, and therefore the signal is classified as clear. The second substate displays similar behavior but with reductions in equity and debt.

The first substate in panel A of Table 6 displays an increase in investment that was financed by debt; however, with no sign of improvement in either the liquidity or earnings power it is almost impossible to predict the future prosperity of the firm. Thus, prior to the dividend announcement, a single item attribute (investment) prevails but with two opposing forces: a positive signal of prosperity from the new project, and a negative sign caused by liquidity and profitability ex-post problems. This is an ex-post highly uncertain case. Investors then look for a clear signal in the form of a decrease or at least no change in dividends released to make the state clearer. Under the same conditions, a dividend increase would worsen liquidity conditions and would not reduce the confusion. In this case a dividend increase resulted in an unclear signal which was associated with a "net" negative market response. The negative effect of liquidity problems overruled the favorable investment news.

The first observation in panel D (Table 6) reflects a mixed investment-agency problem. Incremental investment was financed by both debt and equity. In this example, simultaneous debt financing and new investment are theoretically expected to cause a relative positive reaction while equity, generally, is expected to induce a negative reaction. A stagnating cash or liquidity position and no earnings improvement add to the negative effect. Thus, this was a case which is depicted as unclear prior to the dividend announcement and it remained unclear after the announcement. No change in dividends may have resulted in a clearer state, but dividends were increased, worsening the liquidity condition and resulting in a "net" negative effect. All remaining substates in Tables 4–6 are evaluated in the same way.

Thus far, no claim is made that this subjective classification system is without any error; however, one must note that most of the substates that were examined in this study behaved as expected based on the assigned quality level and news direction. For instance, 29 of the 41 dividend increase signals were expected to result in a positive market reaction. Only 3 of them did not (i.e., 10% prediction error). Twelve dividend increase signals were anticipated to cause price declines, which they did with a single exception. In the case of dividend decrease signals, there was no prediction error in terms of the direction of market reaction. In

*Table 6.* $\overline{CAR}$ Results for Dividend Unclear Signal Hypothesis

| *State of Balance Sheet Changes* | *Sample Points* | *Cumulative Abnormal Returns* | | | |
|---|---|---|---|---|---|
| | | *Before* | *On* | *After* | *Overall* |
| **A. Investment Attribute** | | | | | |
| $\Delta C$=0, $\Delta I$>0, $\Delta B$>0, $\Delta CS$=0, $\Delta RE$=0,$\Delta D$>0 | 6[6] | –1.57<br>(0.25) | –0.27<br>(0.44) | –3.51**<br>(0.07) | –5.35**<br>(0.06) |
| $\Delta C$<0, $\Delta I$>0, $\Delta B$=0, $\Delta CS$<0, $\Delta RE$>0,$\Delta D$=0 | 8[5] | –0.81<br>(0.36) | –1.93<br>(0.20) | –2.39<br>(0.14) | –5.14**<br>(0.06) |
| **B. Financing Attribute** | | | | | |
| $\Delta C$=0, $\Delta I$=0, $\Delta B$>0, $\Delta CS$<0, $\Delta RE$=0,$\Delta D$=0 | 13[10] | –2.81<br>(0.11) | –0.28<br>(0.44) | –1.99<br>(0.20) | –5.07**<br>(0.06) |
| **C. Investment-Financing Attributes** | | | | | |
| $\Delta C$>0, $\Delta I$<0, $\Delta B$<0, $\Delta CS$<0, $\Delta RE$>0,$\Delta D$=0 | 5[4] | 1.58<br>(0.25) | 1.60<br>(0.23) | 2.65<br>(0.12) | 5.83*<br>(0.05) |
| $\Delta C$>0, $\Delta I$>0, $\Delta B$<0, $\Delta CS$=0, $\Delta RE$=0,$\Delta D$=0 | 16[8] | 0.84<br>(0.36) | 1.04<br>(0.30) | 3.05<br>(0.12) | 4.93**<br>(0.08) |
| $\Delta C$>0, $\Delta I$<0, $\Delta B$<0, $\Delta CS$=0, $\Delta RE$=0,$\Delta D$=0 | 6[4] | –0.15<br>(0.47) | 1.23<br>(0.27) | 6.43*<br>(0.03) | 7.51*<br>(0.02) |
| $\Delta C$<0, $\Delta I$>0, $\Delta B$=0, $\Delta CS$=0, $\Delta RE$>0,$\Delta D$=0 | 6[6] | –3.01<br>(0.12) | –2.04<br>(0.19) | –4.09*<br>(0.05) | –9.14*<br>(0.01) |
| $\Delta C$>0, $\Delta I$<0, $\Delta B$>0, $\Delta CS$=0, $\Delta RE$>0,$\Delta D$=0 | 11[8] | –2.07<br>(0.20) | 0.07<br>(0.49) | –2.21<br>(0.17) | –4.21**<br>(0.10) |
| $\Delta C$>0, $\Delta I$>0, $\Delta B$=0, $\Delta CS$<0, $\Delta RE$=0,$\Delta D$=0 | 7[4] | –1.23<br>(0.30) | 1.10<br>(0.29) | –4.58*<br>(0.04) | –4.77**<br>(0.08) |
| $\Delta C$=0, $\Delta I$>0, $\Delta B$=0, $\Delta CS$>0, $\Delta RE$=0,$\Delta D$>0 | 8[4] | –5.20*<br>(0.05) | –0.74<br>(0.35) | 0.82<br>(0.36) | –5.12**<br>(0.07) |
| **D. Investment-Agency Attributes** | | | | | |
| $\Delta C$=0, $\Delta I$>0, $\Delta B$>0, $\Delta CS$>0, $\Delta RE$=0,$\Delta D$>0 | 6[4] | –2.61<br>(0.15) | –1.52<br>(0.25) | –2.77<br>(0.14) | –6.90*<br>(0.03) |
| $\Delta C$=0, $\Delta I$<0, $\Delta B$<0, $\Delta CS$<0, $\Delta RE$=0, $\Delta D$=0 | 5[4] | 1.59<br>(0.24) | 1.14<br>(0.29) | 2.87**<br>(0.07) | 5.59*<br>(0.05) |
| $\Delta C$=0, $\Delta I$>0, $\Delta B$>0, $\Delta CS$>0, $\Delta RE$>0,$\Delta D$=0 | 24[13] | –3.04<br>(0.12) | –1.54<br>(0.24) | –1.30<br>(0.28) | –5.88*<br>(0.05) |
| $\Delta C$>0, $\Delta I$>0, $\Delta B$=0, $\Delta CS$>0, $\Delta RE$>0, $\Delta D$=0 | 5[4] | –2.10<br>(0.19) | –2.59<br>(0.16) | –3.50**<br>(0.07) | –8.19*<br>(0.01) |
| $\Delta C$=0, $\Delta I$>0, $\Delta B$=0, $\Delta CS$>0, $\Delta RE$>0, $\Delta D$=0 | 23[14] | –2.19<br>(0.18) | –1.13<br>(0.29) | –1.48<br>(0.26) | –4.80**<br>(0.09) |
| $\Delta C$<0, $\Delta I$>0, $\Delta B$=0, $\Delta CS$>0, $\Delta RE$>0, $\Delta D$=0 | 26[20] | –1.46<br>(0.25) | –0.92<br>(0.32) | –1.69<br>(0.23) | –4.06**<br>(0.10) |
| $\Delta C$>0, $\Delta I$=0, $\Delta B$=0, $\Delta CS$=0, $\Delta RE$>0, $\Delta D$=0 | 15[10] | –2.56<br>(0.15) | –1.26<br>(0.27) | –0.89<br>(0.34) | –4.70**<br>(0.09) |
| $\Delta C$<0, $\Delta I$=0, $\Delta B$<0, $\Delta CS$>0, $\Delta RE$<0, $\Delta D$=0 | 8[6] | 1.81<br>(0.22) | –5.91**<br>(0.08) | –1.82<br>(0.22) | –5.93*<br>(0.05) |
| $\Delta C$=0, $\Delta I$>0, $\Delta B$>0, $\Delta CS$>0, $\Delta RE$>0, $\Delta D$<0 | 7[6] | 1.57<br>(0.25) | 5.88**<br>(0.08) | –0.01<br>(0.48) | 7.44*<br>(0.02) |
| $\Delta C$=0, $\Delta I$>0, $\Delta B$>0, $\Delta CS$>0, $\Delta RE$=0, $\Delta D$<0 | 8[5] | –2.48<br>(0.16) | –2.02<br>(0.20) | –2.43<br>(0.16) | –6.93*<br>(0.03) |

(continued)

*Table 6. (continued)*

| State of Balance Sheet Changes | Sample Points | Cumulative Abnormal Returns Before | On | After | Overall |
|---|---|---|---|---|---|
| **E. Financing-Agency Attributes** | | | | | |
| $\Delta C<0, \Delta I=0, \Delta B<0, \Delta CS>0, \Delta RE=0, \Delta D>0$ | 19[7] | 1.14 (0.31) | 1.33 (0.26) | 1.58 (0.25) | 4.05** (0.10) |
| $\Delta C<0, \Delta I=0, \Delta B<0, \Delta CS>0, \Delta RE=0, \Delta D=0$ | 100[53] | 3.62** (0.08) | 1.28 (0.27) | 1.30 (0.28) | 6.19* (0.05) |
| **F. Investment-Financing-Agency Attributes** | | | | | |
| $\Delta C<0, \Delta I=0, \Delta B<0, \Delta CS>0, \Delta RE>0, \Delta D>0$ | 8[6] | 1.61 (0.24) | 6.62** (0.07) | 2.50 (0.13) | 10.73* (0.01) |
| $\Delta C<0, \Delta I<0, \Delta B<0, \Delta CS>0, \Delta RE=0, \Delta D=0$ | 14[10] | 0.54 (0.40) | 2.20 (0.18) | 1.78 (0.22) | 4.52** (0.09) |
| $\Delta C>0, \Delta I<0, \Delta B>0, \Delta CS>0, \Delta RE=0, \Delta D=0$ | 8[6] | –2.27 (0.17) | –1.14 (0.29) | –4.21** (0.07) | –7.63* (0.02) |
| $\Delta C>0, \Delta I<0, \Delta B<0, \Delta CS>0, \Delta RE=0, \Delta D=0$ | 11[6] | –1.03 (0.32) | –4.14 (0.11) | –1.99 (0.20) | –7.16* (0.03) |
| $\Delta C>0, \Delta I>0, \Delta B>0, \Delta CS>0, \Delta RE<0, \Delta D=0$ | 7[2] | 1.38 (0.27) | –0.27 (0.44) | 2.98** (0.10) | 4.10** (0.10) |
| $\Delta C>0, \Delta I>0, \Delta B>0, \Delta CS>0, \Delta RE>0, \Delta D<0$ | 10[7] | –0.29 (0.44) | –2.09 (0.19) | –3.22 (0.11) | –5.60** (0.06) |

*Notes:* See Table 4.

addition, one can see that 7 of the 12 dividend decrease signals were expected to cause, and indeed did cause, positive market appreciation.

A general view of the tables shows that the null hypothesis is more often rejected for the whole period than over any subperiods. In some cases, the CAR prior to the dividend announcement is large enough to reject the null hypothesis. This supports the idea that in light of high uncertainty, the market continues its recalculation of the firm value and that this process may not be fully completed before the dividend announcement. This observation does not contradict the theory of efficient market; it only shows that the flow of new information may be gradual and that the process of resolving uncertainty may be slow. The strongest rejection, however, is naturally observed during the announcement days (0,1). Sometimes, the market reaction extends to few days after the announcement. This is especially evident in the case of unclear signals, where it may take the market a few days to gradually receive and assimilate complex information. In fact, Table 6 shows that there was almost no significant market reaction on the announcement days and that stronger and more frequent significant stock price adjustments were made over the postannouncement period (days +2 to +5).[19] When examining clear and unclear signals, almost half the substates significantly reject the null hypothesis. This is consistent with the idea that the relevance of higher quality dividend signals increases in situations where ambiguity dominates.

In general, the results in Table 4 demonstrate that 32% of neutral signals (14 substates) reject the null hypothesis of dividend announcement irrelevance, and in all these cases the market responds as expected.[20] Nevertheless, three substates show prices that behave in contrast to our prediction; two of them are statistically significant. Likewise, four clear (Table 5) and four unclear (Table 6) signals behave unexpectedly.

Most notably, this study reveals some interesting cases that are observed to be relevant to capital structure and agency theories. For instance, increases in equity, when all other items in the balance sheet remain constant, signal strong good news about future moves rather than bad news measured by a strong higher market value over the overall event period (significant at 8%) despite the temporary setback of dividend decrease news (see panel A.4 in Table 4). This reaction to equity dilution contradicts some earlier studies. Despite their tax disadvantage, equity for debt swaps accompanied by dividend increases are perceived by the market as good news significant at the 3% level or less even when cash levels are drained (B.6 Table 5 and F.1 Table 6). When equity-debt swaps are followed by no change in dividend policy, the market responds significantly (at the level of 5%) in favor or disfavor depending on whether there was no reduction or a reduction in retained earnings over the quarter prior to the announcement, respectively (E.2 Table 6 vs. D.8 Table 6). Another interesting case is a debt for equity swap followed by increased dividend, which also induces positive responses (CAR is significant at the 1% level) as shown in panel C.1, table 4. When the same swap is not accompanied by a dividend change signal, the market reevaluation is strongly negative (B.1, Table 6). Furthermore, a simultaneous reduction in both debt and equity levels along with a dividend increase is associated with strong stock appreciation (B.1, Table 4). This holds true despite the deterioration in cash holdings. However, one should be cautious since other factors such as the size of the firm and degree of leverage were not examined. Many other cases can be closely investigated, but space constraints do not allow for further discussion here.

Table 7 displays the percentage rejection of the null hypothesis for each of the panels in Table 1, i.e., for each level of quality, information attribute, and dividend change. For each level of signal quality categorized by the content of the information attribute for a given dividend policy, the first row shows the percentage rejection at the 5% level and the second row displays the incremental rejection rate at the significance level of 10%. For example a 50% rejection followed by a 50% means that 50% of the states in this category have rejected the null hypothesis at the 5% level and that allowing for a significance level of 10% did not increase the rejection rate. One can clearly observe that dividend announcements do contribute to the market stock evaluation process. In fact, with few exceptions, the null hypothesis is frequently rejected at the 5% level and more often at the 10% level.

*Table 7.* Percentage Rejection Of the Null Hypothesis for each Panel of Signal Quality, Information attribute, and Dividend Change Sign

| | *Dividend Change Sign* | | |
|---|---|---|---|
| *Signal Status* | *Dividend Increases (+)* | *Stable Dividends (0)* | *Dividend Decreases (–)* |
| Neutral, investment signal | 50 | 23 | — |
| | 50 | 35 | 33 |
| | (3–7) | (4–6) | (5–15) |
| Neutral, financing signal | 33 | 33 | 100 |
| | 33 | 33 | 100 |
| | (0–11) | (3–7) | (0–15) |
| Neutral, agency signal | 33 | 33 | — |
| | 33 | 33 | — |
| | (2–8) | (3–7) | — |
| Clear, investment signal | – | 14 | 100 |
| | — | 14 | 100 |
| | — | (3–7) | (1–9) |
| Clear, investment-financing signal | – | 40 | — |
| | — | 40 | — |
| | — | (2–8) | — |
| Clear, investment-agency signal | 77 | 33 | — |
| | 77 | 33 | 100 |
| | (4–6) | (3–7) | (0–21) |
| Unclear, investment signal | — | — | — |
| | 100 | 100 | — |
| | (0–22) | (0–21) | — |
| Unclear, financing signal | — | — | — |
| | — | 100 | — |
| | — | (0–18) | — |
| Unclear, investment-financing signal | — | 20 | — |
| | — | 46 | — |
| | — | (2–8) | — |
| Unclear,, investment-agency signal | 14 | 23 | 100 |
| | 29 | 47 | 100 |
| | (2–8) | (4–6) | (0–13) |
| Unclear, financing-agency signal | – | 50 | — |
| | 50 | 50 | — |
| | (5–15) | (3–7) | — |
| Unclear, investment-financing agency signal | 100 | 17 | — |
| | 100 | 31 | 50 |
| | (0–13) | (6–14) | (3–17) |

*Notes:* The 95% confidence interval is in parentheses. The sample period is 1976–1985.

The rejection rate increases with the use of clear signals, especially at the 5% level as well as with unclear signals. Furthermore, rejection is stronger with dividend increases or decreases than when no dividend changes have been made, an observation that is consistent with prior literature. It also seems that there is a tendency to reject the null hypothesis more frequently when fewer confounded items of information are released.

The use of the percentage rejection method requires the specification of a criterion to determine whether the rate of rejection is significant at the 95% confidence interval. Such a method is provided by measuring the chance occurrence percentage.

For that purpose the assumption is that, under the null hypothesis, the outcomes of the hypothesis tests for each of the $N_S$ events (substates) are independent, and the rejection rates would have a binomial distribution with a mean equal to $\alpha$ and a standard deviation $\sigma_\alpha$ equal to $[\alpha(1-\alpha)/N_S]^{1/2}$. Additionally, if we assume that the rejection rates are normally distributed and the test statistics are properly specified, then the rejection rate should fall between $\alpha \pm 2\sigma_\alpha$ approximately 95% of the time. The percentage rejection rate and the confidence intervals for the hypothesis tests categories are found in parentheses in Table 7. For example, the first entry in the table displays the percentage substates rejecting the null hypothesis of zero CAR at the 0.05 level. The second row of the same entry (i.e., neutral, investment signal) reports the *cumulative* percentage rejection at the 0.10 level. The third row of the same entry indicates the confidence interval at the 95% level.

It is clear from Table 7 that none of the rejection rates falls within the 95% confidence interval, which implies that the rate of hypothesis rejection could not have occurred by chance alone in any cell.

## V. CONCLUSIONS

Earlier research by John and Williams (1985), Miller and Rock (1985), and Ambarish et al. (1987) presents the foundations of a dividend signaling equilibrium model. However, direct tests of these models are in the early stage. Moreover, these models neither accommodate all other possible signaling devices nor distinguish conditions of superiority.

An expanded version of the dividend signaling theory is proposed in this paper, relating ex-post accounting signals found in the firm's financial statements to allow testing of dividend signals with multiple qualities and contents.

The level of quality and the information content, along with the sign of the dividend signals are tested. The findings show that firms tend to associate neutral signals with no change in dividend payouts, thus implying less need for dividend payout changes in a clearer environment. Dividend changes are used most often to reveal clear and unclear signals in order to reduce the complexity of the firms' actions. Market reaction to dividend signals depends on the quality as related to both the type (investment, financing, and/or agency) and direction (favorable or unfavorable) of inside information and the magnitude of the dividend change. More important, results show that the direction of the signal (favorable versus unfavorable) depends on the type of information as defined in this paper rather than the sign of dividend change. In other words, not all dividend increases carry good news and not all dividend decreases convey bad news.

The major contribution of this paper is that it provides a new methodology to identify, interpret, and test dividend signals as related to the signals provided in the balance sheet of the firm. This procedure makes it possible to determine whether the same dividend policy administered by the same firm will draw a different market response depending on the signal quality, news direction, dividend change sign, and/or the state of clarity and type of information revealed through the dividend signal. It also allows for further investigations of many anomalies related to capital structure and agency problems. Moreover, it may explain why differences in dividend policies exist across industries and between firms. In addition, this paper lays the foundation for a guideline for investors in assessing the future direction of the stock price in light of the firm's dividend policies. Because the same methodology can be independently applied to stock repurchases or issues, bond repurchases or issues, stock splits, and other signals, it may help resolve some of the anomalous and contradictory empirical findings observations.

In the future, this work can be extended to determine whether the strength of market reaction differs across signal qualities. Also it would be interesting to know the effect on bond prices during the same dividend announcement periods. A theoretical extension, however, is needed to model efficient signaling theory to possibly explain the results reported in this paper. A general equilibrium condition that distinguishes the circumstances under which dividend signals are superior to other signaling devices has yet to be identified.

## ACKNOWLEDGMENTS

This paper is part of the author's dissertation. The author is indebted to the committee chairman, Professor Larry Merville, for his unlimited support and to the committee members, Jim Overdahl, Dan Pieptea, and John Wiorkowski, for their helpful guidance. Also, the author would like to express his appreciation for valuable comments made by anonymous referees of this journal and helpful discussions with David Fowler, Paul Halpern, and participants of the Northern Finance Association Meeting, 1990. All remaining errors are the author's.

## NOTES

1. Earnings announcements are assumed to be made before dividend announcements. See note 10.
2. This scenario can be reversed as shown by Aharony and Swary (1980). However, the sampling criteria used in this paper exclude the events where dividend announcements are made before earnings announcements. Please refer to sampling criteria filter (11) and note 10 for further elaboration.

3. This case is shown later in Table 4 (see panel A.1 vs. A.3).

4. This case is explored in panel A.2 of Table 4.

5. Whether bondholders would allow this wealth transfer to occur or whether this act can serve the ownership interest in the long run is a testable conjecture.

6. For example, if prior quarter dividends are $1.50 per share and current quarter dividends are only $1.55 per share, this positive change does not reflect a very strong signal. In no case in the sample was a dividend change less than 5%. In this study, the changes in dividends per share are relatively large; thus all dividend changes above or below zero are treated as strong, which means the sign of the signal also provides information about its strength.

7. The reason that dollar change in dividends is used rather than percentage change is that the market reaction does not depend on the percentage change of quarterly dividends as shown by Pettit (1976). In addition, all changes in the balance sheet items were also measured in dollars.

8. In the case of changes in *C*, *I*, *B*, or *RE*, a band of ± 5% is placed around the zero (stable) change state to account for classification error. This has the effect of converting 16 infeasible states into feasible states.

9. This process can prove to be judgmental in the sense that different analysts may infer different types, direction and quality. However, results reported later in Tables 4–6 are not biased by this effect since each unique combination of changes in sources and uses of funds (substate) is tested independently, regardless of any classification error. Furthermore, Table 7 demonstrates that any such classification error is minimum.

10. This criterion resulted in only a 3% reduction in the number of observations (121/4,033).

11. Approximately 40% of the firms on the COMPUSTAT tape used in this study announced their earnings after announcing their dividends. Since it is not obvious that earnings-second signals are perfect substitutes for dividends-second signals, they were separated. Future analysis in this area is planned by the author.

12. This practice is consistent with other empirical studies such that of Aharony and Swary (1980) and Eades, Hess, and Kim (1984).

13. In no case did a sampled firm have less than three trading days during the event period including days 0 and 1. Firms that have three or four trading days were few (less than 2%). However, the portfolio of events in each category was standardized on a daily basis to reflect the actual number of firms trading in a particular day.

14. When a firm decides to omit a dividend payment for one or more quarters, an announcement to this effect may or may not come from the firm's board of directors. The CRSP tape does not report this event. Moreover, the CRSP tape occasionally fails to report a dividend payment which is already reported on the COMPUSTAT tape. Hence in both cases these events were collected manually. Omission for two consecutive quarters was dropped from the sample.

15. In 70% of the sample points, the announcement period is no more than seven days. In 15% of the sample, the nonevent period was less than fifteen days and these were dropped from the announcement effects. Longer periods can be contaminated by other noisy events. However, the nonevent period was allowed to be twenty days with no discernible effects on the results.

16. The portfolio is standardized each day $t$ to account for the possibility that the number of sample points could change each day as implied in note 13.

17. This result implies that dividend decreases possess little information beyond what is already known by the market. Also, it is apparent that a zero change in dividends carries little information. Table 3 confirms the idea that the preannouncement and postannouncement periods contain little or no significant amount of new information and that almost always the announcement effect occurs on the day of the announcement or one day later.

18. The total number of substates examined and tested is 147, as shown in Tables 1 and 2. However, Tables 4–6 display only those substates that have observed a statistically significant market reaction to dividend signals (CAR significance level is 10% or better). The remaining cases, including infeasible substates (see note 7), are not reported here for lack of space but are available for interested readers.

19. It will be interesting to further examine unclear signals by extending this analysis to more than two periods in order to trace any future signals used by the firm to turn its state of ambiguity into more clarity. This is left for future research.

20. In an earlier draft of this paper, an expected price change for each substate was predicted and reported; these expectations are dropped from current Tables 4–6. However, in almost 93% of the cases, the predicted price change did conform with the sign of actual price movements over the announcement period.

## REFERENCES

Aharony, J., and Swary, I. (1980). "Quarterly Dividend and Earnings Announcements and Stockholder's Returns: An Empirical Analysis," *Journal of Finance* 35: 1–12.

Ambarish, R., John, K., and Williams, J. (1987). "Efficient Signalling with Dividends and Investments." *Journal of Finance* 42: 321–343.

Asquith, P., and Mullins, Jr., D. (1983). "The Impact of Initiating Dividend Payments on Shareholders' Wealth." *Journal of Business* 56: 77–96.

Asquith, P., and Mullins, Jr., D. (1986). "Signalling with Dividends, Stock Repurchases, and Equity Issues." *Financial Management* 15: 27–44.

Bhattacharya, S. (1979). "Imperfect Information, Dividend Policy and the Bird in Hand Fallacy." *Bell Journal of Economics* 10: 259–270.

Bhattacharya, S. (1980). "Non Dissipative Signaling Structure and Dividend Policy." *Quarterly Journal of Economics* 95: 1–24.

Black, F. (1976). "The Dividend Puzzle." *Journal of Portfolio Management* 5–8.

Brown, S. J., and Warner, J. B. (1985). "Using Daily Stock Returns: The Case of Event Studies." *Journal of Financial Economics* 4: 3–31.

Charest, G. (1978). "Dividend Information, Stock Return and Market Efficiency II." *Journal of Financial Economics* 6: 297–330.

Eades, K., Hess, D., and Kim, H. (1984). "On Interpreting Security Returns During the Ex-Dividend Period." *Journal of Financial Economics* 13: 3–34.

Fama, E., and Babiak, H. (1968). "Dividend Policy: An Empirical Analysis." *Journal of American Statistical Association* 63: 32–61.

Hakansson, N. (1982). "Dividend Policy and Valuation: Theory and Tests." *Journal of Finance* 37: 415–442.

Healy, P. M., and Palepu, K. G. (1988). "Market Rationality and Dividend Announcements." *Journal of Financial Economics* 149–176.

John, K., and Kalay, A. (1982). "Costly Contracting and Optimal Payout Constraints." *Journal of Finance* 37: 457–470.

John, K., and Kalay, A. (1985). "Informational Content of Optimal Debt Contracts." Pp. 133–161 in *Recent Advances in Corporate Finance*, edited by E. Altman and M. Subrahmanyam. Homewood, IL: Irwin.

John, K., and Williams, J. (1985). "Dividends, Dilution, and Taxes: A Signaling Equilibrium." *Journal of Finance* 40: 1053–1070.

Kalay, A., and Lowenstein, U. (1985). "Predictable Events and Excess Returns: The Case of Dividend Announcements." *Journal of Financial Economics* 14: 423–449.

Kane, A., Lee, Y., and Marcus, A. (1984). "Earnings and Dividend Announcements: Is There a Corroboration Effect?" *Journal of Finance* 39: 1091–1099.

Lintner, J. (1956). "Distribution of Income among Dividends, Retained Earnings, and Taxes." *American Economics Review* 46: 97–113.

Makhija, A., and Thompson, H. (1986). "Some Aspects of Equilibrium for a Cross-Section of Firms Signaling Profitability with Dividends: A Note." *Journal of Finance* 51: 249–254.

Miller, M., and Modigliani, F. (1961). "Dividend Policy, Growth and Valuation of Shares." *Journal of Business* 34: 411–433.

Miller, M., and Rock, K. (1985). "Dividend Policy under Asymmetric Information." *Journal of Finance* 40: 1031–1052.

Myers, S., and Majluf, N. (1984). "Stock Issues and Investment Policy When Firms Have Information That Investors Do Not Have." *Journal of Financial Economics* 13: 187–221.

Ofer, A. R., and Siegel, D. R. (1987). "Corporate Financial Policy, Information, and Market Expectations: An Empirical Investigation of Dividends." *Journal of Finance* 42: 889–912.

Ofer, A. R., and Thakor, A. V. (1987). "A Theory of Stock Price Responses to Alternative Corporate Cash Disbursement Methods: Stock Repurchases and Dividends." *Journal of Finance* 42: 365–394.

Pettit, R. (1972). "Dividend Announcements, Security Performances and Capital Market Efficiency." *Journal of Finance* 27: 993–1007.

Pettit, R. (1976). "The Impact of Dividend and Earnings Announcements, A Reconciliation." *Journal of Business* 49: 86–96.

Riley, J. (1979). "Informational Equilibrium." *Econometrica* 47: 331–359.

Ross, S. (1977). "The Determination of Financial Structure: The Incentive Signaling Approach." *Bell Journal of Economics* 8: 23–40.

Wansley, J. W., and Lane, W. R. (1987). "A Financial Profile of the Dividend Initiating Firm." *Journal of Business Finance and Accounting* 14: 425.

Wansley, J. W., Sirmans, C. F., Shilling, J. D., and Lee, Y. J. (1991). "Dividend Change Announcement Effects and Earnings Volatility and Timing." *Journal of Financial Research* 14: 37–50.

Watts, R. (1978). "Systematic Abnormal Returns after Quarterly Earnings Announcements." *Journal of Financial Economics* 6: 127–150.

# ESTIMATING THE STRATEGIC VALUE OF LONG-TERM FORWARD SALE CONTRACTS:

## THE CASE OF R&D

Wayne Y. Lee, Hoje Jo, and Dirk Zwemer

## ABSTRACT

This paper presents an optimal model, a priority pricing auction model, for maximizing expected profit for a research and development organization selling research projects to a group of buyers. It is shown that a priority pricing auction is superior to a single price auction when the dispersion in buyers' reservation prices is not extreme. In addition, comparative statics results indicate that the expected profit and the strategic value of a forward sale is a convex function of the dispersion in buyers' reservation prices.

Advances in Quantitative Analysis of Finance and Accounting,
Volume 2, Part B, pages 77–91.

ISBN: 1-55938-565-0

# I. INTRODUCTION

In the typical capital investment, firms seek buyers for their product only after production capacity has been installed and output produced. In contrast, in industrial projects where large amounts of capital are initially required to install production capacity and where the market for the output produced consists of a small number of buyers, product is contractually sold in advance of actual production. The use of long-term forward sale contracts in these circumstances is advantageous only if it conveys strategic advantages over spot sales.

A recent paper by Parsons (1989) suggests two major strategic advantages. First, the use of long-term forward sale contracts permits the firm (seller) to learn about market demand. Through an auction process, buyers bid for each unit of output. When demand equals potential supply, price clears the market; when less, some potential output is unsold; and when greater, potential output is rationed.[1] The possibility of rationing once production capacity has been installed is critical to the success of the auction. Scarcity relative to demand enables the firm to discriminate across buyers based upon the probability of receiving product and induces buyers to reveal their true reservation values in their bids for output.[2] On average the auction will result in a higher price and a lower quantity of output sold compared to the profit-maximizing "take-it or leave-it" single price solution. But as Harris and Raviv (1981) note, this trade-off of quantity for price yields a higher level of expected profit.

Second, the use of forward sale contracts avoids the ex post bargaining problem. The small number of potential buyers creates an incentive for opportunistic bargaining over prices once production capacity is installed. Making the successful negotiation of forward sale contracts a contingency upon which a firm bases its decision to install capacity allows the firm to better expropriate the value of its investment to its potential customers.

In short, long-term forward sale contracts can improve the efficiency of capital investment decisions—directly, as a result of information revelation and indirectly, by avoiding the incentive for a small number of buyers to engage in ex post opportunistic bargaining.[3] The purpose of this paper is to examine whether the strategic advantages of long-term forward sale contracts for investments in industrial projects carry over to the case of investments in research and development (R&D) as well.

The issue is significant. The ability of American companies to survive and prosper in an increasingly hostile and global marketplace has been a subject of considerable public discussion and debate. Fostering investment in R&D, particularly in high technology, is widely perceived as an important strategic response to this competitive threat. Since investment in R&D is inherently costly and risky, contractual arrangements where the costs and risks of R&D activity are optimally shared by those who have the most to gain from such efforts should result, ceteris paribus, in a higher level of investment in R&D.[4]

Research and development and investments in industrial projects like the development of natural gas fields considered by Parsons (1989) share similarities. Both involve large initial investments, and in both, the number of potential buyers may be small. There are however three crucial differences. First, unlike natural gas development projects, the marginal cost of reproducing and selling information to an additional buyer is zero once the investment in R&D has been made. The costs of investment in R&D largely fixed and there are no capacity constraints which limit the number of potential buyers who can be served after the R&D effort has been undertaken. Second, unlike physical commodities like natural gas, information is a discrete consumption good. It is of value to a buyer only when sold in its entirety. Third, it is well-known that investment in R&D entails high product risk. The effects of product risk in R&D are analyzed in Jo, Lee, and Zwemer (1990).

Taking these differences into account yields two interesting insights. First, the value of a priority pricing auction depends upon the cross-sectional variation in reservation prices across buyers.[5] A priority pricing auction is superior to a single price auction when the dispersion in buyers' reservation prices is not extreme. Where there is a sharp disagreement or a strong consensus among buyers regarding the value of R&D, a priority pricing auction is tantamount to a single price auction. Second, in cases where the dispersion in buyers' reservation prices is moderate, comparative statics results indicate that the expected profit and the strategic value of a forward sale is a convex function of the variance in buyers' reservation prices.

The paper proceeds as follows. In Section II the auction model for R&D is detailed. In Section III numerical examples for a single price auction, a priority pricing auction, and comparative statics results are provided. Section IV provides a discussion. The last section concludes the paper.

## II. AN AUCTION MODEL FOR R&D[6]

Consider a firm which is contemplating an investment in R&D. Estimating the expected cash inflows is a key step in evaluating the profitability of such an investment. How much output should be sold, to whom, and at what price? Moreover, should the product be sold under a spot or long-term forward contract?

As in Parsons (1989) assume that the utility for each potential buyer $i$, $u(d_i, q_i, r_i,)$ can be expressed as a linear function of his cash balance, $d_1$, his decision to purchase information, $q_i \varepsilon (0,1)$, and his reservation price, $r_i$. In particular, if $d$ denotes each buyer's initial wealth endowment, $u(d_i, q_i, r_i) = d - p_i q_i + r_i q_i = d_i + r_i q_i$ is such that at any sales price $p_i$ below the reservation price $r_i$, purchasing a unit of information ($q_i = 1$) increases the buyer's utility. Moreover, assume that each buyer is informed only about his own reservation price, and that each buyer's reservation price $r_i$, is viewed by the seller and other ($j \neq i$) buyers as a random variable. Specifically each buyer's reservation prices can take on discrete values ranging from $x_1$ to $x_k$, where the difference between any two successive values is

$\delta$, and the probability of each buyer's reservation price being any value in the interval $x_1$ to $x_k$ is uniform. Furthermore, in addition to each buyer's wealth endowment, the number of potential buyers, $N$, and the fixed cost of investment in R&D, $c$, are known to both buyers and sellers.

Given a specific realization of $N$-buyer reservation values, let $R = (R_1, \ldots, R_k)$ denote the ranking of reservation prices from highest to lowest. That is, since the same reservation price may be bid by more than one buyer,

$$R_1 \geq R_2 \geq \ldots \geq R_k,$$

where $R_i \in (x_1, \ldots x_k)$. Further suppose that the seller's decision to provide a buyer with a unit of information depends upon the buyer's rank. Specifically, let $T$ denote the optimal number of bids to accept, and $Q$ an artificially imposed scarcity constraint, where $Q \equiv k - T + 1$, such that for any vector of realized (unknown to buyer $i$) reservation prices of buyers other than $i, R_{-i}$,

$$q_i(x_i, R_{-i}) = \begin{cases} 1 \text{ if} \begin{cases} x_i = x_k & \text{, or} \\ x_i \geq x_T \text{ and} \sum_{m=i+1}^{k} n_m(R) < Q, \text{for } i < k \end{cases} \\ 0 \qquad \text{otherwise} \end{cases} \tag{1}$$

where $n_m(R)$ are the number of buyers whose reservation bid prices equal $x_m$ for $m - 1, \ldots, k$. In other words, buyers with reservation values less than $x_T$ do not bid at all, those who bid equal to $x_k$ receive a unit of information and those with reservation bid prices greater than or equal to $x_T$ receive a unit of information, and those less than $x_T$, do not. We show in the following theorem that a priority pricing auction is optimal provided that the priority prices are properly chosen.

*Theorem 1*: For $k \geq T \geq 1$, a priority pricing auction is optimal, where the cutoff rank $T$ is defined as the smallest $j$ for which

$$x_1 + \delta(2j - k - 1) \begin{array}{ll} \geq 0 & \text{for } j \geq T \\ < 0 & \text{for } j < T, \end{array} \tag{2}$$

where $k$ is the number of possible reservation prices and $\delta$ is the difference between reservation prices $x_{i+1}$ and $x_i$. The optimal pricing schedule $(p_T^*, \ldots, p_k^*)$ is

$$p_T^* = x_T, \text{ and}$$

$$p_i^* = x_i - (\delta / z_i^*) \sum_{j=T}^{i-1} z_j^*, \quad \text{for } i = T+1, \ldots, k, \tag{3}$$

where $z_i^*$, the probability of buyer $i$ receiving a unit of information given that $x_i$ is his true reservation price is given by

$$z_i^* = \sum_{j=0}^{Q} [j^N] \, [O - \frac{1}{k}]^j \left[\frac{k - O + 1}{k}\right]^{N-j} \otimes$$

$$\left(1 - \frac{[K - Q]^{N-j}}{k - Q + 1}\right)$$

$$\text{and } Q \equiv k - T + 1. \tag{4}$$

where ⊗ represents Kroeneker product.

*Proof.* Let $r_i$ denote each buyer's declared bid, where $r_i \varepsilon\ (x_1, \ldots, x_k)$. Based on these declared bids, define an allocation rule $d_i(r)$, $q_i(r)$ which satisfies the self-selection and individual rationality conditions, that is, the allocation rule induces each buyer to declare his true reservation price $R_i$ given that all other buyers are declaring their true reservation prices and maximizes each buyer's expected utility. Subject to these constraints, the seller's R&D optimization problem can be stated as

$$\underset{[d_i(R), q_i(R)]}{\text{maximize}} \quad E(\sum_{i=1}^{N} [d - d_i(R)]) - c,$$

where $d_i(R) \geq 0$, $q_i(R) \in (0,1)$ and the budget constraint $\Sigma_{i=1}^{N} d_i(R) \leq N$ is satisfied. Following the steps outlined in Harris and Ravis (1981, pp. 354–355), the seller's expected profit for the R&D problem can be written as

$$E\pi = (N/k)(\sum_{j=1}^{k} [x_1 + \delta(2j - k - 1)]z_j) - c,$$

where $c$, the total fixed cost, is constant. Since the maximand is linear in $z_j$'s, and the coefficients of $z_j$ increase with $j$, the optimal cutoff allocation rank $T$ is the smallest $j$ for which the coefficient of $z_j$ is nonnegative; that is, $T$ is such that

$$x_1 + \delta(2j - k - 1) \begin{matrix} \geq 0 & \text{for } j \geq T \\ < 0 & \text{for } j < T. \end{matrix}$$

In addition, the seller's expected profit is maximized by choosing $z_1, \ldots, z_{T-1} = 0$, and choosing $z_k$ as large as possible, followed by $z_{k-1}$ and so on down to $z_T$.

To make $z_k$ as large as possible, we should give any buyer $i$ who bids the reservation price $x_k$ a unit of information regardless of what other ($j \neq i$) buyers bid, that is, $q_i(x_k, R_{-1}) = 1$ for all $R_{-1}$, where $R_{-1}$ is the vector of unknown (to buyer $i$)

reservation prices of the buyers other than $i$. In Eq. (3), $z_i^* = Eq_i(x_i, R_{-i})$ is the expected output given that $i$'s true reservation price is $x_i$, and $E(\cdot)$ is the expectation taken over the vector of unknown (to buyer $i$) reservation price of the buyers other than $i$, $R_{-i}$. Q.E.D. (See Appendix for the calculation of $z_i^*$.)

As the seller has imperfect information about the private values assigned to the information by the buyers, he or she can discriminate across buyers by adopting the priority pricing auction described in Theorem 1. With a priority pricing auction, the seller does not rely on altruism by the buyers or an external information source to learn the reservation prices of the buyers. In this priority pricing mechanism, buyers with higher reservation prices will choose to pay higher priority prices in exchange for higher probability of obtaining the product.

## III. NUMERICAL EXAMPLE

In this section, we will illustrate single price auction outcomes, priority pricing auction outcomes, and comparative statics results with a numerical example and calculate the expected profit from spot and forward sales and strategic value, the increased value of the expected profit for forward sales relative to spot sales.

Table 1 explains the numerical example. There are 4 buyers, each of which has 6 different sets of 4 reservation values with an average reservation price of 0.5. The planned capital cost of the project is 1 and the operating cost is 0. The buyer reservation values are allowed to have different variances as the dispersion parameter changes. Following Parsons (1989), we assigned the buyer reservation values uniform probability (other distribution can be easily incorporated via the probability factor).

Tables 2 and 3 show the calculations for this example using a single price auction and a priority pricing auction. Column 1 is the row index; there are 35 different combinations in which 4 buyers can be distributed among 4 different reservation values. Columns 2–5 show the number of buyers at each reservation value, which defines $(x_1, x_2, x_3, x_4)$, and column 6 shows the probability of event, $z_i^*$, following Eq. (4). Columns 7 and 8 show the quantity sold and the price, following Eq. (1) and single price of 0.75 for a single price auction and following Eq. (3) for priority pricing auction. Columns 9–11 show the total sales, the quantity sold times the price, the profit, total sales minus the fixed cost of 1, and expected profit with risk under spot sales, probability of event times $\pi$. The equivalent calculation for forward contracts is shown in column 12. Note that negative $\pi$ in the corresponding spot sales shows zero quantity sold. These rows correspond to situations when the seller does not proceed with the R&D project in forward sales. Therefore, there are no situations occurring with negative total profit. As shown in Theorem 1, the expected profit (at bottom right), the sum of the terms in the last two columns, is higher for a priority pricing auction for both spot and forward sales.

*Table 1.* Numerical Example

| *Model Parameters* | | | *Values* |
|---|---|---|---|
| Fixed Cost | | $c$ | 1.00 |
| Number of possible reservation prices | | $k$ | 4 |
| Average reservation price | | $\mu$ | 0.50 |
| Dispersion parameter | | $\delta$ | |
| | Case 1 | High | 1.20 |
| | Case 2 | | 1.00 |
| | Case 3 | | 0.50 |
| | Case 4 | | 0.25 |
| | Case 5 | | 0.18 |
| | Case 6 | Low | 0.10 |
| Number of buyers | | $N$ | 4 |
| Scarcity constraint | | $Q$ | $k-T+1$ |
| Optimal cutoff allocation rank | | $T$ | $\leq k$ |
| | Case 1 | High | 4 |
| | Case 2 | | 3 |
| | Case 3 | | 3 |
| | Case 4 | | 3 |
| | Case 5 | | 2 |
| | Case 6 | Low | 1 |

| | | | | | *Distribution of Buyers' Reservation Prices* | | | |
|---|---|---|---|---|---|---|---|---|
| *Case* | *Dispersion Paramter* $\delta$ | *Mean* | *Std. Dev.* $\sigma$ | *Outcomes Probability* | $x_1$ *0.25* | $x_2$ *0.25* | $x_3$ *0.25* | $x_4$ *0.25* |
| 1 | 1.20 | 0.50 | 1.34 | | –1.3 | –0.1 | 1.1 | 2.3 |
| 2 | 1.00 | 0.50 | 1.12 | | –1.0 | 0.0 | 1.0 | 2.0 |
| 3 | 0.50 | 0.50 | 0.56 | | –0.25 | 0.25 | 0.75 | 1.25 |
| 4 | 0.25 | 0.50 | 0.28 | | 0.125 | 0.375 | 0.625 | 0.875 |
| 5 | 0.18 | 0.50 | 0.20 | | 0.23 | 0.41 | 0.59 | 0.77 |
| 6 | 0.10 | 0.50 | 0.11 | | 0.35 | 0.45 | 0.55 | 0.65 |

To investigate further the superiority of a priority pricing auction to a single price scheme, comparative statics results are reported in Table 4. The first and second panel reporting expected profit from forward and spot sales, respectively, yields two interesting insights. First, a priority pricing auction is superior to a single price auction when the dispersion in buyers' reservation prices is not extreme. Where there is a sharp disagreement or a strong consensus among buyers regarding the

## *Table 2.* Single Price Auction Outcomes

| | *Number of Buyers with Reservation Value* | | | | *Probability of Event* | *Single Price* | | | | *Expected Profit* | |
|---|---|---|---|---|---|---|---|---|---|---|---|
| *Event* | *–0.25* | *0.25* | *0.75* | *1.25* | *Event* | $Q^*$ | $p^*$ | *Total Sales* | $\pi$ | *Spot Sale* | *Forward Sale* |
| 1 | 4 | 0 | 0 | 0 | 1/256 | 0 | 0.75 | 0.00 | –1.00 | –0.004 | 0.00 |
| 2 | 3 | 1 | 0 | 0 | 4/256 | 0 | 0.75 | 0.00 | –1.00 | –0.016 | 0.00 |
| 3 | 3 | 0 | 1 | 0 | 4/256 | 1 | 0.75 | 0.75 | –0.25 | –0.004 | 0.00 |
| 4 | 3 | 0 | 0 | 1 | 4/256 | 1 | 0.75 | 0.75 | –0.25 | –0.004 | 0.00 |
| 5 | 2 | 2 | 0 | 0 | 6/256 | 0 | 0.75 | 0.00 | –1.00 | –0.023 | 0.00 |
| 6 | 2 | 0 | 2 | 0 | 6/256 | 2 | 0.75 | 1.50 | 0.50 | 0.012 | 0.01 |
| 7 | 2 | 0 | 0 | 2 | 6/256 | 2 | 0.75 | 1.50 | 0.50 | 0.012 | 0.01 |
| 8 | 2 | 1 | 1 | 0 | 12/256 | 1 | 0.75 | 0.75 | –0.25 | –0.012 | 0.00 |
| 9 | 2 | 1 | 0 | 1 | 12/256 | 1 | 0.75 | 0.75 | –0.25 | –0.012 | 0.00 |
| 10 | 2 | 0 | 1 | 1 | 12/256 | 2 | 0.75 | 1.50 | 0.50 | 0.023 | 0.02 |
| 11 | 1 | 3 | 0 | 0 | 4/256 | 0 | 0.75 | 0.00 | –1.00 | –0.016 | 0.00 |
| 12 | 1 | 0 | 3 | 0 | 4/256 | 3 | 0.75 | 2.25 | 1.25 | 0.020 | 0.02 |
| 13 | 1 | 0 | 0 | 3 | 4/256 | 3 | 0.75 | 2.25 | 1.25 | 0.020 | 0.02 |
| 14 | 1 | 2 | 1 | 0 | 12/256 | 1 | 0.75 | 0.75 | –0.25 | –0.012 | 0.00 |
| 15 | 1 | 2 | 0 | 1 | 12/256 | 1 | 0.75 | 0.75 | –0.25 | –0.012 | 0.00 |
| 16 | 1 | 1 | 2 | 0 | 12/256 | 2 | 0.75 | 1.50 | 0.50 | 0.023 | 0.02 |
| 17 | 1 | 1 | 0 | 2 | 12/256 | 2 | 0.75 | 1.50 | 0.50 | 0.023 | 0.02 |
| 18 | 1 | 1 | 1 | 1 | 24/256 | 2 | 0.75 | 1.50 | 0.50 | 0.047 | 0.04 |
| 19 | 1 | 0 | 2 | 1 | 12/256 | 3 | 0.75 | 2.25 | 1.25 | 0.059 | 0.05 |
| 20 | 1 | 0 | 1 | 2 | 12/256 | 3 | 0.75 | 2.25 | 1.25 | 0.059 | 0.05 |
| 21 | 0 | 4 | 0 | 0 | 1/256 | 0 | 0.75 | 0.00 | –1.00 | –0.004 | 0.00 |
| 22 | 0 | 3 | 1 | 0 | 4/256 | 1 | 0.75 | 0.75 | –0.25 | –0.004 | 0.00 |
| 23 | 0 | 3 | 0 | 1 | 4/256 | 1 | 0.75 | 0.75 | –0.25 | –0.004 | 0.00 |
| 24 | 0 | 2 | 2 | 0 | 6/256 | 2 | 0.75 | 1.50 | 0.50 | 0.012 | 0.01 |
| 25 | 0 | 2 | 0 | 2 | 6/256 | 2 | 0.75 | 1.50 | 0.50 | 0.012 | 0.01 |
| 26 | 0 | 2 | 1 | 1 | 12/256 | 2 | 0.75 | 1.50 | 0.50 | 0.023 | 0.02 |
| 27 | 0 | 1 | 3 | 0 | 4/256 | 3 | 0.75 | 2.25 | 1.25 | 0.020 | 0.02 |
| 28 | 0 | 1 | 0 | 3 | 4/256 | 3 | 0.75 | 2.25 | 1.25 | 0.020 | 0.02 |
| 29 | 0 | 1 | 1 | 2 | 12/256 | 3 | 0.75 | 2.25 | 1.25 | 0.059 | 0.05 |
| 30 | 0 | 1 | 2 | 1 | 121256 | 3 | 0.75 | 2.25 | 1.25 | 0.059 | 0.05 |
| 31 | 0 | 0 | 4 | 0 | 1/256 | 4 | 0.75 | 3.00 | 2.00 | 0.008 | 0.00 |
| 32 | 0 | 0 | 3 | 1 | 4/256 | 4 | 0.75 | 3.00 | 2.00 | 0.031 | 0.03 |
| 33 | 0 | 0 | 2 | 2 | 6/256 | 4 | 0.75 | 3.00 | 2.00 | 0.047 | 0.04 |
| 34 | 0 | 0 | 1 | 3 | 4/256 | 4 | 0.75 | 3.00 | 2.00 | 0.031 | 0.03 |
| 35 | 0 | 0 | 0 | 4 | 1/256 | 4 | 0.75 | 3.00 | 2.00 | 0.008 | 0.00 |
| | | | | | 1 | | | | | 0.500 | 0.62 |

### Table 3. Priority Pricing Auction Outcomes

| Event | Number of Buyers with Reservation Value –0.25 | 0.25 | 0.75 | 1.25 | Probability of Event | Single Price $Q^*$ | $p^*$ | Total Sales | $\pi$ | Expected Profit Spot Sale | Forward Sale |
|---|---|---|---|---|---|---|---|---|---|---|---|
| 1 | 4 | 0 | 0 | 0 | 1/256 | 0 | 0.000 | 0.00 | –1.00 | –0.004 | 0.00 |
| 2 | 3 | 1 | 0 | 0 | 4/256 | 0 | 0.000 | 0.00 | –1.00 | –0.016 | 0.00 |
| 3 | 3 | 0 | 1 | 0 | 4/256 | 1 | 0.750 | 0.75 | –0.25 | –0.004 | 0.00 |
| 4 | 3 | 0 | 0 | 1 | 4/256 | 1 | 0.847 | 0.85 | –0.15 | –0.002 | 0.00 |
| 5 | 2 | 2 | 0 | 0 | 6/256 | 0 | 0.000 | 0.00 | –1.00 | –0.023 | 0.00 |
| 6 | 2 | 0 | 2 | 0 | 6/256 | 2 | 0.750 | 1.50 | 0.50 | 0.012 | 0.01 |
| 7 | 2 | 0 | 0 | 2 | 6/256 | 2 | 0.847 | 1.69 | 0.69 | 0.016 | 0.01 |
| 8 | 2 | 1 | 1 | 0 | 12/256 | 1 | 0.750 | 0.75 | –0.25 | –0.012 | 0.00 |
| 9 | 2 | 1 | 0 | 1 | 12/256 | 1 | 0.847 | 0.85 | –0.15 | –0.007 | 0.00 |
| 10 | 2 | 0 | 1 | 1 | 12/256 | 2 | 0.799 | 1.60 | 0.60 | 0.028 | 0.02 |
| 11 | 1 | 3 | 0 | 0 | 4/256 | 0 | 0.000 | 0.00 | –1.00 | –0.016 | 0.00 |
| 12 | 1 | 0 | 3 | 0 | 4/256 | 3 | 0.750 | 2.25 | 1.25 | 0.020 | 0.02 |
| 13 | 1 | 0 | 0 | 3 | 4/256 | 3 | 0.847 | 2.54 | 1.54 | 0.024 | 0.02 |
| 14 | 1 | 2 | 1 | 0 | 12/256 | 1 | 0.750 | 0.75 | –0.25 | –0.012 | 0.00 |
| 15 | 1 | 2 | 0 | 1 | 12/256 | 1 | 0.847 | 0.85 | –0.15 | –0.007 | 0.00 |
| 16 | 1 | 1 | 2 | 0 | 12/256 | 2 | 0.750 | 1.50 | 0.50 | 0.023 | 0.02 |
| 17 | 1 | 1 | 0 | 2 | 12/256 | 2 | 0.847 | 1.69 | 0.69 | 0.033 | 0.03 |
| 18 | 1 | 1 | 1 | 1 | 24/256 | 2 | 0.799 | 1.60 | 0.60 | 0.056 | 0.05 |
| 19 | 1 | 0 | 2 | 1 | 12/256 | 3 | 0.782 | 2.35 | 1.35 | 0.063 | 0.06 |
| 20 | 1 | 0 | 1 | 2 | 12/256 | 3 | 0.815 | 2.44 | 1.44 | 0.068 | 0.06 |
| 21 | 0 | 4 | 0 | 0 | 1/256 | 0 | 0.000 | 0.00 | –1.00 | –0.004 | 0.00 |
| 22 | 0 | 3 | 1 | 0 | 4/256 | 1 | 0.750 | 0.75 | –0.25 | –0.004 | 0.00 |
| 23 | 0 | 3 | 0 | 1 | 4/256 | 1 | 0.847 | 0.85 | –0.15 | –0.002 | 0.00 |
| 24 | 0 | 2 | 2 | 0 | 6/256 | 2 | 0.750 | 1.50 | 0.50 | 0.012 | 0.01 |
| 25 | 0 | 2 | 0 | 2 | 6/256 | 2 | 0.847 | 1.69 | 0.69 | 0.016 | 0.01 |
| 26 | 0 | 2 | 1 | 1 | 12/256 | 2 | 0.799 | 1.60 | 0.60 | 0.028 | 0.02 |
| 27 | 0 | 1 | 3 | 0 | 4/256 | 3 | 0.750 | 2.25 | 1.25 | 0.020 | 0.02 |
| 28 | 0 | 1 | 0 | 3 | 4/256 | 3 | 0.847 | 2.54 | 1.54 | 0.024 | 0.02 |
| 29 | 0 | 1 | 1 | 2 | 12/256 | 3 | 0.815 | 2.44 | 1.44 | 0.068 | 0.06 |
| 30 | 0 | 1 | 2 | 1 | 12/256 | 3 | 0.782 | 2.35 | 1.35 | 0.063 | 0.06 |
| 31 | 0 | 0 | 4 | 0 | 1/256 | 4 | 0.750 | 3.00 | 2.00 | 0.008 | 0.00 |
| 32 | 0 | 0 | 3 | 1 | 4/256 | 4 | 0.774 | 3.10 | 2.10 | 0.033 | 0.03 |
| 33 | 0 | 0 | 2 | 2 | 6/256 | 4 | 0.799 | 3.19 | 2.19 | 0.051 | 0.05 |
| 34 | 0 | 0 | 1 | 3 | 4/256 | 3 | 0.847 | 2.54 | 1.54 | 0.024 | 0.02 |
| 35 | 0 | 0 | 0 | 4 | 1/256 | 4 | 0.847 | 3.39 | 2.39 | 0.009 | 0.00 |
| | | | | | 1 | | | | | 0.585 | 0.69 |

*Table 4.* Comparative Statics Results

| | *Optimal Priority Pricing Auction* | | | | *Single Price* | *Optimal Priority Pricing Auction less Single Price* | | | |
|---|---|---|---|---|---|---|---|---|---|
| | *Scarcity Constraint* | | | | | | | | |
| *Dispersion Parameter, δ* | *Q*≤1 | *Q*≤2 | *Q*≤3 | *Q*≤4 | *Q*≤4 | *Q*≤1 | *Q*≤2 | *Q*≤3 | *Q*≤4 |
| **Expected Profit from Forward Sale** | | | | | | | | | |
| 1.20 | 1.616 | | | | 1.616 | 0.000 | | | |
| 1.00 | | 1.241 | | | 1.063 | | 0.178 | | |
| 0.50 | | 0.698 | | | 0.625 | | 0.073 | | |
| 0.25 | | 0.439 | | | 0.406 | | 0.033 | | |
| 0.18 | | | 0.356 | | 0.300 | | | 0.056 | |
| 0.10 | | | | 0.400 | 0.400 | | | | 0.000 |
| **Expected Profit from Spot Sale** | | | | | | | | | |
| 1.20 | 1.300 | | | | 1.300 | 0.000 | | | |
| 1.00 | | 1.179 | | | 1.000 | | 0.179 | | |
| 0.50 | | 0.585 | | | 0.500 | | 0.085 | | |
| 0.25 | | 0.289 | | | 0.250 | | 0.039 | | |
| 0.18 | | | 0.297 | | 0.230 | | | 0.067 | |
| 0.10 | | | | 0.400 | 0.400 | | | | 0.000 |
| **Strategic Value: Expected Profit from Forward Sale minus Expected Profit from Spot Sale** | | | | | | | | | |
| 1.20 | 0.316 | | | | 0.316 | | | | |
| 1.00 | | 0.062 | | | 0.063 | | | | |
| 0.50 | | 0.113 | | | 0.125 | | | | |
| 0.25 | | 0.150 | | | 0.156 | | | | |
| 0.18 | | | 0.059 | | 0.070 | | | | |
| 0.10 | | | | 0.000 | 0.000 | | | | |

value of R&D, a single price auction is tantamount to a priority pricing auction. Second, in cases where the dispersion in buyers' reservation prices is moderate, comparative statics results indicate that the expected profit from forward and spot sales is a convex (u-shaped) function of the variance in buyers' reservation prices. In addition, as expected, expected profit from forward sale is greater than or equal to the expected profit from spot sale for both a priority pricing auction and a single price auction.

The third panel reports the strategic value, which is the difference between expected profit from forward sale and expected profit from spot sale. In contrast with the expected profit, the strategic value is greater in a single price auction than in a priority pricing auction, when the dispersion is not extreme. When the dispersion is extreme, the strategic value of a priority pricing auction is equivalent to that of a single price auction. However, the strategic value of a forward sale again is a convex function of the variance in buyers' reservation prices.

## IV. DISCUSSION

Harris and Raviv (1981) demonstrated that when the supply of a product exceeds the maximum possible demand, a single price mechanism, rather than an auction, maximizes seller's profit. Added value for an auction is driven by competition in the fact of scarcity. Why, then, does the auction proposed in the last section give higher expected profits? One difference in our model, relative to the body of theoretical work on auctions (reviewed by McAfee and McMillan [1987]), is that we do not assume a fixed cost per unit. Rather than a reservation price level, the seller works from a reservation profit level for the project as a whole, which must be met from forward sales commitments before the project is accepted. The reservation profit level may be met by a small number of buyers at a high price or a larger number of buyers at a lower price, so it seems reasonable that the ability to vary price in the face of revealed demand would have value. The nature of forward sales also drives the ability to charge higher prices. In a normal spot auction, buyers are given incentive to bid their true reservation prices by the possibility that the limited supply of product will go to competitors if the buyers underbid. In a forward auction with no supply constraint, buyers are given an incentive to bid their true reservation prices by the possibility that the project will not be carried out if the buyers underbid. The "scarcity" that drives the auction is based not on real or artificial supply constraint but rather on the contingent nature of the product in such forward sales.

The relevance of a PPA as proposed here may appear suspect, given that the real process of arranging sponsorship for a group-funded R&D project is likely to be a complex multistage negotiation. However, an optimal PPA (in terms of the seller's expected profit) will generate an expected profit equal to the best average results possible in a real negotiation under optimal conditions.

## V. CONCLUSIONS

We have demonstrated an optimal model for valuing the expected profit along with the strategic advantage of forward sales over spot sales for R&D projects in the absence of perfect information for the seller about the reservation values of buyers for the project's results. There is a priority pricing auction which is superior to a single price allocation rule for the case of forward and spot sales. In addition, it is demonstrated that the value of a priority pricing auction depends upon the cross-sectional variation in reservation prices across buyers.

# APPENDIX: CALCULATION OF $Z_i^*$

Consider the following probabilities:

$P$ (at least 1 buyer has price $x_k$)

$= 1 - P$ (no buyer has price $x_k$)

$= 1 - \prod_{i=1}^{K} P$ (buyer $i$ does not have price $x_k$)

$$= 1 - \left(\frac{K-1}{K}\right)^N$$

$P$ (at least 1 buyer has price $x_{k-1}$ and buyers with price $x_k$ are 2 or less)

$= P$ (at least 1 buyer has price $x_{k-1} \mid$ buyer with price $x_k = 0$)

• $P$ (buyer with price $x_k = 0$)

$+ P$ (at least 1 buyer has price $x_{k-1} \mid$ buyer with price $x_k = 1$)

• $P$ (buyer with price $x_k = 1$)

$+ P$ (at least 1 buyer has price $x_{k-1} \mid$ buyer with price $x_k = 2$)

• $P$ (buyer with price $x_k = 2$)

$$= \left[1 - \left(\frac{K-2}{K-1}\right)^N\right]\left(\frac{K-1}{K}\right)^N$$

$$+ \left[1 - \left(\frac{K-2}{K-1}\right)^{N-1}\right](N_1)\left(\frac{1}{K}\right)\left(\frac{K-1}{K}\right)^{N-1}$$

$$+ \left[1 - \left(\frac{K-2}{K-1}\right)^{N-2}\right](N_2)\left(\frac{1}{K}\right)^2\left(\frac{K-1}{K}\right)^{N-2}$$

•

•

•

P (at least 1 buyer has price $x_{k-3}$ and buyers with price $x_{k-2}$ or $x_{k-1}$ or $x_k$ are 4 or less)

$$= \left[1 - \left(\frac{K-4}{K-3)}\right)^N\right]\left(\frac{K-3}{K}\right)^N$$

$$+ \left[1 - \left(\frac{K-4}{K-3}\right)^{N-1}\right](N_1)(K^3)^2\left(\frac{K-3}{K}\right)^{N-1}$$

$$+\left[1-\left(\frac{K-4}{K-3}\right)^{N-2}\right](N_2)(K^3)^2\left(\frac{K-3}{K}\right)^{N-2}$$

$$+\left[1-\left(\frac{K-4}{K-3}\right)^{N-3}\right](N_3)(\frac{3}{K})^3\left(\frac{K-3}{K}\right)^{N-3}$$

$$+\left[1-\left(\frac{K-4}{K-3}\right)^{N-4}\right](N_4)(\frac{3}{K})^4\left(\frac{K-3}{K}\right)^{N-4}$$

In general, we can express the probability of event as follows:

$$Z_i^* = \left\{\sum_{j=o}^{Q}[N_j]\left[\frac{0-1}{K}\right]^j\left[\frac{k-0+1}{K}\right]^{N-j}\right\} \otimes$$

$$\left\{1-\left(\frac{K-0}{K-Q+1}\right)^{N-j}\right\}$$

and $Q = K - T + 1$.

## ACKNOWLEDGMENTS

We are grateful to two anonymous referees for their comments. We also thank the Leavev School of Business for research support.

## NOTES

1. The advantages accruing to forward contract negotiation for capital budgeting decisions have been widely treated in the literature from the perspective of the information obtained on future demand. That perspective has been quantatively embodied in "arbitrage" models by Cox, Ingersoll, and Ross (1981) and Brennan and Schwartz (1985), in which the value of the forward contract is the value of the exogenous price risk transferred from seller to buyers. The assumptions of these models are a competitive system in which the equilibrium forward price is the anticipated future spot price. For the type of R&D projects, the product is unique, there is not a competitive market, and the "arbitrage" models are not appropriate.

2. The principal source of strategic advantage for forward sales lies in the ability of the seller to reject the project if the buyer's bid prices do not offer adequate return on the investment. In other words, by bidding less than his reservation price, a buyer may increase his or her chance of receiving the product.

3. Sources of conflict among potential parties to a coalition are, however, unavoidable. Perceptions about the likely success of an R&D effort may vary greatly among potential participants. Moreover, the value of the R&D effort to potential participants may depend upon their differing abilities to implement the resulting technology. Where the conflicts of interest are high and the number of potential participants is small, the incentives for opportunistic bargaining are accentuated. The result may be organizational failure. Sematech, a proposed joint venture to produce high-capacity dynamic memory chips, is a case in point.

4. Interestingly, two very different approaches have been adopted in practice. The electronics industry favors the research consortium approach—Bellcore, SRC and MCC are prime examples. There have, however, been some questions raised about the effectiveness of this approach in recent press (see Liebowitz [1990] for an evaluation of the performance of U.S. research consortia).

In contrast, biotechnology firms have opted for the long-term forward sale of R&D approach, for example, initial public offerings of Bio-Electro Systems, Inc. underwritten by Merrill Lynch Capital Markets in November 1988, as well as Tocor, Inc., underwritten by Paine Webber Inc., and Habrecht & Quist in July 1989. In the first case, Alza Corporation had an option to purchase the results of the R&D at exercise prices ranging from $23 to $57 per share depending upon the date of exercise, approximately 2 to 6 years from inception; in the second case, Centocor Inc., at exercise prices ranging from $24 to $32 per share, again depending upon the date of exercise, approximately 3 to 4 years from inception. In addition, the purchasing corporations, Alza and Centocor, shared in the risk of R&D by providing shareholders in Bio-Electro Systems and Tocor with a warrant to purchase one share of Alza and Centocor, respectively, at a fixed exercise price. The use of forward sale contracts has also been used in the movie film industry. Under a fee arrangement with MCA, Imagine Films Entertainment Inc., an independent production company led by Ron Howard and producer Brian Grazer, receives a per movie production overhead fee whether the movies are hits or bombs. In addition, there is a risk-sharing arrangement with MCA. Imagine receives a contingent interest in the film's profits. If all the films do well, Imagine will get to keep part of the profit. But if one film bombs, a portion of Imagine's profit participation in other films is pledged back to MCA to help it recoup the loss.

While group R&D may be organized in a variety of ways, Souder and Nassar (1990) in a survey of consortium participants find that current opinion favors R&D sponsor pools over more permanent, industry-wide organization joint ventures.

5. Following Harris and Raviv (1981), a priority pricing auction is the one in which various prices are charged and buyers paying higher prices are assigned higher priority in receiving the product.

6. For comparability, we utilize whenever possible the notation used in Parsons (1989) as well as Harris and Raviv (1981) to develop the R&D pricing model in this paper.

## REFERENCES

Brennan, M., and Schwartz, E. (1985). "Evaluating Natural Resource Investments." *Journal of Business* 58: 135–157.

Cox, J., Ingersoll, J., and Ross, S. (1981). "The Relation between Forward Prices and Future Prices." *Journal of Financial Economics* 9: 321–346.

Harris, M., and Raviv, A. (1981). "A Theory of Monopoly Pricing Schemes with Demand Uncertainty." *American Economic Review* 71: 347–365.

Jo, H., Lee, W., and Zwemer, D. (1990). "Forward vs. Spot Sales for Consortium-Funded Research and Development." Working paper, Santa Clara University.

Liebowitz, M. (1990). "U.S. Consortia: How Do They Measure Up?" *Electronic Business* January 22, 1990: 46–52.

McAfee, R., and McMillan, J. (1987). "Auctions and Bidding." *Journal of Economic Literature* 25: 699–738.

Parsons, J. (1989). "Estimating the Strategic Value of Long-Term Forward Purchase Contracts Using Auction Models." *Journal of Finance* 44: 981–1010.

Souder, W., and Nassar, S. (1990). "Choosing an R&D Consortium." *Research Technology Management* (March –April): 35–41.

# OPTIMUM DIVIDEND:

## A REEXAMINATION

Dilip K. Ghosh and Gordian A. Ndubizu

## I. INTRODUCTION

James Walter (1956) established that as long as the rate of return on undistributed earnings of corporations exceeded the rate required by equity investors, zero payout ratio was preferable to any positive payout policy, and in the converse situation, zero plowback ratio was the optimum policy. In a subsequent paper (1963), he reasserted the same result after an extensive and detailed examination of dividend issue. Gordon (1959), however, brought out in revealing fashion the direct relationship between dividend and stock price through simple analytics of valuation principle, and thus proved that the higher the dividend payment, the higher the stock price, and vice versa. When this claim of unchallenged merit of payout policy was at its peak of popularity, Miller and Modigliani (1961) dismissed the Gordon result and established the irrelevance of dividend policy by showing that valuation of shares was independent of if or when dividend was paid in perfect capital market. Several works followed the Miller–Modigliani paper to settle the controversy; some researchers even vindicated the Miller–Modigliani result of irrelevance even

**Advances in Quantitative Analysis of Finance and Accounting,**
**Volume 2, Part B, pages 93–104.**

**ISBN: 1-55938-565-0**

in the presence of market distortions such as taxes. Lintner (1956), however, concluded that "generalized uncertainty" would suffice to ensure that shareholders would not be indifferent to whether cash dividends were increased or decreased by substituting new equity issues for retained earnings to finance given capital budgets.

The examination of the dividend puzzle has followed a number of routes since then. Brennan (1970) has demonstrated that as long as the tax rate on dividend income is greater than the tax rate on capital gains, it will be rational to pay no dividend; but Miller and Scholes (1982) argue that even in the presence of different tax rates, individuals can be indifferent between dividend income and capital gains as they can, by a properly calculated investment design, get away with paying only the lower tax rate. In this sense, a firm's value remains unaffected by dividend policy even in the world of taxes. The issue has been further examined by Black and Scholes (1974), Litzenberger and Ramaswamy (1979), Fehrs, Benesh, and Peterson (1988), Ghosh and Woolridge (1988), Eades (1982), Asquith and Mullins (1983), Jayaraman and Shastri (1988), Woolridge (1982), and Ofer and Thakor (1987).

The second line of research, however, moves along the line of its "signaling" effect. The pioneering work of Ross (1977), followed by Bahattacharya (1979, 1980), Miller and Rock (1985), Ambarish, John, and Williams (1987), and Brickly and McConnell (1987), discusses the impact of dividend announcement policy and how that affects the valuation of a firm. By using the agency theory, Easterbrook (1984) shows that when firms issue dividends they can reduce the shareholders' cost of monitoring managers and also lessen the problems of managers who choose too safe projects. When a firm increases dividend, it becomes more of a need for the firm to go out in the capital market for necessary external funds, which leads to a reduction in agency costs, and that reduction in agency costs tends to increase the firm's share price. Asquith and Mullins (1983) show the positive correlation between dividend payout and stock price. Thus, we find that independent of analytical approaches pursued thus far in the literature on the dividend question, the central issue remains to be one as to whether dividend increases the share price and thus the valuation of the firm.

Recently, Ghosh (1990, 1992a, b) reexamines this question within an intertemporal maximization framework by utilizing the optimum control theory á la Pontryagin et al. (1962). This approach is in fact a modified version of Sau (1969), which is based on two related works of Lintner (1956, 1963), a work by Baumol (1962), and the paper by Jorgensen, Kort, and Van Schijndel (1989). The paper by Lee, Rahman, and Liaw (1990), and an earlier work by Lee and Gupta (1977) are also similar in analytical approach. The problem is set up by maximizing utility over time, subject to the dynamics of equity buildup, and in this utility maximand dividend is taken, as in Sau (1969), as the argument. It is established that utility maximization and value maximization boil down to the same thing in this dynamic structure, and thus this new approach resurrects the old concept of value maximization through a new technique. By formulating the Hamiltonian correctly, the optimum value of the dividend has been established, and thus the main thrust of the existing literature has been nicely unified.

In the same spirit, here we also use an intertemporal utility function in which dividends of successive periods are the arguments. Taking the discrete version of time profile, we avoid much of mathematical complexities involved in the papers just cited, and yet we derive the optimum dividend that is also amenable to empirical testing.

The analytical model is based on the rational dynamic decision-making process of individual investors. We postulate that the typical investor represents all investors and thus, on the flip side of the coin, represents the rational choice of the corporation in the perfect market setting. We, therefore, begin our discussion by assuming that the typical investor demands a dividend at each instant of time since it is with this income he meets his current expenditure. The investor maximizes his utility function, subject to his lifetime wealth constraint, and derives the optimum value of dividend at each instant of time. In Section II, we present the formal analytical structure with this objective in mind. In Section III, we test our theoretical framework with data from Compustat tapes on 15 major corporations, and thus examine how our theory relates to reality.

## II. THE ANALYTICAL STRUCTURE

Assume that the representative investor demands a dividend as an income that he can use to buy baskets of consumption goods and other items on his current expenditure. We postulate that utility is derived from dividends of different periods. That is, formally the investor has the following problem:

$$\max U = U(D_0, D_1, D_2, \ldots\ldots\ldots\ldots, D_T) \tag{1}$$

subject to

$$W_0 \; (\equiv A_0 + \sum_{t=0}^{T} E_t/(1+i)^t = \sum_{t=0}^{T} P_t D_t/(1+i)^t, \tag{2}$$

where $W_0 \equiv$ current wealth (i.e., current value of nonhuman capital, $A_0$) plus present value of current and (expected) future income, $E_t$. $D_t$ is the real dividend at time $t$, and $i$ is the nominal rate of interest, which is held constant, and $T$ is the life expectancy of the investor.

Since by virtue of Fisher's relation:

$$1 + i = (1 + r)(1 + P), \text{ or}$$

$$i = r + P \text{ (by ignoring second order of small, } rP),$$

where $r$ stands for real interest and $P$ measures inflation rate, we can rewrite the budget constraint given by Eq. (2) as follows:

$$W_0 = \sum_{t=0}^{T} D_t/(1+r)^t. \tag{2.1}$$

Consider the intertemporal utility function in more specific functional form as follows:

$$U = \sum_{t=0}^{T} \beta_t\, U(D_t), \tag{1'}$$

where $\beta_{t+1} = \beta_t/(1+\delta)$, $\delta$ being the subjective rate of time preference. If $\beta_0$ is set equal to unity, Eq. (1′) can be expressed as follows:

$$U = \sum_{t=0}^{T} U(D_t)/(1+\delta)^t. \tag{1.1}$$

Now, the maximization of Eq. (1.1), subject to (2.1), means the maximization of the following Lagrangean function:

$$L = \sum_{t=0}^{T} U(D_t)/(1+\delta)^t + \mu\Big(W_0 - \sum_{t=0}^{T} D_t/(1+r)^t\Big). \tag{3}$$

The necessary conditions for the maximum are given then as follows:

$$\frac{\partial L}{\partial D_t} = \frac{U_{Dt}}{(1+\delta)^t} - \frac{1}{(1+r)^t} = 0, \tag{4.1}$$

and

$$\frac{\partial L}{\partial D_{t+1}} = \frac{U_{Dt+1}}{(1+\delta)^{t+1}} - \frac{1}{(1+r)^{t+1}} = 0. \tag{4.2}$$

From Eqs. (4.1) and (4.2) one obtains

$$U_{Dt}/U_{Dt+1} = (1+r)/(1+\delta) \text{ for } t = 0, 1, 2, \ldots\ldots, T-1.$$

$$\therefore \text{ if } r = \delta,\ U_{Dt} = U_{Dt+1} \text{ for } 0 \le t \le T-1.$$

But if $r \neq \delta$, then the percentage change in $D$ per time period, $\lambda$, is approximated by

$$\lambda \approx \sigma(r-\delta)/(1+\delta). \tag{5}$$

Here $\sigma$ is the elasticity of substitution à la Hicks (1946) between the dividend in two successive time periods, which we assume to be constant. However, if $\sigma = 1$, the relation (5) holds *exactly*. This is

$$\lambda = \sigma(r - \delta)/(1 + \delta). \tag{5.1}$$

It can be further established that as $T$ becomes large, the result that the dividend grows at a constant rate $\lambda$, the budget constraint (2.1), and the condition $r > \lambda$ (which must hold for the dividend to increase at a constant rate $\lambda$ with $W_0$ finite) together imply that the optimum current dividend converges to

$$D^*_0 = W_0\,(r - \lambda)/(1 + r), \tag{6}$$

which can be rewritten as

$$D^*_0 = W_0 \cdot \frac{r}{1+r} - W_0 \cdot \frac{\lambda}{1+r}. \tag{6.1}$$

The first term on the right-hand side of Eq. (6.1) can be construed as the *normal* dividend: the rate of dividend, which if continued indefinitely, would have a present value equal to $W_0$. It is the dividend analogous to Farrel's (1959) *normal* income. The second term on the right-hand side of (6.1) adjusts current period dividend relative to normal dividend to allow the time trajectory of dividend to slope upward or downward. If $r > \delta$ (or $r < \delta$), the dividend in the current period will be less than (or greater than) the normal dividend and the optimum dividend will increase (decrease) over time.

Differentiation of Eq. (6.1) with respect to the real rate of interest yields

$$\frac{dD^*_0}{dr} = W_0 \cdot \frac{1}{(1+r)^2} - W_0 \cdot \frac{\sigma}{(1+r)^2} + \frac{dW_0}{dr} \cdot \frac{r-\lambda}{(1+r)}. \tag{7}$$

The first term on the right-hand side of Eq. (7) is the intertemporal equivalent of the Slutsky income effect, and the second term is the dynamic analogue of the Slutsky substitution effect, representing the substitution of future for current dividend, holding normal dividend constant. The third term, on the right, measures the wealth effect, and it represents the change in the current dividend which results from any change in current real wealth triggered by the change in real interest.

If we ignore the wealth effect, the real interest elasticity of dividend, $\varepsilon_r$, equals

$$\varepsilon_r = [(1 - \sigma)/(1 + r)]\cdot[r/(r - \lambda)]. \tag{8}$$

Thus, given $\lambda$, the real interest elasticity of dividend depends on $(1 - \sigma)$ and the balance between income and substitution effects of Eq. (7).

Now, to derive an estimable form of Eq. (2.1), we substitute (5.1) for $\lambda$ into Eq. (6) and use the approximation

$$W_0 = A_0 + bE_0,$$

where $b$ is the parameter that capitalizes current labor income $E_0$ into human wealth $W_0$. Then we obtain

$$D^*_0 = (A_0 + bE_0)\{[1 - \sigma/(1 + \delta)] \cdot [r/(1 + r)]$$

$$+ [\sigma\delta/(1 + \delta)][1/(1 + r)]\}. \tag{9}$$

In conformity with the accepted practice in the received macroeconomic literature, assume that the current dividend is the weighted average of the current optimum dividend and the past actual dividend. That is,

$$D_t = \Theta D^*_t + (1 - \Theta)D_{t-1}, \ \ 0 \leq \Theta \leq 1. \tag{10}$$

Now, by incorporating Eq. (10) into (9) we obtain the following:

$$D_t = \Theta[1 - \sigma/(1 + \partial)][bE_t r/(1 + r)$$

$$+ A_t r/(1 + r)] + [\Theta\sigma\delta/(1 + \delta].$$

$$[bE_t/(1 + r) + A_t/(1 + r)] + (1 - \Theta)D_{t-1}. \tag{11}$$

We then aggregate over all investors in each corporation we study in Section III by substituting the resulting aggregate variables for the microvariables we have considered. The empirical structures discussed below are the simple linearized approximations of the theoretical model derived in Eq. (11).

## III. EMPIRICAL ESTIMATES

To empirically estimate the optimum corporate dividend, Eq. (11) is reduced to

$$D_t = a[bE_t r/(1 + r) + A_t r/(1 + r)]$$

$$+ c[bE_t(1 + r) + A_t(1 + r)] + zD_{t-1}$$

$$+ e_t, \tag{12}$$

where

$$a = [1 - \sigma/(1 + \delta)] \tag{13}$$

$$c = [\Theta\sigma\delta/(1 + \delta)] \tag{14}$$

$$z = (1 - \Theta) \tag{15}$$

$$e = \text{stochastic error term}$$

$$D_t = ab[E_t r/(1 + r) + a[A_t r/(1 + r)] + cb[E_t/(1 + r) + c[A/(1 + r)] + zD_{t-1} + e_t. \quad (16)$$

The important coefficients are $a$, $c$, and $z$. The coefficient $a$ measures the substitution effect, $c$ measures the wealth effect, while $z$ captures the effect of past actual dividend on current real dividend. Coefficients $ab$ and $cb$ are parameters that capitalize current earnings per share into wealth.

The variables utilized to estimate Eq. (16) are defined as follows:

| | | |
|---|---|---|
| $E_t$ | = | earnings per common share at time $t$ |
| $CD_t$ | = | cash dividend per common share at time $t$ |
| $A_t$ | = | assets per common share at time $t$ |
| $D_t$ | = | $(CD * 100)/CPI$ |
| $CPI$ | = | consumer price index, 1972 = 100; obtained from the U.S. Department of Labor, Bureau of Labor Statistics; |
| $r$ | = | $i - P$ |
| $i$ | = | nominal interest rate: three-month treasury bill rate in percent per annum obtained from the Federal Reserve Bank of Philadelphia |
| $P$ | = | change in $CPI$. |

The firm-specific variables (e.g., $E_t$, $CD_t$, and $A_t$) used to estimate Eq. (16) are obtained from the quarterly Compustat tape from 1979 to 1989. The sample of firms and their industrial classification code (SIC) are provided in the Appendix.

Equation (16) was fitted on an individual firm over time as well at a given point of time across the sample firms. The individual results were consistent across firms. Thus, allowing a cross-sectional analysis to be performed on the sample, the SAS Autoreg procedure with the maximum likelihood iterative technique ($NLag = 4$) was used to the structures for autocorrelated error terms. This technique was applied in both the individual and cross-sectional models. The White (1980) test of heteroskedasticity was applied only to the cross-sectional models. The results indicate the absence of heteroskedastic error terms.

## IV. RESULTS

Table 1 reports results of different versions of Eq. (16), explaining the wealth and past dividend effects on current real dividend. The result shows that wealth coefficient ($c$) is positive and significant at the 0.01 level. Similar results are observed in regressions 3 and 4, which examine jointly the effect of wealth and past dividends. These findings indicate that current real dividend is positively

*Table 1.* Estimates of Wealth Effect on Current Real Dividend

| | *Intercept* $\alpha$ | *ab* | *a* | *cb* | *c* | *z* | $R^2$ | *D–W* |
|---|---|---|---|---|---|---|---|---|
| **Regression 1** | | | | | | | | |
| *B*-value | 0.0007 | | | | 0.1256 | | 0.57 | 2.00 |
| *t*-ratio | (4.16) | | | | (12.23) | | | |
| Probability | 0.000 | | | | 0.000*** | | | |
| **Regression 2** | | | | | | | | |
| *B*-value | 0.0013 | | | −0.0054 | 0.1362 | | 0.61 | 1.94 |
| *t*-ratio | (6.34) | | | (−10.36) | (13.70) | | | |
| Probability | 0.000*** | | | 0.000*** | 0.000*** | | | |
| **Regression 3** | | | | | | | | |
| *B*-value | 0.0006 | | | | 0.1285 | 0.0286 | 0.57 | 1.99 |
| *t*-ratio | (2.91) | | | | (11.86) | (0.62) | | |
| Probability | 0.003*** | | | | 0.000*** | 0.538 | | |
| **Regression 4** | | | | | | | | |
| *B*-value | 0.0012 | | | −0.0059 | 0.1324 | 0.1365 | 0.63 | 1.94 |
| *t*-ratio | (5.71) | | | (−11.28) | (13.16) | (3.34) | | |
| Probability | 0.000 | | | 0.000*** | 0.000*** | 0.000*** | | |

*Notes*: $D_t = \alpha + ab[E_t r/(1 + r) + a[A_t r/(1 + r)] + cb[E_t/(1 + r)] + c[A/(1 + r)] + zD_{t-1}$.

$R^2$ = *r*-square; *D-W* = Durbin–Watson statistic.

***Significant at 0.01 level.

influenced by accumulated earnings and past real dividend. However, past real dividend is not significant in regression 3, which implies that actual dividend is robust to the partial adjustment mechanism introduced in Eq. (11).

The effect of return on wealth on current real dividend (substitution effect) is reported in Table 2. The results show that the substitution coefficient is positive and significant in all the cases as predicted. When the past dividend effect was included in regression 7, the model *R*-square increased by 0.01, indicating that the substitution effect dominates the past dividend effect. A similar result is also observed in Table 1, regression 4 for wealth effect. In this case, the *R*-square increased from 0.61 (regression 2) to 0.62 (regression 4). These findings indicate that the estimated current real dividend approximates the optimum dividend formalized in Eq. (9). Thus, the past dividend has a modest effect on current real dividend.

To examine the wealth, substitution, and past dividend effects more completely, Eq. (16) was estimated with and without the partial adjustment (e.g., past dividend).

*Table 2.* Estimates of Return on Wealth (Substitution Effect on Current Real Dividend)

| | *Intercept* $\alpha$ | *ab* | *a* | *cb* | *c* | *z* | $R^2$ | *D–W* |
|---|---|---|---|---|---|---|---|---|
| **Regression 5** | | | | | | | | |
| *B*-value | 0.0001 | | 0.0276 | | | | 0.60 | 1.94 |
| *t*-ratio | (1.02) | | (18.42) | | | | | |
| Probability | 0.307 | | 0.000*** | | | | | |
| **Regression 6** | | | | | | | | |
| *B*-value | 0.0009 | –0.006 | 0.0250 | | | | 0.62 | 1.92 |
| *t*-ratio | (5.07) | (–7.98) | (16.47) | | | | | |
| Probability | 0.000*** | 0.000*** | 0.000*** | | | | | |
| **Regression 7** | | | | | | | | |
| *B*-value | 0.0011 | –0.0008 | 0.0234 | | | 0.0583 | 0.63 | 1.93 |
| *t*-ratio | (5.05) | (–9.39) | (14.72) | | | (1.41) | | |
| Probability | 0.000*** | 0.000*** | 0.000*** | | | 0.159 | | |

*Notes*: $D_t = \alpha + ab[E_t r/(1 + r)] + a[A_t r/(1 + r)] + cb[E_t/(1 + r)] + c[A_t/(1 + r)] + zD_{t-1}$.
$R^2$ = *r*-square; *D-W* = Durbin–Watson statistic.
***Significant at 0.01 level.

Table 3 reports results of different versions of the maximum likelihood regression described in Eq. (16). The past dividend is dropped in regression 8.

The results show that the current real dividend is positively associated with the return on wealth (substitution effect). The substitution coefficient $a$ is positive and significant in both regressions 8 and 9. In contrast, the wealth coefficient $c$ is not significant at the 0.10 level. The result in regression 8 indicates that the substitution effect dominates the wealth effect. Such a result may have implications for firms' valuation since stock price equals the discounted present value of future dividends (Easton and Zmijewski, 1989).

The results in regression 9 provide more complete estimates of Eq. (16). The addition of the past dividend does not change the *R*-square, indicating that the partial adjustment has a very modest effect on current real dividend. However, the coefficient of the past dividend is positive and significant at the 0.05 level. Consistent with regression 8, the coefficient of return on wealth ($a$) is positive and significant. In contrast, the wealth coefficient is not significant at the 0.10 level. Thus, the current real dividend is determined by return on corporate wealth as well as past dividend. However, the return on wealth dominates the past dividend effect. These findings support the intertemporal optimum dividend formalized in Eq. (11).

*Table 3.* Estimates of Current Real Dividend

| | *Intercept* $\alpha$ | *ab* | *a* | *cb* | *c* | *z* | $R^2$ | *D–W* |
|---|---|---|---|---|---|---|---|---|
| **Regression 8** | | | | | | | | |
| *B*-value | 0.0009 | 0.0009 | 0.0223 | –0.051 | 0.0157 | | 0.63 | 1.91 |
| *t*-ratio | (4.86) | (0.36) | (4.53) | (–3.00) | (0.49) | | | |
| Probability | 0.000*** | 0.714 | 0.000*** | 0.002*** | 0.626 | | | |
| **Regression 9** | | | | | | | | |
| *B*-value | 0.0009 | 0.0000 | 0.0167 | –0.053 | 0.0409 | 0.0875 | 0.63 | 1.91 |
| *t*-ratio | (4.71) | (0.01) | (2.87) | (–2.67) | (1.09) | (2.05) | | |
| Probability | 0.000*** | 0.993 | 0.004*** | 0.008*** | 0.277 | 0.041** | | |

*Notes*: $D_t = \alpha + ab[E_t r/(1+r) + a[A_{t\,r}/(1+r)] + cb[E_t/(1+r)] + c[A/(1+r)] + zD_{t-1}$.
$R^2$ = *r*-square; $D - W$ = Durbin–Watson statistic.
***Significant at 0.01 level.
** Significant at 0.05 level.

## APPENDIX: SAMPLE FIRMS AND INDUSTRY MEMBERSHIP

| *Sample Firms* | *SIC* |
|---|---|
| General Motors | 37 |
| Ford | 37 |
| USX | 33 |
| General Electric | 36 |
| Chrysler | 37 |
| Texaco | 29 |
| Chevron | 29 |
| Amoco | 29 |
| Occidental Retro | 29 |
| Atlantic Richfield | 29 |
| Tenneco | 29 |
| Phillips Petroleum | 29 |
| Caterpillar | 35 |
| Sara Lee | NA |
| Weyerhaeuser | 24 |
| Aluminum Co. of America | 33 |
| General Dynamics | 37 |
| International Paper | 26 |
| Georgia Pacific | 24 |
| Conagra Omaha | 20 |

| | |
|---|---|
| Johnson and Johnson | 26 |
| Anheuser-Busch | 20 |
| Unocal | 29 |
| Sun Radner | NA |
| Union Carbide | 28 |

## REFERENCES


Ambarish R., John, K., and Williams, J. (1987). "Efficient Signalling with Dividends and Investments." *Journal of Finance* 42, No. 2 (June): 84–87.

Asquith, P., and Mullins, D. (1983). "The Impact of Initiating Dividend Payments on Shareholders' Wealth." *Journal of Business* 56, No. 1 (January): 77–96.

Baumol, W. J. (1962). "On the Theory of Expansion of the Firm." *American Economic Review* 52 (No. 5).

Bhattacharya, S. (1979). "Imperfect Information, Dividend Policy, and 'The Bird in the Hand' Fallacy." *Bell Journal of Economics* 10, No.1 (Spring): 259–270.

Bhattacharya, S. (1980). "Nondissipative Signalling Structures and Dividend Policy." *Quarterly Journal of Economics* 95, No. 1(December): 1–24.

Black, F., and Scholes, M. S. (1974). "The Effects of Dividend Yield and Dividend Policy on Common Stock Prices and Returns." *Journal of Financial Economics* 1, No. 1 (May): 1–22.

Born, J. A. (1988). "Insider Ownership and Signals: Evidence from Dividend Initiation Announcement Effects." *Financial Management* 7, No.1 (Spring): 38–45.

Brennan, M. J. (1970). "Taxes, Market Valuation, and Corporate Financial Policy." *National Tax Journal* (December).

Brickley, J. A., and McConnell, J. J. (1987). "Dividend Policy." In *The New Palgrave: A Dictionary of Economics*. New York: Stockton Press.

Eades, K. M. (1982). "Empirical Evidence on Dividends as a Signal of a Firm Value." *Journal of Financial and Quantitative Analysis* 17, No. 4 (November): 471–500.

Easterbrook, F. H. (1984). "Two Agency-Cost Explanations of Dividends." *American Economic Review* 74, No. 4 (September): 650–659.

Easton, P., and Zmijewski, M. (1989). "Cross-Sectional Variations in the Stock Market Response to Accounting Earnings Announcements." *Journal of Accounting and Economics.*

Fama, E. F., and Babiak, H. (1968). "Dividend Policy: An Empirical Analysis." *Journal of American Statistical Association* (December).

Farrel, M. J. (1959). "The New Theories of the Consumption Function. *Economic Journal* 69, No. 4: 678–696.

Fehrs, D. H., Benesh, G. A., and Peterson, D. R. (1988). "Evidence of a Relation Between Stock Price Reactions around Changes in Cash Dividends and Yields." *Journal of Financial Research* 11, No. 2 (Summer): 111–124.

Ghosh, D. K. (1990). "Dividend and Growth." *Advances in Quantitative Analysis in Finance and Accounting* 1: 225–229.

Ghosh, D. K. (1992a). "Optimal Capital Structure Redefined." *Financial Review* 27 (August): 411–429.

Ghosh, D. K. (1992b). "Optimum Dividend in an Intertemporal Optimization Framework." Mimeo.

Ghosh C., and Woolridge, J. R. (1988). "An Analysis of Shareholder Reaction to Dividend Cuts and Omissions." *Journal of Financial Research* 11, No. 4 (Winter): 281–294.

Gordon, M. (1959). "Dividends, Earnings and Stock Prices." *Review of Economics and Statistics* 41, No. 2 (May): 99–105.

Hicks, J. R. (1946). *Value and Capital*. Oxford: Clarenden Press.

Jayaraman, N., and Shastri, K. (1988). "The Valuation Impacts of Specially Designated Dividends." *Journal of Financial and Quantitative Analysis* 23, No. 1 (September): 301–312.

Jorgensen, S., Kort, P. H., and van Schijndel, G-J. C. T. (1989). "Optimal Investment, Financing, and Dividends: A Stackelberg Differential Game." *Journal of Economic Dynamics & Control* 13 (July): 339–377.

Lee, C.-F., and Gupta, M. C. (1977). "An Inter-Temporal Approach to the Optimization of Dividend with Pre-Determined Investment: A Further Comment." *Journal of Finance* 32, No. 4 (September): 1358–1361.

Lee, C.-F., Rahman, S., and Liaw, T. P. (1990). "Interaction of Investment, Financing and Dividend Policy: A Control Theory Approach." Presented at the TIMS/ORSA Annual Meetings, Las Vegas, NV, May.

Lintner, J. (1963). "The Cost of Capital and Optimal Financing of Corporate Growth." *Journal of Finance* 18, No. 2 (March): 292–310.

Lintner, J. (1963). "Optimal Dividends and Corporate Growth under Uncertainty." *Quarterly Journal of Economics* 78, No. 1 (November): 49–95.

Litzenberger, R. H., and Ramaswamy, K. (1979). "The Effects of Personal Taxes and Dividends on Capital Assets Prices: Theory and Empirical Evidence." *Journal of Financial Economics* 7, No. 2 (June): 163–196.

Miller, M., and Modigliani, F. (1961). "Dividend Policy, Growth, and the Valuation of Shares." *Journal of Business* 34, No. 4 (October): 411–433.

Miller, M., and Rock, K. (1985). "Dividend Policy under Asymmetric Information." *Journal of Finance* 40, No. 4 (September): 1031–1051.

Miller, M., and Scholes, M. S. "Dividends and Taxes: Some Empirical Evidence." *Journal of Political Economy* (December).

Ofer, A., and Thakor, A. V. (1987). "A Theory of Stock Price Responses to Alternative Corporate Cash Disbursement Methods: Stock Repurchases and Dividends." *Journal of Finance* 42, No. 2 (June): 365–394.

Pontryagin, L. S., Boltyanskii, V. G., Gamkrelidze, R. V., and Mishchenko, F. (1962). *The Mathematical Theory of Optimal Processes*, translated by K. N. Trirogoff. New York: Interscience Publishers, John Wiley & Sons.

Ross, S. A. (1977). "The Determination of Financial Structure: The Incentive Signalling Approach." *Bell Journal of Economics* 8, No. 1 (Spring): 23–40.

Sau, R. K. (1969). "The Optimal Rate of Investment in a Firm." *Journal of Finance* 24, No. 1 (March): 1–12.

Woolridge, J. R. (1982). "The Information Content of Dividend Changes." *Journal of Financial Research* 5, No. 3 (Fall): 237–247.

Walter, J. (1956). "Dividend Policies and Common Stock Prices." *Journal of Finance* 11, No. 1 (March): 29–41.

Walter, J. (1963). "Dividend Policy: Its Influence on the Value of the Enterprise." *Journal of Finance* (May): 280–291.

White, H. (1980). "A Heteroscedasticity-Consistent Covariance Matrix Estimator and a Direct Test for Heteroscedasticity." *Econometrica* 48, No. 2.

# A COMPARISON OF THE FINANCIAL CHARACTERISTICS OF COMPANIES IN THE CORE AND PERIPHERY ECONOMIES

Philip Karpik and Ahmed Riahi-Belkaoui


## ABSTRACT

Models derived from theories of economic dualism postulate a group of dominant "core" industries versus secondary "periphery" industries. Most empirical research relying on financial data fails to distinguish between companies in the core and periphery economies. This study tests for sector differences in firm size, beta, leverage, liquidity, and related financial ratios. Also examined are interaction effects among sector class, fiscal year-end (December versus non-December), and stock exchange listing. Finally, a logistic regression model explaining core versus periphery class membership is developed and tested.


**Advances in Quantitative Analysis of Finance and Accounting,**
**Volume 2, Part B, pages 105–139.**

**ISBN: 1-55938-565-0**

# I. INTRODUCTION

The accounting literature has actively examined the question of how various groupings of firms differ or are similar in terms of financial characteristics. Such groupings or classifications include industry membership (King, 1966), size, similarity of accounting and/or market-based variables (Frecka, 1982), fiscal year-end, and/or stock exchange membership (Smith and Pourciau, 1988). The presence of systematic financial differences among groupings creates difficulties in interpreting empirical research findings. For example, unexpected security price changes and duration of price adjustments were found to be sensitive to certain financial characteristics, such as firm size, that differ systematically between subgroups of companies (Atiase, 1985). Some research examines joint hypotheses of sufficient firm similarity and a predicted financial phenomenon, such as tests of the information transfer hypothesis (Baginski, 1987).

Most empirical research relying on financial data, and COMPUSTAT data in particular, fails to distinguish between firms in the core and periphery sectors. The combination of firms from both sectors in the investigation of economic, financial, accounting, and managerial phenomena may affect the generalizibility of the findings, given that firms in different sectors of the economy may be characterized by systematic differences that impact the measure of the treatment effect. Accordingly, this study examines the differences between the fundamental financial characteristics of firms in the core and periphery sectors of the economy. Section II discusses the rationale behind the stratification in a dual economy. Section III reviews related research. The fourth section presents the research model, followed by sections on the methodology, a discussion of the empirical results, and conclusions.

# II. STRATIFICATION IN A DUAL ECONOMY

Models of sectoral differentiation derived from theories of economic dualism exhibit three main perspectives: (1) theories of a dual economy, (2) dual labor markets, and (3) labor force segmentation (Cain, 1976; Hodson and Kaufman, 1982; Beck, Horan, and Tolbert, 1978). A common characteristic of these three perspectives is the division of the industrial structure of the economy into two distinct sectors (at least in the two sector model) consisting of the *core* and *periphery* sectors. These models, however, present different definitions and conceptualizations of these sectors.

The dual labor market and labor force segmentation literature defines the sectors or segments in terms of the characteristics of labor markets and worker behavior (Harrison, 1974; Spilerman, 1977). Common to both perspectives is the argument that, corresponding to the core and periphery sectors, respectively, there are two separate labor markets: a primary labor market and a secondary labor market, distinguished by the extent to which employment is relatively stable and secure. For example, Piori (1977, p. 93) defines the two sectors as follows:

> The central tenet of the analysis is that the role of employment and of the disposition of manpower in the perpetuation of poverty is best understood in terms of a dual labor market. One sector of the market, which I have termed elsewhere the primary market, offers jobs which possess several of the following traits: high wages, good working conditions, employment stability and job security, equity and due process in the administration of work rules, and chances for advancement. The other, or secondary market, has jobs which, relative to those in the primary sector, are decidedly less attractive. They tend to involve low wages, poor working conditions, considerable variability in employment, harsh and often arbitrary discipline, and little opportunity to advance. The poor are confined to the secondary labor market. The elimination of poverty requires that they gain access to primary employment.

The dual economy perspective as illustrated by writers such as Averitt (1968) and Bluestone, Murphy, and Stevenson (1973), views the economic sectors as structural entities derived from the nature of modern industrial capitalism (Beck et al., 1978). It is often argued that sector differentiation resulted from the creation during the late nineteenth and early twentieth centuries of a core industrial sector dominated by large oligopolistic corporations (Baran and Sweezy, 1966). For example, Averitt (1968, p. 7) characterizes the two sectors as follows:

> The new economy is composed of firms large in size and influence. Its organizations are corporate and bureaucratic; its production processes are vertically integrated through ownership and control of critical raw material supplies and product distributions; its activities are diversified into many industries, regions, and nations. . . . Firms in the large economy serve national and international markets, using technologically progressive systems of production and distribution. . . . We shall call this network of firms the "center."
>
> The other economy is populated by relatively small firms. These enterprises are the ones usually dominated by a single individual or family. The firm's sales are realized in restricted markets. . . . Techniques of production and marketing are rarely up to date as those in the center. . . . Let us designate the firms in the small economy by the term "periphery."

Bluestone et al. (1973, pp. 88–89) provides a similar characterization as follows:

> The core economy includes those industries that comprise the muscle of American economic and political power. . . . Entrenched in durable manufacturing, the construction of trades and, to a lesser extent, the extraction industries, the firms in the core economy are noted for high productivity, high profits, intensive utilization of capital, high incidence of monopoly elements, and a high degree of unionization. What follows normally from such characteristics are high wages. The automobile, steel, rubber, aluminum, aerospace, and petroleum industries are ranking members of this part of the economy. Workers who are able to secure employment in those industries are in most cases, assured of relatively higher wages and better than average working conditions and fringe benefits.

The basic distinction in the dual economy perspective is made in terms of market power, with the core industries characterized as monopolists or oligopolists, and periphery firms as competitors. Other distinctions include financial size, scale of employment, conglomerate organization, long-term planning capabilities, and relationship to government (O'Connor, 1973). The relationship between the two sectors is assumed to be one of dependency, with core firms extracting monopoly profits from the periphery firms to which they sell, demanding "preferred" customer rebates from their suppliers, and the periphery firms existing as satellites of core firms or customers (Hodson and Kaufman, 1982, p. 729). What it implies is that beyond the fringes of the core economy lie a set of industries that lack almost all the advantages normally found in the core firms. Concentrated in agriculture, nondurable manufacturing, retail trade, and subprofessional services, the periphery industries are noted for their small firm size, labor intensity, low profits, low productivity, intensive product market competition, lack of unionization, and low wages. Unlike core firms, the firms in the periphery sector lack the assets, size, and political power to take advantage of economies of scale or spend large sums on research and development.

## III. RELATED RESEARCH

The early literature on dualism was descriptive, focusing on proper definitions of the two sectors as core versus periphery (Averitt, 1968), concentrated versus unconcentrated (Bluestone, 1970), monopoly versus competitive (O'Connor, 1973), and planned versus market economies (Galbraith, 1973). What followed were empirical attempts at understanding the differences between the two sectors using factor analysis and cluster analysis (Oster, 1979; Osterman, 1975).

The basic purpose of empirical research on dualism is to differentiate economic units categorized in a monopoly/core sector versus a competitive/periphery sector on the basis of empirical measures. The earlier attempts to operationalize industry segments by Bibb and Form (1977) and Beck et al. (1978) relied on the narrative description of major industrial sectors as periphery or core sectors by Averitt (1968) or the same description by Bluestone et al. (1973). These early studies were followed by empirical attempts to define industrial sectors by using either a factor analysis of economic and structural data as in the studies by Hodson (1978), Oster (1979), and Tolbert, Horan, and Beck (1980) or a factor analysis followed by cluster analysis. While Hodson (1978), Oster (1979), and Tolbert et al. (1980) were able to identify two sectors, Kaufman et al. (1980) found multiple sectors. All these studies used the industry rather than the firm as the unit of analysis, arguing that firms in industries are similar in technologies and organizational forms and face similar variations in the demands for their products (Bibb and Form, 1977; Spilerman, 1977; Tolbert et al., 1980). In addition, these studies relied on macroeconomic and industry-based variables and data.

This study is also related to research that attempts to explain cross-sectional differences in financial ratios and other financial characteristics. Smith and

Pourciau (1988) find evidence of significant ratio differences between firms having December versus non-December fiscal year-ends and/or a different stock exchange listing. Using univariate tests, they find that non-December year-end firms are significantly smaller, riskier (measured by market beta), and more financially levered relative to December year-end firms.

## IV. THE MODEL

This study differs from previous empirical research on dualism by using the firm as the unit of analysis and firms' financial variables as the explanatory variables. The testable null hypothesis is that of no difference in variables (or ratios) between each sector. Evidence of fundamental differences in the financial characteristics of firms in the two sectors allows the null hypothesis to be rejected. This hypothesis is examined in light of the Smith and Pourciau (1988) findings of significant ratio differences between firms having December versus non-December fiscal year-ends and/or different stock exchange listings.

The first set of tests is similar to the approach of Smith and Pourciau (1988), which is to provide descriptive statistics and univariate tests of differences between the subgroups of interest. Specifically, each variable's descriptive statistics are compared for core versus periphery firms. Then an ANOVA model is used for tests comparing firms classified into core versus periphery sectors, differences in year-end choice, and stock exchange membership. This is modeled as

$$F_i = a_{1i}D_i + A_{2i}Y_i + a_3S_i + a_4D_iY_i + a_5D_iS_i + a_6Y_iS_i + a_7D_iY_iS_i, \quad (1)$$

where

$F_i$ = financial variable (see Table 2 for definitions);
$D_i$ = dummy variable representing the dual economy sector: 0 for core and 1 for periphery (see Table 1 for classifications);
$Y_i$ = dummy variable representing the year-end choice: 0 for December and 1 for non-December;
$S_i$ = dummy variable for stock exchange membership: 0 for New York Stock Exchange (NYSE) and 1 for others (American Stock Exchange [AMX] or OTC).

Unlike Smith and Pourciau's (1988) univariate testing approach, this study's analysis tests for interaction effects. In addition, the ratios and characteristics found to be significant using model (1) are analyzed in a logistic regression model. This logistic model and results are presented in Section IV.C.

# V. RESEARCH METHOD

## A. Data

The sample contains the total usable population of firms from both the primary, secondary and tertiary file and the full coverage file of COMPUSTAT for three noncontiguous years: 1978, 1983, and 1988. These periods are recent enough to be representative of the current economic situation and yet far enough apart to illustrate past conditions. In addition, following Smith and Pourciau's (1988) rationale, these years are current enough to be of value to current research projects and far enough in the past to be of value to those interested in historical time series.

Since there is no single theory of the dual economy, it is not possible to operationalize the concept to develop a unique classification of "core" versus "periphery" firms (Oster, 1979). In this study, firms are grouped into either a core or periphery sector based on a sectoral classification provided by Beck et al. (1978) and illustrated in Table 1. The choice of the Beck et al. (1979) core versus periphery industry classifications is based on their timeliness relative to the fairly similar classifications of Bibb–Form (1977) or Hodson (1977), the ease of operationalizing industry classes into firm specific ones, and their acceptance in the economic literature.[1]

## B. Financial Characteristics

The variables examined include those studied by Smith and Pourciau (1988) and are representative of ratios used in financial analysis (Foster, 1986); they include measures of the following:[2]

1. firm size (total assets, market value of equity, and total revenues),
2. rate of return (return on assets and return on equity),
3. liquidity (current ratio and working capital ratio),
4. leverage (debt/market value of equity and debt/assets),
5. leverage coverage or fixed charge coverage ratio,
6. turnover ratios (sales/inventory and sales/receivables),
7. capital intensity—(gross plant/sales and depreciation/total expenses),
8. price earnings ratio, and
9. beta or market risk.

The specific variable definitions, abbreviations, and their COMPUSTAT data item formulas are listed in Table 2.

Because ratio data are usually skewed and otherwise depart from normality, the upper and lower 1 and 5% of the observations were trimmed to remove extreme outliers and to reduce the observed departures from normality (Foster, 1986, p. 111).

# VI. RESULTS

## B. Descriptive Statistics and ANOVA Results

Table 3 summarizes the univariate statistical characteristics for each variable by sector (core or periphery) for each period, for both raw values and 1% trimmed values. For many variables, removing the upper and lower 1% values considerably changes the measures of distributional characteristics such as the sample mean, skewness, standard deviation, and/or normality measures.[3] The ANOVA results are summarized in Table 4.[4] To the extent that the ANOVA interaction terms are considered unimportant (insignificant and/or not consistent across periods) the main effects are additive and can easily be interpreted as separate factors (Neter and Wasserman, 1974, p. 565). The descriptive statistics and ANOVA results are discussed by financial characteristic or ratio categories. Within the discussion, an effect is considered statistically significant if it has an alpha level of 5% or less.

### *1. Firm Size*

Firm size was measured as (1) market value of equity, (2) total assets, (3) total revenues, (4) market value of equity plus book value of debt, and (5) market value of equity plus book value of debt plus preferred stock. For each of the years examined, Table 3 indicates that the median and mean sizes of the core companies are much larger than those of the periphery companies. Table 4 summarizes the analysis of variance results for selected size measures for each of the three years. Except for the total revenue measure, the main effects for the core/periphery classification, fiscal year-end and stock exchange membership factors are consistently significant. In most cases the second-order interaction of core/periphery distinction with stock exchange membership is significant. Thus the dual sector size effect is influenced by stock exchange membership; this is consistent with the minimum size requirements imposed by the NYSE. The second-order interaction effects of the core/periphery distinction and fiscal year-end are rarely significant. The notable exception is the case of revenue for the 1983 and 1988 ANOVAS. In fact, the significant sector/size interaction effect for total revenue helps explain why revenue's pattern of main effects differs from that of other size measures.

### *2. Rates of Return*

Rate of return was measured as either rate of return on assets or rate of return on common equity. Table 3 shows that with one exception (ROE in 1988), the mean core company rate of return was lower than that of the periphery companies. Without exception, the median of the rate of return measures of the core companies was lower than that of the periphery companies. Table 4 shows that the main effect of core/periphery distinction is significant, with the exception of both return

*Table 1.* Sectoral Classifications

| *Industry Group* | *Sector* |
|---|---|
| Agriculture, forestry, and fisheries | Periphery |
| Mining | |
| Metal mining | Core |
| Coal mining | Core |
| Crude petroleum and natural gas | Core |
| Nonmetallic mining and quarrying | Core |
| Construction | Core |
| Durable manufacturing | |
| Lumber and wood products | Periphery |
| Furniture and fixtures | Periphery |
| Stone, clay, and glass products | Core |
| Metal industries | Core |
| Machinery, except electrical | Core |
| Electrical machinery, equipment, supplies | Core |
| Transportation equipment | Core |
| Professional and photographic equipment | Core |
| Ordnance | Core |
| Miscellaneous durable manufacturing | Periphery |
| Nondurable manufacturing | |
| Food and kindred products | Periphery |
| Tobacco manufacturers | Periphery |
| Textile mill products | Periphery |
| Apparel and other fabricated textiles | Periphery |
| Paper and allied products | Core |
| Printing, publishing, and allied industries | Core |
| Chemical and allied products | Core |
| Petroleum and coal products | Core |
| Rubber and miscellaneous plastic products | Core |
| Leather and leather products | Periphery |
| Not specified nondurable manufacturing | Periphery |
| Transportation | |
| Railroads and railway express service | Core |
| Street railways and bus lines | Core |
| Taxicab service | Core |
| Trucking service | Core |
| Warehousing and storage | Core |
| Water transportation | Core |
| Petroleum and gasoline pipelines | Core |
| Services incidental to transportation | Core |
| Communications | |
| Radio broadcasting and television | Core |
| Telephone (wire and radio) | Core |
| Telegraph (wire and radio) | Core |

*(continued)*

*Table 1. (continued)*

| *Industry Group* | *Sector* |
|---|---|
| Utilities and sanitary services | |
| Electric light and power | Core |
| Gas, steam, and supply systems | Core |
| Electric-gas utilities | Core |
| Water supply | Core |
| Sanitation services | Core |
| Other not specified utilities | Core |
| Wholesale trade | Core |
| Retail trade | Periphery |
| Finance, insurance, and real estate | Core |
| Business and repair services | Periphery |
| Personal services | Periphery |
| Entertainment and recreation services | Periphery |
| Prefessional and related services | Core |
| Public administration | Core |

*Table 2.* Variables and Definitions

| *Definition* | *(Variable) = [COMPUSTAT Data Items]* |
|---|---|
| **Size** | |
| Market value of equity | (*MVE*) = [D24 * D24] |
| Total assets | (*TA*) = [D6] |
| Total revenues | (*TR*) = [D12] |
| MVE + debt + preferred debt | (*MVEP*)= [(D24 * D24) + D9 + D10] |
| **Rate of Return** | |
| Return on assets | (*ROA*) =[D18+(D15 * (1 –D16/D170)) /(D6+D7–D8)] |
| Return on common equity | (*ROE*) = [(D18 D19) / D60] |
| **Liquidity** Current ratio | (*CR*) = [D4 / D5] |
| **Leverage** | |
| Total debt/MV of equity | (*TDMV*)= [(D9 + D34) / (D24 * D25)] |
| L.T. debt/total assets | (*DLTA*)= [D9 / D6] |
| L.T. debt /invested capital | (*DLIC*)= [D9 / D37] |
| Fixed charges coverage ratio | (*FCR*) = [(D170+D15)/(D15+D34+D19)] |
| **Price Earnings Ratio** | (*PE*) = [D24 / D58] |
| **Turnover (Sales)** | |
| Sales inventory turnover | (*SIT*) = [D12 / D3] |
| Sales receivable turnover | (*SRT*) = [D12 / D2] |
| **Capital Intensity** | |
| Gross plant /sales | (*CIS*) = [D7 / D12] |
| Depreciation/total expenses | (*CDS*) = [D14 / (D12 – D13)] |
| **Market Betas** | (*BETA*)= Annual returns (Market model) |

### Table 3. Univariate Characteristics by Dual Class

| CL | YR | N | MEAN | MEDIAN | SKEW | KURT | MIN | MAX | STD DEV | NORM |
|---|---|---|---|---|---|---|---|---|---|---|
| **SIZE: MVE = Market Value of Equity at Year End** | | | | | | | | | | |
| C | 78 | 1988 | 371.629 | 47.9594 | 17.6023 | 401.252 | 0.3660 | 43524 | 1679.77 | 0.412538 |
| C | 83 | 2865 | 596.242 | 73.1267 | 27.1914 | 942.111 | 0.0892 | 136270 | 3449.84 | 0.431402 |
| C | 88 | 2948 | 895.145 | 97.2069 | 10.2628 | 160.614 | 0.0000 | 71875 | 3100.11 | 0.386388 |
| P | 78 | 263 | 163.079 | 30.5760 | 8.2997 | 89.131 | 0.5265 | 6372 | 508.44 | 0.374596 |
| P | 83 | 413 | 317.206 | 69.6850 | 8.9256 | 111.959 | 0.4412 | 13163 | 887.20 | 0.360532 |
| P | 88 | 398 | 601.509 | 92.0602 | 6.1027 | 44.235 | 0.0000 | 17745 | 1785.83 | 0.368125 |
| **SIZE (1% FILTER): MVE1 = Market Value of Equity at Year End** | | | | | | | | | | |
| C | 78 | 1950 | 259.122 | 47.9594 | 4.49230 | 25.343 | 1.1825 | 5111 | 571.74 | 0.325942 |
| C | 83 | 2809 | 399.336 | 73.1267 | 3.94384 | 18.275 | 0.9930 | 7735 | 876.86 | 0.324813 |
| C | 88 | 2890 | 666.879 | 97.2069 | 4.42541 | 23.946 | 0.4144 | 13909 | 1576.67 | 0.336256 |
| P | 78 | 259 | 130.378 | 30.5760 | 4.52994 | 23.898 | 1.1250 | 2175 | 293.13 | 0.329626 |
| P | 83 | 405 | 256.771 | 69.6850 | 4.02203 | 20.736 | 1.5890 | 4183 | 499.75 | 0.304808 |
| P | 88 | 392 | 493.611 | 92.0602 | 5.24419 | 34.809 | 0.2647 | 12262 | 1239.40 | 0.345296 |

| CL | YR | N | MEAN | MEDIAN | SKEW | KURT | MIN | MAX | STD DEV | NORM |
|---|---|---|---|---|---|---|---|---|---|---|
| **SIZE: TA = Total Assets at Year End** | | | | | | | | | | |
| C | 78 | 2325 | 1104.75 | 84.690 | 12.8627 | 219.181 | 0.086 | 103327 | 4790.6 | 0.408817 |
| C | 83 | 2922 | 1648.17 | 100.018 | 11.2093 | 164.908 | 0.256 | 149530 | 7223.8 | 0.409776 |
| C | 88 | 3055 | 2778.06 | 183.661 | 9.9814 | 131.252 | 0.088 | 207666 | 11139.1 | 0.401530 |
| P | 78 | 307 | 301.76 | 45.713 | 9.3405 | 110.423 | 0.542 | 15262 | 1119.85 | 0.393972 |
| P | 83 | 423 | 440.67 | 68.320 | 16.5086 | 307.158 | 1.207 | 46176 | 2415.19 | 0.427808 |
| P | 88 | 416 | 903.20 | 146.167 | 15.6567 | 283.857 | 0.129 | 77952 | 4166.81 | 0.414209 |
| **SIZE (1% FILTER): TA1 = Total Assets at Year End** | | | | | | | | | | |
| C | 78 | 2279 | 738.43 | 84.690 | 4.8815 | 30.6206 | 0.805 | 18611.4 | 1822.56 | 0.342843 |
| C | 83 | 2864 | 1067.43 | 100.018 | 5.0458 | 31.6771 | 1.301 | 27199.0 | 2831.53 | 0.353265 |
| C | 88 | 2995 | 1900.21 | 183.661 | 4.5677 | 24.5319 | 1.234 | 46616.5 | 4980.70 | 0.351502 |
| P | 78 | 301 | 217.36 | 45.713 | 5.1283 | 32.5186 | 1.417 | 4833.00 | 549.46 | 0.347154 |
| P | 83 | 415 | 276.08 | 68.320 | 4.2537 | 21.0153 | 2.387 | 4901.34 | 615.97 | 0.328400 |
| P | 88 | 408 | 626.19 | 146.167 | 3.5805 | 13.8244 | 2.858 | 8158.67 | 1302.36 | 0.316105 |

Table 3. (continued)

| CE | YR | N | MEAN | MEDIAN | SKEW | KURT | MIN | MAX | STD DEV | NORM |
|---|---|---|---|---|---|---|---|---|---|---|
| **SIZE: TR = Total Revenue at Year End** | | | | | | | | | | |
| C | 78 | 2321 | 734.19 | 91.941 | 12.1622 | 190.433 | 0.000 | 63221 | 3068.6 | 0.405453 |
| C | 83 | 2921 | 1030.55 | 93.094 | 11.9372 | 174.148 | 0.001 | 88561 | 4671.7 | 0.412760 |
| C | 88 | 3036 | 1355.17 | 157.040 | 11.5475 | 183.329 | 0.000 | 121085 | 5257.6 | 0.398298 |
| * | | | | | | | | | | |
| P | 78 | 307 | 543.66 | 88.907 | 6.2340 | 47.571 | 0.397 | 17946 | 1710.6 | 0.375386 |
| P | 83 | 422 | 674.00 | 85.078 | 9.1260 | 108.744 | 0.453 | 35883 | 2473.6 | 0.392696 |
| P | 88 | 413 | 1213.61 | 231.373 | 7.7160 | 80.937 | 0.037 | 50251 | 3749.0 | 0.373080 |
| **SIZE (1% FILTER): TR1 = Total Revenue at Year End** | | | | | | | | | | |
| C | 78 | 2275 | 495.008 | 91.941 | 4.17020 | 21.1521 | 0.227 | 10154.9 | 1120.14 | 0.329348 |
| C | 83 | 2863 | 661.074 | 93.094 | 4.54633 | 25.2659 | 0.230 | 14669.2 | 1622.06 | 0.341853 |
| C | 88 | 2976 | 955.890 | 157.040 | 4.36296 | 23.0580 | 0.176 | 19404.5 | 2240.40 | 0.334842 |
| * | | | | | | | | | | |
| P | 78 | 301 | 419.597 | 88.907 | 4.77660 | 25.7013 | 1.050 | 8155.0 | 1086.10 | 0.349983 |
| P | 83 | 414 | 488.988 | 85.078 | 5.01947 | 29.8848 | 1.312 | 11574.0 | 1254.56 | 0.348740 |
| P | 88 | 405 | 947.440 | 231.373 | 4.43380 | 23.2305 | 2.872 | 18478.3 | 2203.64 | 0.334093 |
| **SIZE: SZEP = Market Value of Equity + Book Value of Debt + Pref. Stock** | | | | | | | | | | |
| CL | YR | N | MEAN | MEDIAN | SKEW | KURT | MIN | MAX | STD DEV | NORM |
| C | 78 | 1988 | 594.78 | 80.761 | 18.7017 | 483.790 | 0.400750 | 77108 | 2529.03 | 0.407095 |
| C | 83 | 2864 | 855.53 | 101.027 | 21.0427 | 575.938 | 0.113250 | 136111 | 4174.37 | 0.418817 |
| C | 88 | 2942 | 1383.03 | 162.894 | 10.9841 | 181.739 | 0.297236 | 115533 | 4781.49 | 0.386220 |
| * | | | | | | | | | | |
| P | 78 | 263 | 247.854 | 49.434 | 7.3803 | 71.470 | 0.80950 | 8412.2 | 712.15 | 0.364332 |
| P | 83 | 413 | 415.413 | 92.261 | 10.9038 | 159.193 | 0.58825 | 21100.0 | 1299.66 | 0.374795 |
| P | 88 | 397 | 850.028 | 147.548 | 6.0767 | 46.399 | 0.27475 | 25294.2 | 2349.73 | 0.358811 |

Table 3. (continued)

| CE | YR | N | MEAN | MEDIAN | SKEW | KURT | MIN | MAX | STD DEV | NORM |
|---|---|---|---|---|---|---|---|---|---|---|
| **SIZE (1% Filter): SZEP1 = Equity + Debt + Preferred Stock** | | | | | | | | | | |
| C | 78 | 1950 | 432.83 | 80.761 | 4.0802 | 20.2285 | 1.95250 | 7606.9 | 932.06 | 0.321939 |
| C | 83 | 2808 | 595.86 | 101.027 | 3.9689 | 18.8565 | 1.40125 | 11209.9 | 1330.13 | 0.327467 |
| C | 88 | 2884 | 1036.50 | 162.894 | 4.0404 | 19.3842 | 0.99045 | 19633.8 | 2318.29 | 0.329620 |
| * | | | | | | | | | | |
| P | 78 | 259 | 202.78 | 49.434 | 4.2442 | 20.9359 | 1.27000 | 3174.6 | 438.20 | 0.322808 |
| P | 83 | 405 | 325.88 | 92.261 | 4.1313 | 21.9200 | 3.04600 | 5354.1 | 638.46 | 0.306554 |
| P | 88 | 391 | 708.73 | 147.548 | 4.5277 | 24.9751 | 2.24375 | 13679.0 | 1616.30 | 0.331019 |
| **RATE OF RETURN: ROA = Return on Asets** | | | | | | | | | | |
| *CE* | *YR* | *N* | *MEAN* | *MEDIAN* | *SKEW* | *KURT* | *MIN* | *MAX* | *STD DEV* | *NORM* |
| C | 78 | 2183 | 0.0647363 | 0.0597925 | 14.790 | 340.56 | −1.025 | 3.22191 | 0.133665 | 0.2742 |
| C | 83 | 2737 | 0.0379688 | 0.0521540 | 4.063 | 181.71 | −2.843 | 3.84909 | 0.189476 | 0.2628 |
| C | 88 | 2827 | 0.0290964 | 0.0478506 | −30.355 | 1395.46 | −14.770 | 4.70760 | 0.333367 | 0.3180 |
| * | | | | | | | | | | |
| P | 78 | 306 | 0.0667693 | 0.0666476 | −3.982 | 33.854 | −0.5799 | 0.23035 | 0.066006 | 0.1832 |
| P | 83 | 415 | 0.0478957 | 0.0644298 | −10.282 | 146.635 | −2.3983 | 0.43086 | 0.157174 | 0.3047 |
| P | 88 | 405 | 0.0346126 | 0.0502910 | −8.741 | 130.250 | −2.2942 | 0.80541 | 0.154694 | 0.2520 |
| **RATE OF RETURN (1% Filter): ROA1 = Return on Assets** | | | | | | | | | | |
| C | 78 | 2141 | 0.0629001 | 0.0597925 | −0.8397 | 4.7483 | −0.1898 | 0.19569 | 0.043535 | 0.0913 |
| C | 83 | 2683 | 0.0401974 | 0.0521540 | −2.5492 | 11.2301 | −0.5031 | 0.22899 | 0.076163 | 0.1744 |
| C | 88 | 2771 | 0.0356324 | 0.0478506 | −2.2341 | 9.0906 | −0.4917 | 0.26086 | 0.082698 | 0.1649 |
| * | | | | | | | | | | |
| P | 78 | 300 | 0.0695412 | 0.0666476 | −0.9280 | 6.1613 | −0.2110 | 0.20764 | 0.046254 | 0.1095 |
| P | 83 | 407 | 0.0564552 | 0.0644298 | −3.1598 | 16.5725 | −0.4725 | 0.20750 | 0.071494 | 0.2047 |
| P | 88 | 397 | 0.0409070 | 0.0502910 | −1.8198 | 5.3357 | −0.3321 | 0.20069 | 0.075625 | 0.1558 |

Table 3. (continued)

**RATE OF RETURN: ROE = Return on Equity**

| CL | YR | N | MEAN | MEDIAN | SKEW | KURT | MIN | MAX | STD DEV | NORM |
|---|---|---|---|---|---|---|---|---|---|---|
| C | 78 | 2318 | 0.162808 | 0.136033 | 44.530 | 2094.61 | –9.14 | 83.7696 | 1.78194 | 0.42713 |
| C | 83 | 2919 | 0.018664 | 0.107396 | –29.764 | 1298.66 | –59.36 | 18.7217 | 1.35408 | 0.38001 |
| C | 88 | 3028 | –0.047803 | 0.110262 | –45.137 | 2280.96 | –208.11 | 17.1537 | 4.06313 | 0.40907 |
| * | | | | | | | | | | |
| P | 78 | 307 | 0.126760 | 0.156654 | –6.5520 | 55.093 | –2.885 | 0.738 | 0.2942 | 0.29413 |
| P | 83 | 421 | 0.111768 | 0.135620 | 1.7281 | 104.848 | –8.656 | 12.591 | 0.9515 | 0.35940 |
| P | 88 | 412 | 0.783884 | 0.115167 | 20.1162 | 407.196 | –16.916 | 328.139 | 16.2140 | 0.47388 |

**RATE OF RETURN (1% Filter): ROE1 = Return on Equity**

| CL | YR | N | MEAN | MEDIAN | SKEW | KURT | MIN | MAX | STD DEV | NORM |
|---|---|---|---|---|---|---|---|---|---|---|
| C | 78 | 2272 | 0.130798 | 0.136033 | –1.1426 | 10.0891 | –0.7003 | 0.79236 | 0.117669 | 0.12631 |
| C | 83 | 2861 | 0.059603 | 0.107396 | –3.2094 | 17.1838 | –1.7672 | 0.87309 | 0.223266 | 0.20977 |
| C | 88 | 2968 | 0.066620 | 0.110262 | –1.9059 | 21.2532 | –3.0865 | 2.29279 | 0.367821 | 0.22234 |
| * | | | | | | | | | | |
| P | 78 | 301 | 0.144792 | 0.156654 | –4.7103 | 34.2563 | –1.3054 | 0.48795 | 0.167123 | 0.20497 |
| P | 83 | 413 | 0.120460 | 0.135620 | –2.7843 | 29.6804 | –2.0741 | 1.43027 | 0.248755 | 0.23704 |
| P | 88 | 404 | 0.063646 | 0.115167 | –2.1213 | 18.2864 | –3.1077 | 2.35636 | 0.422893 | 0.22783 |

**LIQUIDITY: CR = Current Ratio**

| CL | YR | N | MEAN | MEDIAN | SKEW | KURT | MIN | MAX | STD DEV | NORM |
|---|---|---|---|---|---|---|---|---|---|---|
| C | 78 | 1989 | 2.42105 | 2.04716 | 21.8065 | 620.50 | 0.00798 | 112.50 | 3.4984 | 0.283124 |
| C | 83 | 2867 | 3.73003 | 2.15682 | 47.8537 | 2339.33 | 0.00011 | 1719.25 | 35.0723 | 0.457806 |
| C | 88 | 3229 | 2.64146 | 1.86870 | 11.6788 | 201.14 | 0.02060 | 103.60 | 4.2175 | 0.276542 |
| * | | | | | | | | | | |
| P | 78 | 265 | 2.01619 | 1.91503 | 1.03751 | 1.3345 | 0.40428 | 5.3535 | 0.87253 | 0.103024 |
| P | 83 | 413 | 2.31583 | 1.91930 | 3.83032 | 22.5991 | 0.11561 | 16.7024 | 1.77741 | 0.19048 |
| P | 88 | 476 | 2.00131 | 1.72558 | 2.91155 | 14.1371 | 0.13093 | 11.1999 | 1.32833 | 0.14810 |

Table 3. (continued)

**LIQUIDITY (1% Filter): CR1 = Current Ratio**

| *CL* | *YR* | *N* | *MEAN* | *MEOIAN* | *SKEW* | *KURT* | *MIN* | *MAX* | *STD DEV* | *NORM* |
|---|---|---|---|---|---|---|---|---|---|---|
| C | 78 | 1989 | 2.22961 | 2.04716 | 1.35908 | 3.1266 | 0.49118 | 8.1880 | 1.09881 | 0.08077 |
| C | 83 | 2867 | 2.66560 | 2.15682 | 2.72092 | 10.3616 | 0.31465 | 16.6408 | 2.01409 | 0.16406 |
| C | 88 | 3229 | 2.35129 | 1.86870 | 3.30813 | 15.3841 | 0.23404 | 17.0582 | 1.92856 | 0.17840 |
| * | | | | | | | | | | |
| P | 78 | 265 | 2.00269 | 1.91503 | 0.87519 | 0.57877 | 0.63405 | 4.61330 | 0.81694 | 0.09278 |
| P | 83 | 413 | 2.23920 | 1.91930 | 2.27635 | 6.97985 | 0.32778 | 9.68158 | 1.40375 | 0.16535 |
| P | 88 | 476 | 1.94687 | 1.72558 | 1.68019 | 5.03295 | 0.33760 | 8.72362 | 1.08413 | 0.11578 |

**LEVERAGE: TDMV = TOTAL DEBT/MARKET VALUE EQUITY**

| *CL* | *YR* | *N* | *MEAN* | *MEDIAN* | *SKEW* | *KURT* | *MIN* | *MAX* | *STD DEV* | *NORM* |
|---|---|---|---|---|---|---|---|---|---|---|
| C | 78 | 1988 | 1.7146 | 1.00853 | 9.8023 | 142.59 | 0 | 64.9 | 3.13 | 0.292213 |
| C | 83 | 2864 | 1.0596 | 0.49199 | 13.3384 | 256.16 | 0 | 58.8 | 2.47 | 0.334018 |
| C | 88 | 2934 | 74.8021 | 0.71182 | 32.4521 | 1115.13 | 0 | 78506.6 | 2034.56 | 0.497200 |
| * | | | | | | | | | | |
| P | 78 | 263 | 2.168 | 1.04844 | 14.2015 | 218.58 | 0.029 | 114.1 | 7.25 | 0.384088 |
| P | 83 | 413 | 0.741 | 0.44437 | 4.1212 | 25.62 | 0.000 | 9.4 | 0.97 | 0.221727 |
| P | 88 | 396 | 194.713 | 0.76451 | 19.8997 | 395.999 | 0.000 | 76472.8 | 3842.82 | 0.511950 |

**LEVERAGE (1% FILTER): TDMV1 = TOTAL DEBT/MARKET VALUE EQUITY**

| | | | | | | | | | | |
|---|---|---|---|---|---|---|---|---|---|---|
| C | 78 | 1946 | 1.50496 | 1.01013 | 2.49849 | 8.4060 | 0.000 | 11.985 | 1.61466 | 0.175800 |
| C | 83 | 2807 | 0.89854 | 0.49270 | 2.85082 | 10.6642 | 0.000 | 8.279 | 1.14122 | 0.215594 |
| C | 88 | 2878 | 1.64358 | 0.71411 | 5.66001 | 40.2773 | 0.000 | 39.981 | 3.43893 | 0.316417 |
| * | | | | | | | | | | |
| P | 78 | 259 | 1.69585 | 1.04844 | 2.61683 | 9.0889 | 0.071 | 13.896 | 1.94741 | 0.202036 |
| P | 83 | 405 | 0.68441 | 0.44437 | 2.12598 | 5.5768 | 0.025 | 4.361 | 0.71357 | 0.177611 |
| P | 88 | 390 | 1.38772 | 0.76451 | 3.17743 | 12.8267 | 0.036 | 12.571 | 1.81439 | 0.228172 |

Table 3. *(continued)*

**LEVERAGE: DLTA = DEBT/TOTAL ASSETS**

| CL | YR | N | MEAN | MEDIAN | SKEW | KURT | MIN | MAX | STD DEV | NORM |
|---|---|---|---|---|---|---|---|---|---|---|
| C | 78 | 2325 | 0.201545 | 0.173719 | 4.6578 | 81.060 | 0 | 4.23412 | 0.193805 | 0.14918 |
| C | 83 | 2921 | 0.181840 | 0.138830 | 15.0730 | 494.906 | 0 | 8.27710 | 0.233781 | 0.21834 |
| C | 88 | 3054 | 0.214929 | 0.168244 | 13.4661 | 328.473 | 0 | 8.86967 | 0.299027 | 0.23614 |
| * | | | | | | | | | | |
| P | 78 | 307 | 0.216725 | 0.208101 | 0.74217 | 1.0043 | 0 | 1.07269 | 0.170716 | 0.10213 |
| P | 83 | 423 | 0.180847 | 0.138673 | 1.00215 | 0.5104 | 0 | 0.87578 | 0.168832 | 0.14205 |
| P | 88 | 416 | 0.254077 | 0.213977 | 5.59700 | 61.9988 | 0 | 3.80620 | 0.281961 | 0.18377 |

**LEVERAGE (1% FILTER): DLTA1 = DEBT/TOTAL ASSETS**

| CL | YR | N | MEAN | MEDIAN | SKEW | KURT | MIN | MAX | STD DEV | NORM |
|---|---|---|---|---|---|---|---|---|---|---|
| C | 78 | 2066 | 0.215531 | 0.194541 | 0.68572 | 0.0768 | 0.00 | 0.73832 | 0.156938 | 0.07718 |
| C | 83 | 2584 | 0.192069 | 0.159036 | 0.86045 | 0.1320 | 0.00 | 0.69967 | 0.157389 | 0.11121 |
| C | 88 | 2695 | 0.223710 | 0.197951 | 0.96583 | 0.7983 | 0.00 | 0.90792 | 0.178077 | 0.10209 |
| * | | | | | | | | | | |
| P | 78 | 271 | 0. 236922 | 0.230103 | 0.33866 | –0.7228 | 0.00 | 0.61510 | 0.151367 | 0.07232 |
| P | 83 | 373 | 0.197277 | 0.173175 | 0.78917 | –0.1811 | 0.00 | 0.64921 | 0.157214 | 0.10479 |
| P | 88 | 373 | 0.261801 | 0.235038 | 0.72134 | 0.0027 | 0.00 | 0.87836 | 0.190983 | 0.08320 |

**LEVERAGE: DLIC = DEBT (LONG TERM)/ INVESTED CAPITAL**

| CL | YR | N | MEAN | MEDIAN | SKEW | KURT | MIN | MAX | STD DEV | NORM |
|---|---|---|---|---|---|---|---|---|---|---|
| C | 78 | 2309 | 200.713 | 0.286567 | 48.052 | 2309.00 | –4.91 | 462725 | 9629.66 | 0.50730 |
| C | 83 | 2914 | 0.254 | 0.222762 | –27.055 | 1190.45 | –48.33 | 20 | 1.15 | 0.40838 |
| C | 88 | 3049 | 0.234 | 0.291995 | –47.174 | 2468.58 | –240.54 | 39 | 4.60 | 0.46805 |
| * | | | | | | | | | | |
| P | 78 | 307 | 0.328 | 0.314553 | 4.2198 | 43.171 | 0.000 | 3.503 | 0.2940 | 0.13208 |
| P | 83 | 423 | 0.299 | 0.221450 | 16.7847 | 321.394 | –0.772 | 13.585 | 0.6932 | 0.33087 |
| P | 88 | 416 | 0.360 | 0.324208 | –0.2998 | 17.064 | –2.748 | 2.807 | 0.3897 | 0.16334 |

Table 3. (continued)

| CL | YR | N | MEAN | MEDIAN | SKEW | KURT | MIN | MAX | STD DEV | NORM |
|---|---|---|---|---|---|---|---|---|---|---|
| **LEVERAGE (1% FILTER): DLIC1 = DEBT (LONG TERM)/INVESTED CAPITAL** | | | | | | | | | | |
| C | 78 | 2041 | 0.328317 | 0.311671 | 0.4969 | –0.0650 | 0.000 | 1.02146 | 0.2024 | 0.04479 |
| C | 83 | 2565 | 0.294140 | 0.253494 | 0.6933 | –0.0908 | 0.000 | 1.07681 | 0.2140 | 0.08512 |
| C | 88 | 2989 | 0.321499 | 0.291995 | 0.8343 | 0.6605 | –0.037 | 1.45012 | 0.2644 | 0.10731 |
| * | | | | | | | | | | |
| P | 78 | 271 | 0.351763 | 0.350700 | 0.1471 | –0.8947 | 0.002 | 0.8713 | 0.20927 | 0.07187 |
| P | 83 | 372 | 0.294832 | 0.266336 | 0.5333 | –0.6873 | 0.000 | 0.9194 | 0.21891 | 0.10056 |
| P | 88 | 408 | 0.358847 | 0.324208 | 0.5279 | –0.4745 | –0.140 | 1.2401 | 0.28507 | 0.10150 |
| **LEVERAGE COVERAGE: FCR = FIXED CHARGES COVERAGE RATIO** | | | | | | | | | | |
| *CL* | *YR* | *N* | *MEAN* | *MEDIAN* | *SKEW* | *KURT* | *MIN* | *MAX* | *STD DEV* | *NORM* |
| C | 78 | 2231 | 1234.64 | 1.64490 | 17.3305 | 324.03 | –539 | 454422 | 18521.8 | 0.505817 |
| C | 83 | 2808 | 1214.94 | 1.29354 | 30.5782 | 1120.88 | –5187 | 1036252 | 25033.0 | 0.502760 |
| C | 88 | 2919 | 710.51 | 0.95753 | 22.3983 | 541.16 | –54467 | 384369 | 13851.9 | 0.502548 |
| * | | | | | | | | | | |
| P | 78 | 294 | 39.362 | 2.43248 | 11.9297 | 151.811 | –494.0 | 4494 | 320.8 | 0.444174 |
| P | 83 | 401 | 94.314 | 2.14191 | 13.9345 | 212.282 | –1475.3 | 17746 | 1056.8 | 0.471170 |
| P | 88 | 400 | 708.599 | 1.32581 | 19.2492 | 377.983 | –640.6 | 231646 | 11741.7 | 0.495808 |
| **LEVERAGE (1% FILTER): FCR1 = FIXED CHARGES COVERAGE RATIO** | | | | | | | | | | |
| C | 78 | 2190 | 8.58387 | 1.64490 | 9.0341 | 92.885 | –3.178 | 545.308 | 37.8557 | 0.383196 |
| C | 83 | 2752 | 7.32937 | 1.29354 | 7.8801 | 72.404 | –31.158 | 429.500 | 31.5740 | 0.371262 |
| C | 88 | 2861 | 4.48916 | 0.95753 | 13.3900 | 224.654 | –22.590 | 529.393 | 23.5695 | 0.367669 |
| * | | | | | | | | | | |
| P | 78 | 290 | 15.7719 | 2.43248 | 7.7221 | 68.876 | –2.351 | 684.44 | 61.6336 | 0.386988 |
| P | 83 | 393 | 10.9523 | 2.14191 | 8.1191 | 84.766 | –14.015 | 505.06 | 38.4178 | 0.343499 |
| P | 88 | 392 | 13.4748 | 1.32581 | 10.3791 | 120.822 | –8.278 | 1006.67 | 76.5087 | 0.409178 |

Table 3. (continued)

**PRICE EARNINGS: PE = PRICE/EARNINGS**

| *CL* | *YR* | *N* | *MEAN* | *MEDIAN* | *SKEW* | *KURT* | *MIN* | *MAX* | *STD DEV* | *NORM* |
|---|---|---|---|---|---|---|---|---|---|---|
| C | 78 | 1981 | 8.9162 | 6.8966 | −2.8944 | 373.732 | −1187.5 | 962.5 | 46.3265 | 0.387053 |
| C | 83 | 2844 | 14.1302 | 10.7599 | 6.1777 | 178.448 | −1100.0 | 1975.0 | 88.1707 | 0.319538 |
| C | 88 | 2903 | 10.5137 | 9.5745 | 6.8751 | 196.916 | −837.5 | 1750.0 | 70.7212 | 0.321413 |
| * | | | | | | | | | | |
| P | 78 | 263 | 9.3377 | 7.0175 | 11.5152 | 163.032 | −37.50 | 315.63 | 21.3589 | 0.326925 |
| P | 83 | 411 | 18.5322 | 13.8804 | 2.5226 | 37.068 | −306.25 | 425.00 | 41.6057 | 0.265473 |
| P | 88 | 386 | 19.3128 | 11.8968 | 8.3385 | 88.253 | −225.00 | 1238.60 | 95.3995 | 0.371701 |

**PRICE EARNINGS (1% FILTER): PE1 = PRICE/EARNINGS**

| *CL* | *YR* | *N* | *MEAN* | *MEDIAN* | *SKEW* | *KURT* | *MIN* | *MAX* | *STD DEV* | *NORM* |
|---|---|---|---|---|---|---|---|---|---|---|
| C | 78 | 1943 | 8.4087 | 6.8966 | 3.27199 | 18.4861 | −22.50 | 72.500 | 8.2065 | 0.206778 |
| C | 83 | 2788 | 12.6244 | 10.7599 | 2.57271 | 19.3063 | −115.63 | 262.500 | 29.2508 | 0.199435 |
| C | 88 | 2845 | 9.4828 | 9.5745 | 0.96471 | 12.9883 | −117.05 | 165.833 | 22.8161 | 0.199210 |
| * | | | | | | | | | | |
| P | 78 | 259 | 8.2508 | 7.0175 | 2.91584 | 20.1187 | −26.79 | 64.063 | 8.1926 | 0.214519 |
| P | 83 | 403 | 17.6347 | 13.8804 | 2.93553 | 17.0896 | −65.63 | 206.200 | 25.6302 | 0.220648 |
| P | 88 | 380 | 14.2382 | 11.8968 | 7.53673 | 79.4717 | −156.25 | 600.000 | 49.4381 | 0.309878 |

**SALES RECEIVABLE TURNOVER: SRT = SALES/RECEIVABLES**

| *CL* | *YR* | *N* | *MEAN* | *MEDIAN* | *SKEW* | *KURT* | *MIN* | *MAX* | *STD DEV* | *NORM* |
|---|---|---|---|---|---|---|---|---|---|---|
| C | 78 | 2026 | 31092.3 | 6.52311 | 19.4583 | 407.250 | 0.000 | 10211249 | 421694 | 0.471256 |
| C | 83 | 2594 | 73997.4 | 6.15618 | 19.2605 | 115.265 | 0.027 | 24425008 | 921116 | 0.467986 |
| C | 88 | 2687 | 9365.7 | 5.79061 | 28.8161 | 920.066 | 0.000 | 7934055 | 212183 | 0.505773 |
| * | | | | | | | | | | |
| P | 78 | 300 | 10062 | 12. 1647 | 9.1061 | 94.656 | 0.518 | 866560 | 68861 | 0.506933 |
| P | 83 | 408 | 231426 | 9.0726 | 20. 1777 | 407.420 | 0.681 | 89707056 | 444202 | 0.492438 |
| P | 88 | 401 | 174900 | 9.6865 | 20.0153 | 400.738 | 0.245 | 68875056 | 3439857 | 0.515184 |

Table 3. (continued)

| CL | YR | N | MEAN | MEDIAN | SKEW | KURT | MIN | MAX | STD DEV | NORM |
|---|---|---|---|---|---|---|---|---|---|---|
| **SALES RECEIVABLE TURNOVER (1% FILTER): SRT1 = SALES/RECEIVABLES** | | | | | | | | | | |
| C | 78 | 1986 | 2813.3 | 6.5231 | 9.3068 | 99.893 | 1.039 | 268763 | 1815.0 | 0.495713 |
| C | 83 | 2544 | 10614.9 | 6.1562 | 9.0958 | 96.223 | 0.946 | 970565 | 66665.1 | 0.484286 |
| C | 88 | 2635 | 9.8 | 5.7906 | 29.0155 | 937.871 | 0.112 | 2448 | 65.0 | 0.440774 |
| * | | | | | | | | | | |
| P | 78 | 294 | 4269.2 | 12.1647 | 9.7271 | 103.578 | 1.141 | 383205 | 31231.3 | 0.507032 |
| P | 83 | 400 | 5030.4 | 9.0726 | 12.7693 | 185.279 | 1.269 | 761140 | 46834.4 | 0.513261 |
| P | 88 | 393 | 45.6 | 9.6865 | 3.6515 | 16.457 | 0.777 | 604 | 83.5 | 0.295675 |
| **SALES INVENTORY TURNOVER: SIT = SALES/INVENTORY** | | | | | | | | | | |
| C | 78 | 1772 | 4862.9 | 4.13391 | 42.0798 | 1771.13 | 0.011 | 8309503 | 197418 | 0.503154 |
| C | 83 | 2191 | 9316.9 | 4.07719 | 46.7616 | 2188.07 | 0.000 | 19317504 | 412823 | 0.504506 |
| C | 88 | 2173 | 25728.6 | 4.38785 | 44.3146 | 2019.21 | 0.031 | 38132528 | 833131 | 0.499552 |
| * | | | | | | | | | | |
| P | 78 | 254 | 1430.6 | 6.06010 | 15.7927 | 250.755 | 0.066 | 332578 | 20927 | 0.512301 |
| P | 83 | 335 | 5474.9 | 5.64672 | 17.4172 | 311.945 | 0.147 | 1367245 | 75962 | 0.508691 |
| P | 88 | 338 | 23814.3 | 6.75412 | 9.4244 | 98.747 | 0.026 | 2201298 | 175988 | 0.514705 |
| **SALES INVENTORY TURNOVER (1% FILTER): SIT1 = SALES/INVENTORY** | | | | | | | | | | |
| C | 78 | 1738 | 7.2156 | 4.13391 | 4.8724 | 31.305 | 0.663 | 107.0 | 10.393 | 0.267505 |
| C | 83 | 2148 | 7.6035 | 4.07719 | 4.6065 | 27.680 | 0.424 | 113.0 | 11.576 | 0.267550 |
| C | 88 | 2131 | 34.9472 | 4.38785 | 24.5755 | 637.578 | 0.563 | 15735.6 | 534.579 | 0.474357 |
| * | | | | | | | | | | |
| P | 78 | 250 | 16.84 | 6.06010 | 6.1580 | 47.721 | 0.854 | 372 | 36.8 | 0.331883 |
| P | 83 | 329 | 460.37 | 5.64672 | 17.9483 | 324.147 | 1.213 | 132230 | 7313.8 | 0.495002 |
| P | 88 | 332 | 9436.16 | 6.75412 | 9.0742 | 85.325 | 1.102 | 771683 | 74086.2 | 0.518398 |

Table 3. (continued)

**CAPITAL INTENSITY CIS = GROSS PLANT/SALES (OR TOTAL REVENUE)**

| CL | YR | N | MEAN | MEDIAN | SKEW | KURT | MIN | MAX | STD DEV | NORM |
|---|---|---|---|---|---|---|---|---|---|---|
| C | 78 | 2179 | 1.25168 | 0.366984 | 30.9894 | 1078.37 | 0 | 401.00 | 10.4596 | 0.452373 |
| C | 83 | 2737 | 2.42317 | 0.437857 | 50.8966 | 2630.95 | 0 | 3189.00 | 61.5409 | 0.484296 |
| C | 88 | 2822 | 1.50661 | 0.441544 | 26.8312 | 893.10 | 0 | 285.23 | 7.4496 | 0.419865 |
| * | | | | | | | | | | |
| P | 78 | 306 | 0.42365 | 0.242396 | 4.7726 | 33.312 | 0.000 | 5.859 | 0.5739 | 0.235347 |
| P | 83 | 415 | 0.51217 | 0.285203 | 5.0445 | 35.854 | 0.000 | 7.902 | 0.7446 | 0.249987 |
| P | 88 | 405 | 0.58715 | 0.316230 | 11.2703 | 166.554 | 0.008 | 20.730 | 1.2592 | 0.322870 |

**CAPITAL INTENSITY (1% FILTER): CTS1 = GROSS PLANT/SALES**

| CL | YR | N | MEAN | MEDIAN | SKEW | KURT | MIN | MAX | STD DEV | NORM |
|---|---|---|---|---|---|---|---|---|---|---|
| C | 78 | 2085 | 0.79443 | 0.375647 | 2.56024 | 6.9065 | 0.001 | 7.164 | 1.0708 | 0.259965 |
| C | 83 | 2624 | 0.93388 | 0.453625 | 2.85402 | 9.7209 | 0.001 | 9.651 | 1.2794 | 0.252105 |
| C | 88 | 2668 | 1.13617 | 0.460382 | 3.15413 | 11.3525 | 0.004 | 13.034 | 1.7850 | 0.271854 |
| * | | | | | | | | | | |
| P | 78 | 300 | 0.38820 | 0.242396 | 2.48883 | 7.4387 | 0.018 | 2.5902 | 0.4050 | 0.212560 |
| P | 83 | 407 | 0.46580 | 0.285203 | 2.91430 | 10.8264 | 0.032 | 3.6803 | 0.5208 | 0.207466 |
| P | 88 | 397 | 0.49736 | 0.316230 | 3.16105 | 12.9904 | 0.023 | 3.8602 | 0.5523 | 0.203961 |

**CAPITAL INTENSITY: CDS = DEPRECIATION/TOTAL EXPENSES**

| CL | YR | N | MEAN | MEDIAN | SKEW | KURT | MIN | MAX | STD DEV | NORM |
|---|---|---|---|---|---|---|---|---|---|---|
| C | 78 | 2153 | 0.06125 | 0.028383 | 16.5471 | 403.97 | 0 | 4.7868 | 0.16235 | 0.352980 |
| C | 83 | 2711 | 0.11677 | 0.036035 | 49.7607 | 2542.14 | 0 | 85.8568 | 1.67418 | 0.472197 |
| C | 88 | 2796 | 0.09835 | 0.040362 | 12.2302 | 232.08 | 0 | 6.7379 | 0.26079 | 0.353041 |
| * | | | | | | | | | | |
| P | 78 | 307 | 0.041764 | 0.019770 | 8.526 | 92.975 | 0.000 | 1.2511 | 0.095436 | 0.332794 |
| P | 83 | 420 | 0.065512 | 0.026614 | 10.790 | 153.671 | 0.000 | 3.0759 | 0.190478 | 0.365388 |
| P | 88 | 410 | 0.115622 | 0.032581 | 10.036 | 123.214 | 0.001 | 6.7678 | 0.459001 | 0.401464 |

Table 3. *(continued)*

**CAPITAL INTENSITY (1% FILTER): CDS1 = DEPRECIATION/TOTAL EXPENSES**

| | | | | | | | | | | |
|---|---|---|---|---|---|---|---|---|---|---|
| C | 78 | 2051 | 0.052191 | 0.029227 | 3.5310 | 15.067 | 0.0003 | 0.51935 | 0.068645 | 0.23541 |
| C | 83 | 2592 | 0.070059 | 0.036799 | 3.9026 | 17.750 | 0.0000 | 0.82449 | 0.105598 | 0.25724 |
| C | 88 | 2661 | 0.082980 | 0.041757 | 4.2777 | 22.563 | 0.0000 | 1.18258 | 0.130953 | 0.27006 |
| * | | | | | | | | | | |
| P | 78 | 301 | 0.034560 | 0.019770 | 4.9286 | 34.103 | 0.0031 | 0.49242 | 0.048757 | 0.25917 |
| P | 83 | 412 | 0.052224 | 0.026614 | 4.9039 | 27.357 | 0.0025 | 0.77327 | 0.092602 | 0.29578 |
| P | 88 | 403 | 0.077705 | 0.032489 | 5.7676 | 36.865 | 0.0038 | 1.58651 | 0.183894 | 0.34389 |

**BETA: BETAE (EQUAL WEIGHTED INDEX, ANNUAL 7 TO 14 YEARS) [MARKET MODEL]**

| *CL* | *N* | *MEAN* | *MEDIAN* | *SKEW* | *KURT* | *MIN* | *MAX* | *STD DEV* | *NORM* |
|---|---|---|---|---|---|---|---|---|---|
| C | 2599 | 0.9805 | 0.75418 | 2.96123 | 24.2771 | −3.9542 | 16.6277 | 1.25446 | 0.11041 |
| * | | | | | | | | | |
| P | 355 | 1.2912 | 0.97095 | 4.53645 | 35.3993 | −2.2681 | 17.3868 | 1.60985 | 0.15557 |

**BETA (1% FILTERED) BETAE1 (EQUAL WEIGHTED, $N = 7$ TO 14 YRS)**

| *CL* | *N* | *MEAN* | *MEDIAN* | *SKEW* | *KURT* | *MIN* | *MAX* | *STD DEV* | *NORM* |
|---|---|---|---|---|---|---|---|---|---|
| C | 2547 | 0.9436 | 0.75418 | 1.10575 | 1.8023 | −1.2388 | 5.2011 | 0.98162 | 0.09120 |
| * | | | | | | | | | |
| P | 349 | 1.2199 | 0.97095 | 1.97318 | 7.5102 | −1.0305 | 8.0821 | 1.13594 | 0.10966 |

**BETA: BETAV (VALUE WEIGHTED INDEX, $N = 7$ TO 14 YEARS) [MARKET MODEL]**

| *CL* | *N* | *MEAN* | *MEDIAN* | *SKEW* | *KURT* | *MIN* | *MAX* | *STD DEV* | *NORM* |
|---|---|---|---|---|---|---|---|---|---|
| C | 2599 | 1.1926 | 0.93823 | 1.56994 | 16.8037 | −11.586 | 17.8673 | 1.67084 | 0.118162 |
| * | | | | | | | | | |
| P | 355 | 1.4321 | 1.08152 | 1.87945 | 17.3464 | −10.189 | 18.1307 | 2.03815 | 0.116871 |

**BETA: BETAB1 (1% FILTER): (VALUE WEIGHTED, $N = 7$ TO 14 ANNUAL RETS.)**

| *CL* | *N* | *MEAN* | *MEDIAN* | *SKEW* | *KURT* | *MIN* | *MAX* | *STD DEV* | *NORM* |
|---|---|---|---|---|---|---|---|---|---|
| C | 2547 | 1 | 0.93823 | 1.06631 | 1.9841 | −2.0337 | 6.6289 | 1.2937 | 0.096595 |
| * | | | | | | | | | |
| P | 349 | 1.3973 | 1.08152 | 1.3454 | 3.0203 | −3.0269 | 8.3511 | 1.55879 | 0.094257 |

*Notes:* Dual class (CL): C = core, P = periphery. SEW = skewness , KURT = kurtosis, MIN = minimum, MAX = maximum, NORM = normality.

*Table 4.* ANOVA of Variables (1% Trimmed) by Dual Class, Stock Exchange, and Fiscal Year-end

**SIZE (1% FILTER): MVE1 = MARKET VALUE OF EQUITY**

| | Model Information | | | | Main Effects | | | Interaction Effects | | | |
|---|---|---|---|---|---|---|---|---|---|---|---|
| YEAR | DF | F VAL | (PR>F) | R-SQR | Di | Si | Yi | Di*Si | Di*Yi | Si*Yi | Di*Si*Yi |
| 1978 | 2206 | 53.10 | (.0001) | .1446 | 12.10# | 275.59# | 96.87# | 3.84+ | 0.00 | 0.00 | 0.00 |
| 1983 | 3213 | 96.97 | (.0001) | .1747 | 6.88* | 583.74# | 123.89# | 3.65@ | 1.64 | 0.00 | 0.00 |
| 1988 | 3279 | 71.65 | (.0001) | .1329 | 2.95 | 0.08 | 424.70# | 86.82# | 5.56+ | 12.09# | 0.00 |

**SIZE (1% FILTER): TA1 = TOTAL ASSETS**

| | Model Information | | | | Main Effects | | | Interaction Effects | | | |
|---|---|---|---|---|---|---|---|---|---|---|---|
| YEAR | DF | F VAL | (PR>F) | R-SQR | Di | Si | Yi | Di*Si | Di*Yi | Si*Yi | Di*Si*Yi |
| 1978 | 2579 | 69.62 | (.0001) | .1593 | 19.84# | 299.19# | 176.21# | 3.16@ | 2.33 | 0.00 | 0.00 |
| 1983 | 3278 | 84.47 | (.0001) | .1531 | 33.08# | 367.24# | 200.48# | 16.13# | 0.00 | 0.00 | 0.00 |
| 1988 | 3402 | 73.09 | (.0001) | .1309 | 26.01# | 334.15# | 164.28# | 14.72# | 0.00 | 0.00 | 0.00 |

**SIZE (1% FILTER): TR1 = TOTAL REVENUE**

| | Model Information | | | | Main Effects | | | Interaction Effects | | | |
|---|---|---|---|---|---|---|---|---|---|---|---|
| YEAR | DF | F VAL | (PR>F) | R-SQR | Di | Si | Yi | Di*Si | Di*Yi | Si*Yi | Di*Si*Yi |
| 1978 | 2575 | 60.57 | (.0001) | .1417 | 1.61 | 0.2049 | 350.27# | 89.19# | 2.15 | 3.15@ | 0.00 |
| 1983 | 3276 | 86.28 | (.0001) | .1559 | 3.67+ | 0.0556 | 506.55# | 105.13# | 8.25* | 7.81* | 0.00 |
| 1988 | 3380 | 72.38 | (.0001) | .1306 | 0.10 | 466.11# | 56.58# | 1.90 | 15.62# | 0.00 | 0.00 |

**SIZE (1% FILTER): SZEP1 = MVE + BOOK VALUE DEBT + PREFERRED STOCK**

| | Model Information | | | | Main Effects | | | Interaction Effects | | | |
|---|---|---|---|---|---|---|---|---|---|---|---|
| YEAR | DF | F VAL | (PR>F) | R-SQR | Di | Si | Yi | Di*Si | Di*Yi | Si*Yi | Di*Si*Yi |
| 1978 | 2206 | 66.07 | (.0001) | .1738 | 15.32# | 315.27# | 126.83# | 4.67+ | 0.00 | 9.48* | 0.00 |
| 1983 | 3212 | 115.85 | (.0001) | .2019 | 13.89# | 648.57# | 161.04# | 9.40+ | 0.00 | 0.00 | 0.00 |
| 1988 | 3272 | 85.76 | (.0001) | .1553 | 4.24+ | 506.87# | 105.18# | 5.72+ | 12.10# | 0.00 | 0.00 |

Table 4. *(continued)*

**RETURNS (1% FILTER): ROA1 = RETURN ON ASSETS**

| | *Model Information* | | | | *Main Effects* | | | *Interaction Effects* | | | |
|---|---|---|---|---|---|---|---|---|---|---|---|
| *YEAR* | *DF* | *F VAL* | *(PR>F)* | *R-SQR* | *Di* | *Si* | *Yi* | *Di*Si* | *Di*Yi* | *Si*Yi* | *Di*Si*Yi* |
| 1978 | 2440 | 2.68 | (.0091) | .0077 | 7.10* | 3.99+ | 0.12 | 1.68 | 2.29 | 4.91+ | 0.00 |
| 1983 | 3089 | 11.91 | (.0001) | .0263 | 13.78# | 63.36# | 0.71 | 2.79@ | 2.60@ | 3.63@ | 0.00 |
| 1988 | 3167 | 20.53 | (.0001) | .0435 | 1.30 | 127.34# | 15.54# | 0.86 | 3.84+ | 0.00 | 0.00 |

**RETURNS (1% FILTER): ROE1 = RETURN ON EQUITY**

| | *Model Information* | | | | *Main Effects* | | | *Interaction Effects* | | | |
|---|---|---|---|---|---|---|---|---|---|---|---|
| *YEAR* | *DF* | *F VAL* | *(PR>F)* | *R-SQR* | *Di* | *Si* | *Yi* | *Di*Si* | *Di*Yi* | *Si*Yi* | *Di*Si*Yi* |
| 1978 | 2572 | 5.51 | (.0001) | .0148 | 20.47# | 12.51# | 0.73 | 2.04 | 3.65@ | 0.00 | 0.00 |
| 1983 | 3273 | 12.22 | (.0001) | .0255 | 21.58# | 59.05# | 0.01 | 2.72@ | 2.28 | 3.36@ | 0.00 |
| 1988 | 3371 | 7.66 | (.0001) | .0157 | 0.23 | 48.15# | 3.78+ | 0.81 | 4.11+ | 0.00 | 0.00 |

**LIQUIDITY (1% FILTER): CR1 = CURRENT RATIO**

| | *Model Information* | | | | *Main Effects* | | | *Interaction Effects* | | | |
|---|---|---|---|---|---|---|---|---|---|---|---|
| *YEAR* | *DF* | *F VAL* | *(PR>F)* | *R-SQR* | *Di* | *Si* | *Yi* | *Di*Si* | *Di*Yi* | *Si*Yi* | *Di*Si*Yi* |
| 1978 | 2262 | 10.53 | (.0001) | .0317 | 7.26* | 35.89# | 19.71# | 8.22* | 9.19* | 0.00 | 0.00 |
| 1983 | 2843 | 19.55 | (.0001) | .0460 | 14.50# | 85.95# | 25.41# | 17.23# | 10.71# | 0.00 | 0.00 |
| 1988 | 2793 | 14.81 | (.0001) | .0359 | 9.84* | 66.85# | 22.57# | 8.93* | 7.80* | 0.00 | 0.00 |

**LEVERAGE (1% FILTER): TDMV1 = TOTAL DEBT/MARKET VALUE OF EQUITY [MVE]**

| | *Model Information* | | | | *Main Effects* | | | *Interaction Effects* | | | |
|---|---|---|---|---|---|---|---|---|---|---|---|
| *YEAR* | *DF* | *F VAL* | *(PR>F)* | *R-SQR* | *Di* | *Si* | *Yi* | *Di*Si* | *Di*Yi* | *Si*Yi* | *Di*Si*Yi* |
| 1978 | 2205 | 1.12 | (.3481) | .0036 | 1.48 | 0.97 | 4.26+ | 0.00 | 0.85 | 0.11 | 0.30 |
| 1983 | 3212 | 5.68 | (.0001) | .0123 | 8.80* | 7.64* | 20.73# | 7.03* | 0.00 | 2.92@ | 0.00 |
| 1988 | 3267 | 1.11 | (.3529) | .0024 | 0.85 | 2.42 | 0.01 | 0.53 | 2.47 | 2.02 | 0.00 |

Table 4. (continued)

**LEVERAGE (1% FILTER): DLTA1 = DEBT (LONG TERM)/TOTAL ASSETS**

| | *Model Information* | | | | *Main Effects* | | | *Interaction Effects* | | | |
|---|---|---|---|---|---|---|---|---|---|---|---|
| *YEAR* | *DF* | *F VAL* | *(PR>F)* | *R-SQR* | *Di* | *Si* | *Yi* | *Di*Si* | *Di*Yi* | *Si*Yi* | *Di*Si*Yi* |
| 1978 | 2336 | 2.50 | (.0148) | .0074 | 6.09* | 4.72+ | 0.38 | 2.31 | 0.17 | 1.89 | 1.93 |
| 1983 | 2956 | 1.57 | (.1394) | .0037 | 1.24 | 3.56@ | 0.70 | 0.48 | 0.67 | 1.67 | 2.68@ |
| 1988 | 3068 | 3.52 | (.0009) | .0080 | 14.74# | 3.54@ | 1.47 | 0.69 | 4.63+ | 0.00 | 0.06 |

**LEVERAGE (1% FILTER): DLIC1 = DEBT (LONG TERM)/INVESTED CAPITAL**

| | *Model Information* | | | | *Main Effects* | | | *Interaction Effects* | | | |
|---|---|---|---|---|---|---|---|---|---|---|---|
| *YEAR* | *DF* | *F VAL* | *(PR>F)* | *R-SQR* | *Di* | *Si* | *Yi* | *Di*Si* | *Di*Yi* | *Si*Yi* | *Di*Si*Yi* |
| 1978 | 2311 | 1.52 | (.1551) | .0046 | 3.86+ | 2.17 | 0.58 | 1.46 | 1.20 | 0.00 | 1.60 |
| 1983 | 2936 | 3.66 | (.0006) | .0087 | 0.05 | 12.64# | 13.03# | 1.39 | 0.96 | 0.00 | 0.00 |
| 1988 | 3396 | 10.75 | (.0001) | .0217 | 9.33* | 45.58# | 19.11# | 3.89@ | 6.57* | 0.00 | 0.00 |

**LEVERAGE COVERAGE (1% FILTER): FCR1 = FIXED CHARGES COVERAGE RATIO**

| | *Model Information* | | | | *Main Effects* | | | *Interaction Effects* | | | |
|---|---|---|---|---|---|---|---|---|---|---|---|
| *YEAR* | *DF* | *F VAL* | *(PR>F)* | *R-SQR* | *Di* | *Si* | *Yi* | *Di*Si* | *Di*Yi* | *Si*Yi* | *Di*Si*Yi* |
| 1978 | 2477 | 1.86 | (.0718) | .0052 | 3.88+ | 5.57+ | 0.14 | 0.00 | 3.16@ | 0.29 | 0.33 |
| 1983 | 3144 | 2.03 | (.0482) | .0045 | 1.46 | 10.88# | 1.52 | 0.20 | 0.00 | 0.00 | 0.59 |
| 1988 | 3252 | 2.10 | (.0405) | .0045 | 5.61+ | 2.70@ | 6.25* | 0.00 | 0.00 | 0.00 | 0.70 |

**PRICE EARNINGS (1% FILTER): PE1 = SHARE PRICE/EPS**

| | *Model Information* | | | | *Main Effects* | | | *Interaction Effects* | | | |
|---|---|---|---|---|---|---|---|---|---|---|---|
| *YEAR* | *DF* | *F VAL* | *(PR>F)* | *R-SQR* | *Di* | *Si* | *Yi* | *Di*Si* | *Di*Yi* | *Si*Yi* | *Di*Si*Yi* |
| 1978 | 2199 | 1.85 | (.0748) | .0059 | 0.00 | 6.07* | 5.55+ | 0.39 | 0.80 | 0.00 | 1.59 |
| 1983 | 3189 | 3.16 | (.0024) | .0069 | 13.64# | 2.62@ | 9.62* | 0.00 | 0.00 | 0.00 | 1.17 |
| 1988 | 3224 | 0.65 | (.7188) | .0014 | 0.99 | 0.90 | 0.98 | 0.39 | 0.64 | 0.01 | 0.59 |

Table 4. (continued)

**TURNOVER (1% FILTER): SRT1 = SALES/RECEIVABLE TURNOVER**

| | *Model Information* | | | | *Main Effects* | | | *Interaction Effects* | | | |
|---|---|---|---|---|---|---|---|---|---|---|---|
| *YEAR* | *DF* | *F VAL* | *(PR>F)* | *R-SQR* | *Di* | *Si* | *Yi* | *Di*Si* | *Di*Yi* | *Si*Yi* | *Di*Si*Yi* |
| 1978 | 2279 | 5.55 | (.0001) | .0168 | 0.00 | 2.29 | 0.41 | 1.00 | 6.82* | 23.71# | 4.62+ |
| 1983 | 2941 | 3.98 | (.0002) | .0094 | 2.53 | 14.61# | 0.68 | 1.46 | 0.00 | 6.22* | 2.57@ |
| 1988 | 3027 | 43.47 | (.0001) | .0915 | 261.50# | 0.00 | 25.81# | 5.42# | 0.00 | 0.68 | 8.89* |

**TURNOVER (1% FILTER): SIT1 = SALES/INVENTORY TURNOVER**

| | *Model Information* | | | | *Main Effects* | | | *Interaction Effects* | | | |
|---|---|---|---|---|---|---|---|---|---|---|---|
| *YEAR* | *DF* | *F VAL* | *(PR>F)* | *R-SQR* | *Di* | *Si* | *Yi* | *Di*Si* | *Di*Yi* | *Si*Yi* | *Di*Si*Yi* |
| 1978 | 1985 | 9.81 | (.0001) | .0335 | 43.05# | 0.64 | 6.05* | 0.00 | 8.48* | 1.13 | 9.49* |
| 1983 | 2475 | 10.35 | (.0001) | .0285 | 44.98# | 0.41 | 10.18# | 0.06 | 11.08# | 0.00 | 6.07* |
| 1988 | 2460 | 3.59 | (.0007) | .0101 | 1.48 | 1.07 | 0.24 | 2.49 | 8.26* | 1.74 | 9.86* |

**CAPITAL INTENSITY (1% FILTER): CIS1 = PLANT (GROSS)/SALES**

| | *Model Information* | | | | *Main Effects* | | | *Interaction Effects* | | | |
|---|---|---|---|---|---|---|---|---|---|---|---|
| *YEAR* | *DF* | *F VAL* | *(PR>F)* | *R-SQR* | *Di* | *Si* | *Yi* | *Di*Si* | *Di*Yi* | *Si*Yi* | *Di*Si*Yi* |
| 1978 | 2386 | 27.45 | (.0001) | .0747 | 36.87# | 36.66# | 145.39# | 1.13 | 0.00 | 0.00 | 0.00 |
| 1983 | 3033 | 18.25 | (.0001) | .0405 | 43.56# | 1.90 | 81.84# | 0.00 | 0.00 | 13.60# | 0.00 |
| 1988 | 3067 | 17.17 | (.0001) | .0378 | 45.30# | 0.05 | 86.70# | 0.14 | 0.00 | 4.46+ | 0.43 |

**CAPITAL INTENSITY (1% FILTER): CDS1 = DEPRECIATION/TOTAL EXPENSES**

| | *Model Information* | | | | *Main Effects* | | | *Interaction Effects* | | | |
|---|---|---|---|---|---|---|---|---|---|---|---|
| *YEAR* | *DF* | *F VAL* | *(PR>F)* | *R-SQR* | *Di* | *Si* | *Yi* | *Di*Si* | *Di*Yi* | *Si*Yi* | *Di*Si*Yi* |
| 1978 | 2353 | 8.64 | (.0001) | .0251 | 19.35# | 2.04 | 49.97# | 0.00 | 0.00 | 0.00 | 1.03 |
| 1983 | 3006 | 5.96 | (.0001) | .0137 | 11.07# | 6.91* | 18.91# | 2.55 | 0.00 | 5.70+ | 0.81 |
| 1988 | 3065 | 8.52 | (.0001) | .0191 | 11.26# | 0.05 | 47.12#* | 1.42 | 0.00 | 2.30 | 3.20@ |

Table 4. *(continued)*

**RISK (1% FILTER): BETAE1 = BETA (ANNUAL, EQUAL WTD. 7YR + OBS—YEARS (1975–1988))**

| | *Model Information* | | | | *Main Effects* | | | *Interaction Effects* | | | |
|---|---|---|---|---|---|---|---|---|---|---|---|
| *YEAR* | *DF* | *F VAL* | *(PR>F)* | *R-SQR* | *Di* | *Si* | *Yi* | *Di*Si* | *Di*Yi* | *Si*Yi* | *Di*Si*Yi* |
| 75–88 | 2895 | 16.29 | (.0001) | .0380 | 13.11# | 61.00# | 67.10# | 0.00 | 0.00 | 0.00 | 1.59 |

**RISK (1% FILTER): BETAV1 = BETA (ANNUAL, VALUE WTD., 7YR + OBS—YEARS (1975–1988))**

| | *Model Information* | | | | *Main Effects* | | | *Interaction Effects* | | | |
|---|---|---|---|---|---|---|---|---|---|---|---|
| *YEAR* | *DF* | *F VAL* | *(PR>F)* | *R-SQR* | *Di* | *Si* | *Yi* | *Di*Si* | *Di*Yi* | *Si*Yi* | *Di*Si*Yi* |
| 75–88 | 2895 | 12.81 | (.0001) | .03010 | 5.51+ | 51.55# | 47.14# | 0.00 | 0.00 | 0.00 | 1.01 |

*Notes:* *F values* (*F* VAL) for overall model and all effects (*DF*: degrees of freedom).

Class Level Information

| *Class* | *Values* | |
|---|---|---|
| Di (dual class): | O = CORE. | 1 = PERIPHERY |
| Si (stock exchange): | O = NYSE, | 1 = AMX \| OTC |
| Yi (fiscal year-end): | O = DEC. FYR | 1 = NON-DEC. FYR. |

Significance levels [(PR>F)]: #<0.001>. *<0.01>, +<0.05>, @<0.10>.

measures in 1988. Without exception the main effect of stock exchange membership is significant, while the main effect for fiscal year-end is generally not significant. The second-order interactions for rates of return were generally not significant.

### 3. *Liquidity*

Liquidity was measured by the current ratio. Table 3 shows that for each of the three years, the median and the mean of the current ratio are higher for the core companies than for the periphery companies. Table 4 summarizes the analysis of variance results for each of the three years. In all cases the main effect of the core/periphery distinction, fiscal year-end, and stock exchange membership, and the second-order interactions between core/periphery distinction and the fiscal year-end and stock exchange membership are significant.

### 4. *Leverage*

Measures of leverage include (1) total debt/market value of equity, (2) long-term debt/total assets, (3) long-term debt/invested capital, and (4) the fixed coverage ratio. Table 3 shows that for each of the leverage measures used, the means and the medians of the core companies were lower than those of the periphery companies. The overall model information reported in Table 4 indicates that none of the alternate leverage measures is consistently well explained—in terms of significant $F$ values—by the tested ANOVA models. Keep in mind that it is not meaningful to interpret specific main and/or interaction effects when the overall model is not significant. The main effect of the core/periphery distinction was generally significant, with the exception of each leverage measure's 1983 effects. The main effect of stock exchange membership was generally significant, whereas the main effect of fiscal year-end was generally not. The second-order interactions were rarely significant.

### 5. *Price-Earnings Ratio*

Table 3 indicates the mean and median price earnings ratio, for the core companies are lower than those for the periphery companies in each of the three years. Table 4's summary of the analysis of variance results shows that the ANOVA models produce significant results only in 1983. For that year, the main effects of both the core/periphery distinction and fiscal year-end are significant. All the second- and third-order interactions were not significant.

### 6. *Turnover*

Measures of turnover include inventory turnover and receivables turnover. Table 3 shows that for both turnover measures used, the mean and median of the core companies were greater than those of the periphery companies in each period. From Table 4, it can be seen that the ANOVA models for turnover are unique in having consistently significant third-order effects. This indicates a complex relationship among the levels of the independent variables, making the interpretation of second-order interactions and individual main effects difficult. Note that, other than the third-order effects, each turnover measure's pattern of effect significance differs substantially over the three periods. For example, the main effect of the core/periphery distinction was significant for the receivable measure only in 1988, whereas the inventory measure was significant in 1978 and 1983, but not in 1988. To further complicate matters, the second-order interaction term significance varies over periods and differs between turnover measures. Finally, the much smaller sample sizes for inventory turnover relative to receivable turnover indicates the possibility of substantially different samples and/or populations. Thus the interpretation of the main or second-order effects for the turnover measures is quite complex and possibly is neither stable nor comparable.

### 7. *Capital Intensity*

Capital intensity was measured as gross plant and equipment over sales and depreciation over total expenses. Table 3 shows that for both capital intensity measures used, the mean and median of the companies in the core sector are greater than those of the companies in the periphery sector. The main effect of the core/periphery distinction is consistently significant for both measures. The main effect of the stock exchange membership was significant in only one of three periods for each measure. The main effect of the fiscal year-end was significant in all cases. With only a few exceptions, the second-order interaction terms were insignificant.

### 8. *Market Beta*

Market betas were generated using annual returns (a minimum of 7 and a maximum of 14 observations were required) based on the market model. Betas were based on annual returns (a) to be consistent with the other ratios, (b) to overcome the lack of monthly returns data for the smaller firms, especially in earlier periods, and (c) because annual betas are not biased by size as are shorter period betas (Puneet, Kothari, and Wasley, 1989). Market betas were computed for the entire period for each of the firms.[5] Table 3 summarizes the distributional characteristics of market beta for the years examined. The mean and median betas of the periphery companies are significantly larger than those of the core companies. Table 4 shows that all the main effects were highly significant, while none of the interaction terms was significant.

## B. Discussion of Univariate and ANOVA Results

As summarized in Table 5, the measures of size, liquidity, capital intensity, and market beta had consistently significant main effects for both the core/periphery dimension and the fiscal year-end dimension. In addition, size, liquidity, price earnings ratio, and beta had consistently significant main effects on the stock exchange membership dimension. In the case of leverage ratios, price earnings ratios, turnover measures, and rates of return, the three main effects were significant in only some of the years. These results show that (1) there are financial and accounting variables that systematically differ between the core and periphery sectors, the fiscal year-end classes, and stock exchange membership, and (2) that the results on leverage and liquidity not only confirm earlier findings in the literature (Smith and Pourciau, 1988; Titman and Wessels, 1988), but also indicate

*Table 5.* Summary of ANOVA Model Main Effects[a]

| | | *Di Effect by Year* | | | *Si Effect by Year* | | | *Yi Effect by Year* | | |
|---|---|---|---|---|---|---|---|---|---|---|
| *Variable* | *Symbol* | *78* | *83* | *88* | *78* | *83* | *88* | *78* | *83* | *88* |
| Market value of equity | *MVE* | * | * | | * | * | | * | * | * |
| Total assets | *TA* | * | * | * | * | * | * | * | * | * |
| Total revenues | *TR* | | * | | | | * | * | * | * |
| MVE + debt + pref. stock | *MVEP* | * | * | * | * | * | * | * | * | * |
| Return on assets | *ROA* | * | * | | * | * | * | | | * |
| Return on equity | *ROE* | * | * | | * | * | * | | | * |
| Current ratio | *CR* | * | * | * | * | * | * | * | * | * |
| Total debt/*MV* of equity | *TDMV* | ? | * | ? | ? | * | ? | ? | * | ? |
| L.T. debt/total assets | *DLTA* | * | ? | * | * | ? | | | ? | |
| L.T. debt/invested cap. | *DLIC* | ? | | * | ? | * | * | ? | * | * |
| Fixed charges coverage | *FCR* | ? | | * | ? | * | | ? | | * |
| Price earnings | PE | ? | * | ? | ? | | ? | ? | * | ? |
| Sales receivable *T*/over | *SRT* | | | * | | * | | | | * |
| Sales inventory *T*/over | *SIT* | * | * | | | | | * | * | |
| Gross plant/sales | *CIS* | * | * | * | * | | | * | * | * |
| Deprec./total expenses | *CDS* | * | * | * | | * | | * | * | * |
| *Market beta (total period)* | | | (1) | | | (1) | | | (1) | |
| Beta: equal weighted | *BETAE* | | * | | | * | | | * | |
| Beta: value weighted | *BETAV* | | * | | | * | | | * | |

*Notes:* [a]See Table 4 for details.

*Main effects: Di*: dual class, where 0 = core and 1 = periphery; *Si*: stock exchange, where 0 = *NYSE* and 1 = other (OTC, AMX, and so on); *Yi*: fiscal year-end, where 0 = Dec. year-end and 1 = non-Dec. year-end.

*Significance levels*: *significant at alpha < 0.05 or less; ?: parameter coefficients meaningless because model nonsignificant.

*Table 6.* Summary of ANOVA Model Interaction Effects[a]

| | | *Second-Order Interaction Effects* | | | | | | | | | *Third* | | |
|---|---|---|---|---|---|---|---|---|---|---|---|---|---|
| | | *Di * Si by Year* | | | *Di * Si by Year* | | | *Si * Yi by Year* | | | *Di * Si * Yi by Year* | | |
| Variable | *Symbol* | *78* | *83* | *88* | *78* | *83* | *88* | *78* | *83* | *88* | *78* | *83* | *88* |
| Market value of equity | *MVE* | * | | * | | | * | | | * | | | |
| Total assets | *TA* | | * | * | | | | | | | | | |
| Total revenues | *TR* | * | * | | | * | * | * | * | | | | |
| *MVE* + debt + pref. stock | *MVEP* | * | * | * | | | * | * | | | | | |
| Return on assets | *ROA* | | | | | | * | * | | | | | |
| Return on equity | *ROE* | | | | | | * | | | | | | |
| Current ratio | *CR* | * | * | * | * | * | * | | | | | | |
| Total debt/*MV* of equity | *TDMV* | ? | * | ? | ? | | ? | ? | | ? | ? | | ? |
| L.T. debt/total assets | *DLTA* | | ? | | | ? | * | | ? | | | ? | |
| L.T. debt/invested cap. | *DLIC* | ? | | | ? | | * | ? | | | ? | | |
| Fixed charges coverage | *FCR* | ? | | | ? | | | ? | | | ? | | |
| Price earnings | *PE* | ? | | ? | ? | | ? | ? | | ? | ? | | ? |
| Sales receivable *T*/over | *SRT* | | | * | * | | | * | * | | * | | * |
| Sales inventory *T*/over | *SIT* | | | | * | * | * | | | | * | * | * |
| Gross plant/sales | *CIS* | | | | | | | | * | * | | | |
| Deprec./total expenses | *CDS* | | | | | | | | * | | | | |
| Market beta (total period) | | | (1) | | | (1) | | | (1) | | | (1) | |
| Beta: equal weighted | *BETAE* | | | | | | | | | | | | |
| Beta: value weighted | *BETAV* | | | | | | | | | | | | |

*Notes:* [a]See Table 4 for details.

*Definition of effects:* *Di*: dual class, where 0 = core and 1 = periphery; *Si*: stock exchange, where 0 = *NYSE* and 1 = other (OTC, AMX, and so on); *Yi*: fiscal year-end, where 0 = Dec. year-end and 1 = non-Dec. year-end.

*Significance levels:* *significant at alpha < 0.05 or less; ?: parameter coefficients meaningless because model nonsignificant.

that the capital structure decisions and accounting return dimensions are complex phenomena in need of further theoretical and empirical investigations.

As summarized in Table 6, the interaction effects, both second and third order, are consistently significant only for the two turnover ratios and some of the size measures. The interaction effects are generally insignificant or not consistently significant for the other factors. These results show that the consistent and significant main effects obtained earlier are generally separate phenomena, underscoring the separate importance of either (1) the core/periphery distinction, (2) the fiscal year-end choice, or (3) stock exchange membership rather than the more difficult to interpret combined effects.

## C. Multivariate Logistic Regression Analysis

Logistic regression was used to test the significance of a model explaining the core/periphery classification as a function of a set of financial characteristics or ratios. The analysis was performed only on the 1988 data. Table 7 presents the Pearson correlation matrix for 1988.[6] The greatest correlation between variables used in the regression analysis was 0.3416, the correlation between the current ratio and the fixed charges (coverage) ratio. Most of the other variables exhibited correlations significant at alpha levels of 0.0001 or less. This can adversely affect the interpretation of the regression coefficients. When independent variables provide redundant information relative to the dependent variable, the individual coefficient's significance levels are usually underestimated. In some cases, the sign of the coefficient may be reversed versus relationship. There is no general agreement on what constitutes a high level of multicollinearity. The method suggested by Johnston (1972) is to calculate the coefficient of multiple correlation $R^2$ between each variable and all the others. This provides an estimate of the degree to which each independent variable is related to all other variables as a group. The largest multiple correlation was for the current ratio with a value of 0.2303, which is reasonably low. This degree of intercorrelation among the variables suggests that

*Table 7.* Correlation among Logistic Model Explanatory Variables Analysis for 1988 Using Variables Truncated with a 5% Filter

| | *Pearson Correlation Coefficients [N = 1,424] /( PROB > \|R\| Under HO:RHO=O)/* | | | | | | |
|---|---|---|---|---|---|---|---|
| *Variables*[a] | *BETAE* | *TA_5* | *CR_5* | *DLTA_5* | *FCR_5* | *PE_5* | *CIS_5* |
| *BETAE* | 1.00000 | — | | | | | |
| Beta (equal weighted) | * | | | | | | |
| *TA 5* | –0.17742 | 1.00000 | — | | | | |
| Total assets | (0.0001) | * | | | | | |
| *CR 5* | 0.09656 | –0.26283 | 1.00000 | — | | | |
| Current ratio | (0.0003) | (0.0001) | * | | | | |
| *DLTA 5* | 0.00323 | 0.03999 | –0.15392 | 1.00000 | — | | |
| Debt/assets | (0.9031) | (0.1315) | (0.0001) | * | | | |
| *FCR 5* | –0.06505 | 0.01467 | 0.34161 | –0.28618 | 1.00000 | — | |
| Fixed charges ratio | (0.0141) | (0.5803) | (0.0001) | (0.0001) | * | | |
| *PE 5* | –0.10990 | 0.09171 | 0.11930 | –0.10050 | 0.21498 | 1.00000 | — |
| Price earnings | (0.0001) | (0.0005) | (0.0001) | (0.0001) | (0.0001) | * | |
| *CIS_5* | –0.16138 | 0.25638 | –0.27858 | 0.22355 | –0.06713 | –0.01097 | 1.00000 |
| Capital intensity | (0.0001) | (0.0001) | (0.0001) | (0.0001) | (0.0113) | (0.6792) | * |
| Multiple R2[b] | 0.0581 | 0.1347 | 0.2303 | 0.1220 | 0.2077 | 0.0656 | 0.1578 |

*Notes:* [a]Variables are defined in Table 2.
[b]*R2i* is the coefficient of multiple determination between variable *i* and all other independent variables.

Table 8. Logistic Model of Dual Economy Classes Data for 1988 ($N = 1{,}423$)[a]

| *Variable* | *Expected Sign* | *Coef. Beta* | *Std. Error* | *Chi-Square* | *Prob. <* |
|---|---|---|---|---|---|
| Intercept | ? | −1.23846 | 0.31144 | 15.81 | −0.0001 |
| *BETA_E* | + | +0.14140 | 0.06132 | 5.32 | 0.0211 |
| *TA_5* | − | −0.00004 | 0.00005 | 0.61 | 0.4347 |
| *CR_5* | − | −0.53702 | 0.11459 | 21.96 | 0.0001 |
| *DLTA_5* | + | 1.66442 | 0.45076 | 13.63 | 0.0002 |
| *FCR_5* | + | 0.09031 | 0.02576 | 12.29 | 0.0005 |
| *PE_5* | + | 0.02213 | 0.00886 | 6.24 | 0.0125 |
| *CIS_5* | − | −1.29823 | 0.24480 | 28.12 | 0.0001 |

*Notes:* [a]Model parameters: independent variable coefficients.
See Table 2 for variable definitions. Note independent variables were truncated using a 5% filter, except for Beta, which is already adjusted (normalized to the population mean) to reduce departures from normality.
Dependent variable (dual) = 0 if core ($N = 1{,}257$), and 1 if periphery class ($n = 167$).
Model chi-square statistic = 72.96 with $d.f. = 7$; probability under $H_0 < 0.00001$.

a multivariate approach is appropriate for examining the simultaneous effect of the variables on the core/periphery distinction. The specific statistical methodology used is the maximum likelihood logistic regression.

A logistic regression model of the following form is estimated:[7]

$$\ln(P_{cs}/1 - P_{cs}) = b_0 + b_1BE + b_2TA + b_3CR + b_4DLTA \qquad (2)$$

$$+ b_5FCR + b_6PE + B_7CIS,$$

where (see Table 2 for detailed definitions) $b_j$ = regression coefficients; *BE* = beta (equal weighted index [annual returns] in the market model); *TA* = total assets; *CR* = current ratio; *DLTA* = long-term debt/total assets; *FCR* = fixed coverage ratio; *PE* = price earnings ratio; and *CIS* = gross plant/sales.

Table 8 presents the results of the logistic model using the complete sample of firms in the core and periphery sectors for 1988.[8] The overall model was significant at alpha < 0.00001. Six of the seven variables had coefficients of the expected sign and significance levels at alpha < 0.05. These coefficients are consistent with periphery firms being riskier, having lower current ratios, decreased levels of capital intensity, while having greater leverage and higher levels of fixed charge coverage. Only size as measured by total assets (*TA*) was not significant, though the negative coefficient is consistent with periphery firms being smaller than core firms.[9]

The model results indicate that accounting ratios are relevant to tests of the dual economy paradigm that allows a distinction between firms in the core and periphery sectors.

## VII. CONCLUSIONS

Most empirical research relying on published financial data fails to distinguish between companies in the core and periphery sectors. This study investigates whether the distinction between firms in the core and periphery sectors can be made on the basis of accounting variables. Both univariate and multivariate tests were used. The methodology differs from previous studies in economics and sociology by using the firm rather than the industry as the unit of analysis and relying on firm specific accounting data rather than industry-based data. The univariate analysis and ANOVA identified firm size, turnover ratios, capital intensity, and market beta as factors that delineate between firms in the core and periphery sectors. The multivariate logistic model identified a significant set of accounting variables (systematic risk, current ratios, debt leverage, fixed charge coverage, and capital intensity ratios) in a test of the dual economy paradigm. These results point to the need to consider the dual nature of the economy, the core versus periphery sectors.

These results have potentially important implications for both intraindustry research in finance and accounting and interdisciplinary research among finance, accounting, and economics.

With regard to intraindustry research in finance and accounting, the results may have implications for models or analysis requiring sufficient similarity between firms to examine a particular economic phenomenon. Given the evidence of information transfer in cases of sufficient similarity between firms (Baginski, 1987), the results in this study suggests a testable hypothesis that such information transfers may occur within sectors, core or periphery. Thus information released by a firm (firms) in a given sector generates unexpected share price revisions for another firm (other firms) in the same sector. Analysis of the information transfer hypothesis may be extended to consider the cases of firms classified as similar according to sector (core or periphery) and other attributes, such as risk class.

With regard to interdisciplinary research in finance, accounting, and economics, the findings of significant differences between the core versus periphery sector firms point to the need for controlling for this factor or performing separate financial analysis for each sector when using accounting data. Prediction models based on accounting data need to consider not only the differences in size and industry but also differences in economic sectors. Failure to recognize these differences may limit the explanatory and predictive powers of these models. This study also provides evidence that accounting and financial variables at the firm level may be useful in testing general economic theories such as economic dualism.

## ACKNOWLEDGMENTS

The authors are grateful to James Bannister, Ron Picur, and participants in the UIC Accounting Workshop for their helpful comments in the development of this paper.

## NOTES

1. This classification method is subject to various qualifications. The characteristics of industries and/or firms may not be uniquely attributable to a binomial distribution. For example, it is assumed that all industry members are collectively classed as either core or periphery, and firms are classified into a single industry by their primary line of business. However, industries may not be homogeneous and firms can have several lines of business. Furthermore, industry relationships and therefore dual classifications may change over time because of changes in technology, foreign competition, and other factors.

2. Other variants of the reported ratios were also tested, including log transformations, total debt instead of long-term debt, and so on; these alternate ratios are not shown since they are highly correlated with those reported.

3. Univariate parametric (*t*-tests of means) and nonparametric (tests of median equality and Wilcoxon signed-rank tests) tests were conducted on untrimmed as well as one and five percent trimmed variables. The less restrictive nonparametric tests provided somewhat lower significance levels but otherwise similar results relative to parametric tests. Each set of tests showed increased significance levels as the degree of trimming (0, 1, and then 5%) increased. The individual univariate results are not reported since they are consistent with the ANOVA main effect results reported in Table 4.

4. ANOVA results were generally similar when generated for raw variables, 1 and 5% trimmed variables, though there was increased overall model significance as the degree of trimming increased. The ANOVA model is reasonably robust against departures from normality; therefore the reported analysis on the 1% trimmed variables was considered both apt and representative of alternate variable results.

5. Both equally and value weighted betas were generated and evaluated with generally similar results; thus only equally weighted beta results are reported.

6. Correlations were also calculated for the other periods using rank orders; they are not reported since they are similar to the reported matrix.

7. The probability of a firm in the core sector is $P_{CS}$ while the probability that it will be in the periphery sector is $1 - P_{CS}$. The predicted value of the dependent variable is therefore the maximum likelihood estimate of the natural logarithm of the odds that the firm in question is in the core sector.

8. The logistic model was also run with sales inventory turnover (*SIT*) and/or sales receivable turnover (*SRT*) variables; the overall results are not materially different. Though these terms were statistically significant at a 0.05 level, including either turnover measure considerably reduced the subsample of periphery firms, thereby reducing the overall power of the model.

9. Several factors may explain the lack of significance for the size term. Total assets are highly correlated with the current ratio and capital intensity measure. Another likely explanation is that firms issuing publicly traded equity and that are included in the COMPUSTAT files tend to be larger and more successful; thus there is a bias against periphery firms which are likely to be smaller and less successful.

## REFERENCES

Atiase, R. K. (1985). "Predisclosure Information, Firm Capitalization, and Security Price Behavior around Earnings Announcements." *Journal of Accounting Research* 23: 21–26.

Averitt, R. T. (1968). *The Dual Economy: The Dynamics of American Industry Structure.* New York: Horton.

Baginski, S. P. (1987). "Intraindustry Information Transfers Associated with Management Forecasts of Earnings." *Journal of Accounting Research* (Autumn): 196–216.

Baran, P. A., and Sweezy, P. M. (1966). *Monopoly Capital.* New York: Monthly Review Press.

Bavishi, B. F., Choi, F., and Shawky, H. (1981). "Analyzing the Financial Ratio of the World's 1000 Leading Industrial Companies." *Business International* (New York).

Beck, E. M., Horan, P. N., and Tolbert II, C. M. (1978). "Stratification in a Duel Economy: A Sectoral Model of Earnings Determination." *American Sociological Review* 43: 704–720.

Bibb, R., and Form, W. (1977). "The Effects of Industrial, Occupational, and Sex Stratification on Wages in Blue-Collar Markets." *Social Forces* 55: 974–996.

Bluestone, B. (1970). "The Tripartite Economy: Labor Markets and the Working Poor." *Poverty and the Human Resource Abstracts* 5: 15–35.

Bluestone, B., Murphy, W. M., and Stevenson, M. (1973). *Low Wages and the Working Poor*. Ann Arbor: Institute of Labor and Industrial Relations, University of Michigan.

Blume, M., and Stambaugh, R. (1983). "Biases in Computed Returns: An Implication to the Size Effect." *Journal of Financial Economics* 12: 387–404.

Bourgeois, J., Haines, G. H., and Sommers, M. S. (1980). "Defining an Industry." Pp. 120–133 in *Market Measurement and Analysis*, edited by D. B. Montgomery and D. R. Wittink. Cambridge, MA: Marketing Science Institute.

Bowen, R. M., Daley, L. A., and Huber, C. C. (1982). "Evidence on the Existence and Determinants of Inter-Industry Differences in Leverage." *Financial Management* (Winter): 10–20.

Brown, P., and Ball, R. (1967). "Some Preliminary Findings on the Association Between the Earnings of a Firm, Its Industry, and the Economy." *Empirical Research in Accounting: Selected Studies Supplement to Journal of Accounting Research*, pp. 55–77.

Brown, P., Kleidon, A. W., and Marsh, T. A. (1983). "New Evidence on the Nature of Size Related Anomalies in Stock Prices." *Journal of Financial Economics* 12: 33–56.

Cain, G. C. (1976). "The Challenge of Segmented Labor Market Theories to Orthodox Theory: A Survey." *Journal of Economic Literature* 14: 1215–1257.

Foster, G. (1986). *Financial Statement Analysis*, 2d ed. Englewood Cliffs, NJ: Prentice-Hall.

Frecka, T. J. (1982). "The Effects of Complex Capital Structure on the Market Values of Firms." *Financial Review* (September): 86–111.

Galbraith, J. K. (1973). *Economics and the Public Purpose*. Boston: Houghton Mifflin.

Harrison, B. (1973). "The Theory of the Dual Economy." Pp. 269–282 in *The Worker in Post Industrial Capitalism*, edited by B. Silverman and M. Yanovitch. New York: Free Press.

Hodson, R. (1978). "Labor in the Monopoly, Competitive and State Sectors of Production." *Politics and Society* 8: 429–480.

Hodson, R., and Kaufman, R. L. (1982). "Economic Dualism: A Critical Review." *American Sociological Review* 47 (December): 727–739.

Johnston, J. (1972). *Econometrics Methods*. New York: McGraw-Hill.

Keim, D. B. (1983). "Size Related Anomalies and Stock Return Seasonality: Further Empirical Evidence." *Journal of Financial Economics* 12: 13–32.

King, B. F. (1966). "Market and Industry Factors in Stock Market Price Behavior." *Journal of Business* 39: 139–190.

Kinney, W. R. (1986). "Empirical Accounting Research Design for Ph.D. Students." *Accounting Review* 61: 338–350.

Neter, J., and Wasserman, W. (1974). *Applied Linear Statistical Models*. Homewood, IL: Richard D. Irwin.

O'Connor, J. (1973). *The Fiscal Crisis of the State*. New York: St. Martin's Press.

Olsen, C., and Dietrich, J. R. (1985). "Vertical Information Transfers: The Association between Retailers' Sales Announcements and Suppliers' Security Returns." *Journal of Accounting Research* (Supplement): 144–166.

Oster, G. (1979). "A Factor Analytic Test of the Theory of the Dual Economy." *Reviews of Economics and Statistics* 61: 33–39.

Osterman, P. (1975). "An Empirical Study of Labor Market Segmentation." *Industrial and Labor Relations Review* 28: 508–523.

Piori, M. (1977). "The Dual Labor Market: Theory and Implications." *Problems in Political Economy: An Urban Perspective*. Lexington, MA: Health, pp. 93–97.

Puneet, H., Kothari, S. P., and Wasley, C. (1989). "The Relation between the Return Interval and Betas: Implication for the Size Effect." *Journal of Financial Economics* 23: 79–100.

Reinganum, M. R. (1981). "Misspecification of Capital Asset Pricing: Empirical Anomalies Based on Earnings Yields and Market Values." *Journal of Financial Economics* 9: 19–46.

Smith, D. B., and Pourciau, S. (1988). "A Comparison of Financial Characteristics of December and Non-December Year-end Companies." *Journal of Accounting and Economics* 10: 335–344.

Spilerman, S. (1977). "Careers, Labor Market Structure, and Socioeconomic Achievement." *American Journal of Sociology* 93: 551–593.

Titman, S., and Wessels, R. (1988). "The Determinants of Capital Structure Choice." *Journal of Finance* 43 (March): 1–20.

Tolbert, C., Horan, P., and Beck, E. M. (1980). "The Structure of Economic Segmentation: A Dual Economy Approach." *American Journal of Sociology* 85: 1095–1116.

Tse, S. (1988). "Attributes of Industry, Industry Segment and Firm-Specific Information in Security Valuation." *Contemporary Accounting Research* 5, No. 2 (Spring): 592–614.

Watts, R. L., and Zimmerman, J. L. (1986). *Positive Accounting Theory*. Englewood Cliffs, NJ: Prentice-Hall.

# VENTURE CAPITAL FINANCE:

## REVIEW AND SYNTHESIS

Edgar Norton

## I. INTRODUCTION

Financial theory and empirical work in finance typically (either implicitly or explicitly) involve large established firms. Relatively little has been written, from the viewpoint of financial theory, on the venture capital (VC) process. The study of venture capital is the study of finance at the "knife's edge." Perhaps only bankruptcy can rival venture capital for the role played by financial concerns. Agency costs, information asymmetries, unique products, and intangible assets are important considerations in the venture capital financing decision.

The purpose of this paper is to give an overview of venture capital finance from the distinct perspectives of both the venture capitalist and the entrepreneur. We will see that "mainstream" finance theory creditably explains many aspects of the venture capital process. In other areas, however, finance theory falls short in explaining and even contradicts some of the events in the venture capital process.

The format of the paper is as follows. Section II reviews the application of finance theory to venture capital. Section III discusses risk, return, and market efficiency

**Advances in Quantitative Analysis of Finance and Accounting,**
**Volume 2, Part B, pages 141–165.**

**ISBN: 1-55938-565-0**

issues in venture capital. Section IV discusses the anticipated termination of the venture capital process—the initial public offering of a firm. The final section offers a concluding overview and comments for future research.

## II. FINANCIAL THEORY AND VENTURE CAPITALISTS

Modern finance theory has much to say about how VC deals should be financially structured. Unfortunately, most discussions of capital structure theory take place in the context of a (public) corporation. The typical VC deal may involve a firm whose capital structure has previously been comprised of the savings and borrowings of the entrepreneurial team or contributions from informal investors (Bruno and Tyebjee, 1985; Wetzel, 1987). The addition of a VC investor places a formal capital structure on the firm, complete with restrictions, and may remove control of the firm from the hands of the entrepreneurs and place it into the hands of the VC investors. In this section we examine the implications of capital structure theory for venture capital investments.

### A. Asymmetric Information

In few other business situations is asymmetric information so clearly evident. Asymmetries may exist in two places. First, asymmetric information will exist between the VC firm and the entrepreneurial team. The VC firm must examine the proposed product, technology, and market before investing. The VC firm must also do background checks on the team members to ensure the quality, ethics, and fortitude of the team. The team members know their qualities and abilities; the VC must determine that information for himself and qualitatively evaluate it.

A second source of asymmetric information can arise, rudely put, between the entrepreneurial team and reality. The team *believes* that it knows its abilities, talent, and fortitude. The team *believes* that its proposed idea is marketable and presumably highly profitable and attractive to potential investors. The job of the VC, in its role as a financial intermediary and through the means of due diligence, is to determine if there exist gaps between the entrepreneurial team's beliefs and market reality. By reducing information asymmetries between the team and market reality, the VC informs the team of potential technical, personnel, and market trouble spots and gives the team greater insight into the views of potential investors; that is, the proposed venture may not be as attractive and potentially profitable as the team had envisioned.

Papers by Myers and Majluf (1984) and Giammarino and Lewis (1988) address the impact that information asymmetry has on a firm's financing choices. Neither paper addresses the second source of asymmetry (between the entrepreneurial team and reality), but they do provide insights into the effect that asymmetric information between the team and VC investors may have on financing structure.

The paper by Myers and Majluf has been discussed and summarized in several venues (Myers, 1984; Thakor, 1989); the interested reader is advised to consult these discussions or the original paper for a review of the theoretical framework. Our discussion below will focus on the framework's "missing links" as far as venture capital investments are concerned.

Several aspects of the Myers and Majluf (M&M) paper may be of dubious applicability to the venture capital market. First, M&M assume that managers know more about the value of the firm than outside investors. Given the second source of information asymmetry discussed above, this may not be true in the "typical" venture capital deal (Adler, 1987). After their due diligence work, the venture capitalists may know more than management about the market and profit potential of the firm's proposed product.

Second, M&M conclude that as a result of the market's lack of information on the firm's investment opportunities, the market places a low valuation on the firm's equity. In the context of the model, a firm may choose to pass up positive net present value (NPV) projects due to this low valuation. In the VC market, however, the team may not have that choice. For the firm to continue to develop the team's product, financing is sorely needed, even if the cost is high (Peterson, Shulman, and Darroch, 1987).

Third, M&M conclude that their model explains the preference of debt over equity financing in the "financing pecking order." Again, the VC market poses some problems for this conclusion. First, owing to the level of intangible assets present in most prospective VC deals, unsecured debt is not a viable avenue for investor involvement. Second, debt service takes precious cash flow from the firm. Such cash can be better used to earn higher returns if it is retained and reinvested in the firm to finance future growth and success. Thus interest-paying debt is not an attractive source of capital for VC deals (Sahlman, 1988).

Finally, one conclusion from the M&M model is that equity issues send a signal of poor future prospects to the financial market. M&M argue that this explains why empirical studies show that stock prices decline after management announces a new equity issue. This result is curious from the perspective of an entrepreneurial firm going public in an initial public offering (IPO); such equity issues are usually thought of sending the good news of a successful venture being passed from the venture capital or private market to the public market. Additionally, the security of choice in the VC market appears to be a type of equity—convertible preferred (Sahlman, 1988). The fact that a venture capitalist is willing to invest precious capital to assist a growing firm should send a positive signal regarding the future of the firm, counter to M&M's argument. The signaling implications of M&M's theory also run counter to the need of high growth firms to maintain financial flexibility. Cornell and Shapiro (1988) suggest that high growth firms should use equity financing to maintain flexibility.

Giammarino and Lewis (G&L) assume, like M&M, that managers are better informed than the capital markets about the value of the firm and its investment opportunities. G&L focus their analysis on new equity issues by the firm in a setting in which the price of the equity issue is negotiated, as in a negotiated underwriting or private placement. Thus, despite the assumption that the team is better informed than the VC, the setting of the G&L model is more appropriate to the venture capital investment process.

The analysis of G&L results in some conclusions which differ from those of M&M. First, G&L find that a form of credit rationing may occur in a game involving mixed strategies. The financier may agree to purchase the securities of only a portion of the firms seeking financing, despite their apparent similarity from the financier's perspective. Another result of G&L's model is that new equity issues are not necessarily perceived by the market to signal poor-quality investment projects. Once the market realizes (in G&L's model) that the firm is high quality, the stock price rises. This result may help explain underpricing in IPO markets.

Giammarino and Lewis's model still falls short of explaining the financing choices available in the venture capital process. The model still maintains that management has information superiority over the venture capitalist. Additionally, in the model, financial slack plays a role in determining which projects receive financing and which ones do not; in the VC market, slack is a moot point.

In the game played by the firm and financier in the G&L model, the financier cannot distinguish high and low quality firms; therefore low quality firms can try to fool the financier by asking a high price for its new equity issue. In reality, many more deals are rejected than accepted. As a result of the due diligence process, the VC obtains market and technical information which enables it to determine the attractiveness of an investment. Unless one wishes to assume the due diligence process results in an arbitrary collection of information which randomizes the VC decision process, it is safe to say the VC can determine the differences between an attractive investment and an unattractive investment with a fair degree of reliability.[1] Otherwise, investment pools of funds would be developed to invest in venture capital deals with only a minimal amount of background investigation.[2]

We have briefly reviewed several recent models of information asymmetry in the capital market. As we have shown, they fall short of approximating the issues inherent in venture capital and the appropriate setting of the venture capital investment process. Perhaps the major omission of these and other models is the double information asymmetry present in the VC market and the role that a costly due diligence process plays in reducing information asymmetries. Indeed, such a due diligence process may grant the potential investor (the venture capitalist) an information advantage over the entrepreneurial team, contrary to the assumption of many information asymmetry models.

### B. Signaling

Entrepreneurial teams may be able to signal venture capitalists regarding future firm prospects in order to obtain funding—at a good price—for their venture.

MacMillan, Siegel, and SubbaNarasimha (1985) report the findings from a survey of venture capitalists on criteria considered in evaluating deals. Five of the ten top-ranked criteria dealt with an aspect of the entrepreneurial team, including items such as "capable of sustained intense effort," "thoroughly familiar with market," and "demonstrated leadership in past." They interpret the emphasis that VCs place on evaluating the team's business plan as due to the belief that the quality of the plan signals the quality of the entrepreneurial team. The completeness of the market, technical, and financial analysis indicates diligence on the part of the team. They also help the VC consider whether the team has the capabilities to match the demands outlined in the business plan. Wilson (1985) also indicates the value of a business plan in the venture capitalist's evaluation of the team.

Wilson (1985) emphasizes the importance of referrals to signal quality to venture capitalists, as does an empirical study by Tyebjee and Bruno (1984a). Tyebjee and Bruno's survey indicates that deals coming from a respected referral source (e.g., investment broker with a good track record, another venture capitalist, a respected accounting firm or bank) are more likely to receive funding than "cold calls."[3] Thus a reference from a respected source should be a positive signal to a venture capitalist considering the deal.

Tyebjee and Bruno's (1984b) results suggest other positive signals for an entrepreneurial team to send venture capitalists. Entrepreneurs who are full-time with the venture are more likely to get funding than those who "hedge" personal financial risk by working only part-time with the venture. In terms of financing needed, Tyebjee and Bruno found that small deals are the least favored by venture capitalists, as a result of their small impact on overall portfolio returns. Large deals are also not favored, owing to the risk of such deals going sour. Medium-size deals (involving an investment by a venture capitalist in the $0.5 million to $1.5 million range) are most favored by venture capitalists.

In terms of entrepreneurial background, Tyebjee and Bruno (1984b) found that VCs prefer a general management background to narrow functional specialization. Cooper and Bruno (1977) found that venture investment success was related to two or more individuals founding the firm. At least one founder should have experience in the market or technology addressed by the entrepreneurial firm and have prior experience in large (more than 500 employees) firms. Van der Ven, Hudson, and Schroeder (1984) found that venture success is related to having one person in command without the firm being a one-man show. There needs to be active involvement by top officers and board members in decision making.

For an explicitly finance-based signal, the team can show its support of a project and desire to make the project work by exhausting many other financing sources before seeking venture capital support (Plummer, 1987). The team can signal confidence in the project and itself by raising as much money as it can from personal savings, borrowing against personal and business assets, borrowing or receiving investment funds from family and friends, and seeking capital from informal investors or "angels" (Wetzel, 1987).

Sahlman (1988) states that venture capitalists can get information regarding the team's confidence in itself, its business plan, and financial projections by offering the entrepreneur different deal terms and observing the team's response. Sahlman concludes that the ability of the team to signal its abilities and beliefs creditably may help the team receive funding.

A final signal which could be shown in the business plan is that the target market is a high growth market. Rea's (1989) results indicate that business factors are more important in successful seed financing negotiations than product characteristics. Rea finds that a market that offers great opportunities for rapid growth is a more important venture capitalist consideration than team completeness and specific product characteristics. The biggest reason for negotiation failure resulted from a business plan where too many things could go wrong. As mentioned in the beginning of this section, the thoroughness of a business plan sends a strong signal to potential investors of the quality of the team and the team's ability to put forth the intense effort needed for a successful venture capital investment.

Positive VC market signals, from this review of venture capital research, include an introduction to a venture capitalist by a respected referral source, a financial commitment on behalf of the team, a team comprised of persons with appropriate experience and leadership skills, and a well-prepared business plan showing thorough analysis, including risk and contingency analysis. These factors indicate the team has carefully thought out its plan of action and is both financially and personally committed to the plan. This helps to reduce, from the VCs perspective, the possibility of a self-serving entrepreneurial team taking advantage of the investor's money and goodwill. Though VCs monitor their investments closely, often sit on boards, have input on major decisions, and may own the majority equity stake in the firm, such signals reduce the possibility of the VC having to play nursemaid to an entrepreneurial team whose character and abilities he or she does not fully trust.

In the finance literature the issuance of debt is often thought of as a positive signal (Grossman and Hart, 1982; Myers and Majluf, 1984; Ross, 1977). The use of debt as a signal in VC deals is limited, however, by the intangible assets of most entrepreneurial projects and the fact that debt reduces the cash flow that can be reinvested in the firm. The use of debt as a signal appears to be limited by the amount of borrowing on personal assets the team has done in order to raise money needed to continue the venture.

## C. Agency Costs

Few other financial settings contain as many potential agency cost problems as venture capital investments. The principals (venture capitalists) entrust funds to the agent (the entrepreneurial management team) in the hopes that the agent will be able to successfully develop, produce, and market a product that will lead to an attractive return (40% or better) (Plummer, 1987) on the principals' investment.

Many times the investment is backed only by intangible assets and trust in the ethics and abilities of the entrepreneurial team. If there ever were a need for monitoring and bonding agents, the venture capital market is it. Brophy (1986) identifies the venture capital market as an exciting research arena where complex securities and monitoring systems are used as "devices to achieve the equivalent of the 'discipline of the marketplace' in situations where agency risk exists and in which no trading in the firm's securities occur (p. 138)."

### *i. Financing Structure*

The "security of choice" in many venture capital deals is preferred stock (Norton and Tenenbaum, 1992). Preferred stock offers a preference over cash flow and assets that common equity does not, and, unlike debt, preferred stock may not drain cash flow from the growing firm.

Formerly the security of choice was common equity (Wilson, 1985).[4] Common equity, however, provides no extra security to the investor; it places the principal and agent on a level financial playing field. If losses occur, both principal and agent share in proportion to their common equity ownership; if gains occur, they share in proportion to ownership. If the deal involves the entrepreneurial team giving up majority control of the firm, the VC will have to absorb the majority of any losses of the failed enterprise. It may also hurt the incentives facing the entrepreneurial team; why should they work hard so the VC can receive the lion's share of the profits? If the common equity deal allows the team to maintain majority ownership of the firm, the incentive for profits problem is corrected. The venture capitalist, however, faces large monitoring costs to ensure that the team does not take advantage of the minority position of the financing source.

By taking a preferred equity position, one can mitigate many of these problems. The venture capitalist will have a preferred claim (vis-à-vis the team) on the firm's cash flow in case of success and a preferred claim on the firm's assets in case of failure. Preferred stock arrangements typically include conversion provisions so the VC can participate to a greater extent in the firm's success. To enable the VC to exercise greater control over the team, redeemable and puttable provisions may also be written into the financing agreement. Typical preferred stock agreements will also specify voting rights for preferred shareholders and board composition (King, 1988; Testa, 1987).[5] Typically VCs will require that majority control (more than 50% of voting equity) reside in either one outside investor or a syndicate of outside investors (Plummer, 1987). Preferred stock is thus a good tool for venture capitalists to use to help shift risk away from the investor and toward the entrepreneurial team.

Brennen and Schwartz (1988) argue that convertible securities are a good "conflict resolution" tool between firms and investors. Though they do not explicitly discuss venture capital, the main thrust of their reasoning is appropriate for VC investments. They show that by combining a straight security (such as preferred stock or debt) whose value is negatively affected by risk with an option whose value relates positively with risk, the value of the overall package is relatively insensitive to differences in risk perceptions between issuers and investors. The use of a financing vehicle such as convertible preferred stock allows the two sides to agree on a price despite different perceptions regarding potential firm returns, risks, management ability, and management ethics.

Financing structure can also be used to mitigate agency problems relating to future rounds of financing for the growing firm. A danger facing the venture capitalist is that if the firm does poorly (or at least less well than projected), future financing rounds may result in future investors purchasing part of the firm for a cheaper price than that paid by the venture capitalist, thus diluting the original VC's position. Antidilution provisions can address and correct this potential agency cost by adjusting the earlier investors' price and proportionate ownership. One example is a "rachet-down" provision which retroactively reduces the price paid by early investors if the firm raises money in the future at a lower price.

Another way to protect early investors is to include rights of first refusal on subsequent offerings, preemptive rights, or rights of prior negotiation in the investment agreement. Thus investors can seek to maintain or increase their proportionate ownership of a successful firm or protect themselves from dilution in distress situations.

### *ii. People Issues*

Much of the success of a venture capital investment results from the talent and foresight of the entrepreneurial team as well as the interactions between team members and the venture capitalist. Unfortunately, one of the biggest question marks confronting a venture capital deal is in regard to these very attributes. Constant monitoring and interfacing with the entrepreneurial team may be necessary to protect the VC's investment and to help guide the team to success.

MacMillan, Siegel, and SubbaNarasimha (1985) sought to gain insight into how venture capitalists evaluate possible investments. Their survey results show that of the ten items ranked highest by the survey respondents, five dealt with the entrepreneur's experience or personality.[6] As the business plan presented to prospective investors shows little of the entrepreneur's character, why do venture capitalists place such great emphasis on the business plan? MacMillan, Siegel, and SubbaNarasimha (1985) conclude that the document provides insight into whether the entrepreneur is fit to lead the proposed enterprise, based upon the nature of the five characteristics reflected in the plan.

In addition to reviewing the business plan and meeting the entrepreneurial team members, venture capitalists must do "due diligence" work before they commit money to a team (Hall and Hofer, 1989; King, 1988). Such due diligence work involves explicit research costs in an effort to lower future agency costs. Due diligence involves background checks on team members, reviews of past experience and duties, and discussions with outside consultants on the viability and market potential of the proposed project. Patent searches are needed to ensure that the proposed technology or product does not infringe existing patents. Likewise, the VC must ensure that the team did not use the facilities or work time of former employers to develop the technology or recruit the entrepreneurial team.

A survey by MacMillan, Kulow, and Khoylian (1989) provides insight regarding VCs' monitoring of their investments. The survey sought information on the degree of VC involvement in a number of activities with their portfolio firms. The survey also asked the VCs in what activities would they like to increase or decrease their involvement. Not surprisingly, areas for increased involvement included those that have major impacts on the portfolio firm's success. Areas for greater monitoring and input include formulating business strategy and market plans, acting as a sounding board for the entrepreneurial team, replacing management personnel, interviewing and selecting the management team, and monitoring operating performance. All these activities would result in higher explicit costs of actively monitoring the team. However, not being more heavily involved in these activities leads to implicit agency costs resulting from poor team decisions, slower growth, and lower profitability.

Sapienza and Timmons (1989) studied the interactions between VCs and their investment firms. They found that more frequent interaction between the VC and entrepreneur lead to more favorable perceptions regarding the effectiveness of the VC. They also discovered that the more open the interaction between the VC and entrepreneur, the higher the level of perceived VC effectiveness. Measures of VC effectiveness were positively related to venture performance.[7]

To conclude this section on agency costs, we see that the financial structure typically used in VC deals reflects a desire on the part of venture capitalists to reduce agency costs. Likewise, the evaluation of the entrepreneurial team by the VC and interactions of the VC with the team are a means to reduce implicit agency costs. Such actions also reduce the possibility of an investment going sour as the VC substitutes explicit monitoring costs for future agency costs.

## D. Static Trade-off Theory

The static trade-off hypothesis states that in making capital structure decisions firms balance the future benefits of the debt interest tax deduction with potential future bankruptcy costs (Kraus and Litzenberger, 1973; Scott, 1976). Although empirical evidence implies bankruptcy costs—and hence the static trade-off hypothesis—are of little use to financial officers (Norton, 1989; Pinegar and Wilbricht, 1989; Warner, 1977), this model still plays a prominent role in theory and textbooks. The empirical studies referenced above focus, for the most part, on larger firms. Venture capital-backed firms are much smaller and riskier investments than *Fortune* 500 firms. Perhaps the greater possibility of failure and the venture capitalist's prior experience with failed firms and turnaround situations have impacts on the financing structure of portfolio firms.

Information regarding bankruptcy of venture-backed investments is scarce. Kane (1989) reports that 40% of venture-backed firms result in investment losses and another 30% are "living dead"; these are firms that move "sideways" and consume management time and energy but do not make much money. Landry (1989) reports that 34.5% of venture-backed deals lost money, with 11% of all deals resulting in total losses. Chiampou and Kallet (1989) report that venture capital returns from 55 private firms averaged 17.5% from 1978 to 1987, with a standard deviation of 37.6%. They report that the younger funds in their sample (those in operation between 3 and 6 years) had a failure rate of 35.3%. The default rate on assets for the S&P 500 was 4.5% over the same time period (Chiampou and Kallet, 1989). The higher perceived and empirical risk of venture capital lead one to hypothesize that VC-backed firms should not make much use of debt in their financing structures.[8]

Long and Malitz (1985) found that firms with greater amounts of intangible assets use less debt in their capital structures. Given the lack of tangible assets for the typical VC-backed firm, this implies that most venture capital investments will involve equity. This appears to be the case (Norton and Tenenbaum, 1992; Plummer, 1987; Wilson, 1985).

Tax factors also dictate that venture-backed firms should use little debt. In order to take advantage of the tax deductibility of interest, the venture-backed firm needs to generate taxable income. Plummer (1987) observes that venture-backed firms pay little corporate income tax. Thus venture-backed firms have little economic incentive to use debt financing.

Based on risk and tax arguments, the conclusions of the static trade-off theory are in line with empirical observations in the venture capital market. However, as discussed above, there are many other possible explanations (information asymmetries, agency costs) for the observed financing behavior of venture capitalists. Given the low or zero taxable incomes of many venture-backed investments, leasing may be an attractive way to finance asset acquisition as the entrepreneurial firm can pass along certain tax advantages to the lessor.[9]

### E. Uniqueness

Titman (1984) and Titman and Wessels (1988) propose that firms producing "unique" or specialized products will use less debt in their capital structures. Such firms can impose great implicit costs on their suppliers, distributors, and customers should bankruptcy or liquidation occur. To reduce the potential of exposing "stakeholders" to these costs, the firm should use less debt financing.

Cornell and Shapiro (1987) use similar arguments in their discussion of stakeholders. The use of debt by a firm should be directly related to the amount of "organizational capital" or reputation a firm has with its various stakeholders.

Whereas Titman's (1984) model is in the context of a possible bankruptcy filing, Cornell and Shapiro take a more general view of the impact of stakeholders' implicit claims on the financing and investment decisions of a firm.[10]

These concepts can be applied to venture capital. Venture capital firms, for the most part, seek to produce unique or specialized products. The potential for serving a product niche, opening new distribution channels, or being the first mover in an industry is what attracts venture capital investment. Suppliers of materials to the venture-backed firm may need to undertake investment to serve the needs of the firm. Customers and distributors must be found for a firm whose short-term existence may be somewhat questionable. The views of the above researchers lead to the conclusion that venture-backed firms should use a minimal amount of debt financing as debt financing increases the potential for failure and nonreceipt of implicit claims by stakeholders.

## F. Transactions Costs

Williamson (1988) postulates that capital-raising decisions should be made in the context of the type of asset to be financed.[11] Developing a theory of finance based on transactions cost economics, Williamson argues that "asset specificity" determines whether debt or equity financing should be used. Debt is a financing structure that relies on rules. Thus redeployable assets should be financed using debt. In case of failure, lenders can exercise their claim on the firm's assets and take possession of them for later resale. Assets that are highly specific to the firm or production process will be more difficult to convert to cash in the resale market; thus the greater the specificity of the assets, the greater should be the use of equity financing. Equity financing allows the use of discretion by managers to achieve a value-maximizing solution. Since debt relies on rules to govern the lender-borrower relationship, it is not conducive to a value-maximizing solution in case of financial distress. By focusing on "rules" (debt) versus "discretion" (equity), Williamson argues that financing decisions relate not so much to different financing instruments but rather to different governance structures (Williamson, 1988, p. 576).[12]

In venture capital finance, particularly early stage deals, assets—many intangible—are firm specific. In case of failure, the investor will be left with little, if anything, to salvage. Williamson's analysis indicates that equity will be the major source of financing in venture capital deals. However, Williamson discusses only two types of financing in his paper: debt and equity. A third financing possibility, "dequity," is analyzed by Williamson and rejected as not being a viable source of financing. Dequity is a financing/governance structure combining features of both debt and equity. As described by Williamson, dequity contains the aspects of debt (rules) which are perceived, on average, to be beneficial. However, when these constraints interfere with value-maximizing activities, the board of directors (or some similar oversight body) can waive the rules and allow discretionary behavior.

Williamson argues that the major problem with such a governance scheme is that promises by the board to behave responsibly and in the best interests of all lack credibility: "Those who enjoy discretion can be expected to exercise it in their favor" (Williamson, 1988, p. 582). Thus Williamson implies that a governance structure implied by preferred stock may not be an optimal financing arrangement. Williamson does not mention "preferred stock" in his paper, but his description of "dequity" can be construed to refer to many of the characteristics of preferred equity financing. Additional work is needed before the preferred equity financing arrangements of many venture capital deals can be justified by Williamson's analysis.

## G. Option Pricing Theory

The venture capital investor is investing in an idea and in people more than in tangible assets. As a result of the importance of future events for firm value, option pricing theory has several applications in the valuation of venture capital deals. Much of the discussion below is based on Sahlman (1988).

The typical venture capital deal goes through several financing stages. At each financing stage—spaced from several months to a year or so apart—more information is available for the entrepreneurial team and investors to evaluate. Venture capitalists seek to control risk (Driscoll, 1974; MacMillan, Siegel, Subba-Narasimha, 1985). At the seed or start-up financing round, the venture capitalist has many unanswered questions about the character, ability, and stick-to-it-ive-ness of the entrepreneurial team; about the ability of the team to fill any missing links in its composition; and about the technical, production, and market risks facing the proposed venture. As time progresses, some of these questions get answered or at least additional information is supplied to better evaluate them. Team members are hired, fired, or voluntarily leave; technical hurdles are passed or stumbled upon; prototypes are built and the technology appears to be successful or to require additional work; production problems and market studies are evaluated. By staging financing commitments over time (as opposed to giving the entrepreneur a lump sum at the seed stage), the venture capitalist has a chance to evaluate and reevaluate the growing collection of knowledge he/she is acquiring about the firm, team, product, and market. By staging capital commitments over time the venture capitalist is "investing" in options: the option to abandon the project and the option to revalue the project. Likewise, the entrepreneurial team also can potentially benefit from the option to revalue the project: if the team is successful, it can benefit from this option by increasing the project's valuation. As information regarding the product, market, and team skills becomes evident to investors, the higher valuation they place on the firm also represents a reduction in the cost of capital to the firm. As a result of lesser information asymmetries, reduced agency costs, lesser risk, and the transformation of intangible assets into tangible assets, the costs of financing the firm decrease.

The value of the option to abandon is the difference in the expected net present value of a deal with staged commitments compared to a deal without staged commitments (Sahlman, 1988, p. 30). By preserving the option to back out of a deal once additional information becomes available after the initial commitment of funds, the venture capitalist is able to increase the expected net present value of the deal. The value of the option to abandon (and hence the expected NPV of a deal) increases the greater the amount of uncertainty about future cash flows; the greater the amount of time the VC has to decide to abandon; and the higher the ratio of the project's liquidation value to its net present value of additional (latter stage) investment.

The second option available in a staged commitment process is the option to revalue a deal or the option for future flexible pricing. Rather than make an all-or-nothing decision to invest or abandon based on available new information, the venture capitalist may be willing to pursue the deal, but at a lower price. Or perhaps the information received since the prior capital infusion was far above expectations and the entrepreneur wants to receive a better price on subsequent investments. By maintaining the option to revalue the deal, flexible investment pricing can occur in future capital commitments and thus have benefits for both the venture capitalist and the entrepreneur.

Given the level of uncertainty concerning future cash flows and the typically long-time horizons necessary for the venture capitalist's concerns to be addressed, option pricing theory holds promise for its ability to value such risky investments and to explain certain aspects of observed deal structure.

## III. MARKET EFFICIENCY AND VENTURE CAPITAL INVESTMENT

A result of an efficient market in investments is a trade-off between risk and return. Higher risk investments need to compensate investors with higher expected returns. If investment markets are efficient and investors make informed decisions, the long-run ex-post returns for high risk investments should be greater than those of low risk investments. This necessary condition appears to be true for the venture capital market.

Bygrave et al. (1989) review nine studies of returns to venture capital investment which cover the period from 1946 to 1985. The studies referenced involved either individual firms or publicly held venture capital firms, primarily SBICs.[13] As the majority of venture capital firms are private limited partnerships and are not SBICs, this earlier literature on returns may not give us a good picture of the returns earned in the venture capital market.

Fortunately, Bygrave et al. do provide us with analysis on a new, proprietary data base. Venture Economics is an industry research group that collects data from venture capital firms. Bygrave et al. analyzed the Venture Economics data base for the period 1978–1984.[14] Given the typical ten-year life of a venture capital limited partnership, their results are preliminary at best. The median average annual rate of return for a five-year old firm was 25%; the median average annual rate of return for a three-year old firm was 13%. Rates of return will depend not only upon the age of the partnership but also upon when the partnership was founded. The Venture Economics data base allows returns to be examined based upon the year of fund formation; this is important as partnership returns are affected by "hot" and "cold" venture capital markets as well as "hot" and "cold" IPO markets. Many prior studies conglomerated returns of both young and mature funds in their return calculations. If entry is an indication of attractive returns, the venture capital market must be attractive to investors. From only 2 new and follow-on partnerships formed in 1977, 87 were formed in 1983. Funds committed to these partnerships increased from $20 million in 1977 to $3.4 billion in 1983 (Bygrave et al., p. 103). The preliminary results of Bygrave et al. hint at a reduction in returns over time as more and more money chases fewer attractive deals.

Chiampou and Kallett (1989) looked at a sample of 55 privately held venture capital funds. Their results indicate that a 17.5% return was earned on the sample; but for those firms that were more than six years old, the average annual return was 24.4%. An appendix to their paper indicates many private funds have average returns of well over 20% per year. Their analysis, however, is not on par with the quality and detail of Bygrave et al. (1989). Chiampou and Kallet's small sample size led them to combine funds by age (three to six years old and more than six years old) rather than examine the funds on the basis of founding year. As the research of Bygrave et al. (1989) indicate, fund returns are sensitive to the year in which a fund was started and the calendar year in which the returns are calculated.

In addition to reporting returns, Chiampou and Kallet also report risk measures (standard deviations, dispersions, and default rates) for their sample. However, their attempts to measure the risk of their small sample of immature venture capital funds have several drawbacks. Venture capital differs from typical capital market investments on many fronts; for example, venture capital investments are less liquid and thus more difficult to "mark to the market" and are, by their nature, long-term investments. The typical venture fund experiences a J-curve effect where, in the first few years, bad deals become evident and are written off; attractive returns may not become evident until some years pass. The typical life is ten years for a venture capital investment pool; the lifetime of the funds in C&K's sample is not long enough to derive meaningful conclusions concerning risk or the relationship between risk and return. As Bygrave (1988, p. 187) states, "Comparisons of risk/returns of venture capital funds at intermediate stages in their lives . . . have little validity for making investment decisions."

But may pockets of inefficiency exist in venture capital? Given the characteristics of the market and the uncertainty inherent in VC deals, perhaps a superior analyst can succeed to a greater extent than his or her peers. In a less efficient market, the payoff for expertise is greater and the penalty for inexperience or incompetence is greater.

Roulac (1986) contains some insights which are applicable to venture capital market efficiency. Roulac discusses sources of inefficiency in the real estate market but his insights can be applied to the venture capital market as well.

Among the sources of inefficiency which can be applied to venture capital is transaction infrequency. Even a successful investment has capital commitments staged over time; marking to the market is at best a process of estimation. As a result of illiquidity and the inability to compare one deal to another, mispricing may occur.

A second potential source of inefficiency is deal uniqueness. Every investment opportunity will involve different markets, technologies, levels of expertise (at both the venture capitalist and team level), and team composition, abilities, and drive. In contrast to investments in stocks and bonds, returns and success in venture capital are very much affected by the initiative, energy, creativity, and foresight of the entrepreneurial team. As MacMillan, Siegel, and SubbaNarasimha (1985) point out, the venture capitalist is very much investing in people; the evaluation of the team is a very important—and difficult—factor in venture capital investing.

A third source of potential inefficiency is the extended time horizon. The typical venture capital limited partnership has a life of ten years. Deals which the venture capitalist realizes are failing or that are going sideways (the "living dead," in VC parlance) cannot easily be sold or liquidated in a secondary market. Just a few successful deals comprise the bulk of the venture capitalist's return. In one study, DeHudy, Fast, and Pratt (1981) examined the portfolios of five venture capital firms and found that 3.2% of the investments were responsible for 31% of the total return. If superior analysis can be used to better identify these winning long-term investments, venture capital returns can rise dramatically.

A final source of potential inefficiency is the pricing process. Venture capitalists invest a given amount of money in a deal in exchange for a stated percentage ownership. Thus an investment of $1 million for 60% of a firm implies a firm valuation of ($1,000,000/0.60) or $1,666,666.67. The specific dollar amount invested is subject to negotiation, as is the specific percentage ownership figure. Without a liquid market to guide the pricing process, negotiation skills are important. As Sahlman and Stevenson (1985) show, even "expert" venture capitalists can become overly euphoric over the potential of a new technology or new market.

The venture capital market meets at least one necessary condition for efficiency: its higher perceived risk leads to higher returns. As the above discussion indicates, however, the appropriate means by which to measure "risk" in the venture capital market is subject to some debate. There also appear to be several sources of inefficiency in the venture capital market. Perhaps the advent of better analytical techniques and team evaluation procedures will be able to profitably exploit several of these sources.

## IV. IPO—END OF A SUCCESSFUL VENTURE CAPITAL DEAL

An initial public offering is often thought of as the desired end of a venture capital investment. Though merger or acquisition of the portfolio firm is also a possibility, market valuations are higher for IPOs than for acquisitions. In 1985 the average *P/E* ratio for an IPO was 20.4 as compared to the average *P/E* implicit in an acquisition of 18.0 (Plummer, 1987). However, much can also be stated in favor of an acquisition by a larger company. In an acquisition, the team receives shares in a firm which may have greater market liquidity than would the shares of a firm experiencing an IPO.

Many textbooks (e.g., Reilly, 1989) and academic articles (e.g., Ibbotson, Sindelar, and Ritter, 1988; Smith, 1986; Tinic, 1988; Young and Zaima, 1988) review theory and the empirical data regarding IPOs and aftermarket performance. Empirical studies show that, on average, abnormal short-run profits are possible if the stock is purchased at the offer price.[15] Aftermarket purchases, however, result in returns in line with risk. For whatever reason (and theorists propose many) IPOs are, on average, underpriced; but market efficiency seems to be the guiding rule in the aftermarket. The article by Ibbotson et al. indicates that IPOs are underpriced to a lesser extent for larger firms or in situations involving a "reverse LBO."

Downes and Heinkel (1982) empirically tested the Leland–Pyle (1977) hypothesis. The hypothesis states that greater insider equity retention during an IPO sends a positive signal to the financial markets. This positive signal should result in higher *P/E* multiples at IPO. "Insiders" were defined by Downes and Heinkel to be all parties owning stock in the firm prior to IPO. Their empirical results were in line with their signaling explanation: firms in which insiders retained higher levels of percentage ownership achieved larger IPO earnings multiples. The ability of dividends to signal value was not supported by the Downes and Heinkel tests. Downes and Heinkel propose that this negative finding results from IPO investors seeking capital gains rather than income.

McBain and Kraus (1989) construct a test very similar to that of Downes and Heinkel. McBain and Kraus argue from the perspective of agency theory that high insider ownership at IPO resolves several agency cost problems that arise when ownership and control are separated. Their empirical results indicate, as expected, the level of insider ownership after the IPO was positively related to the earnings multiple at IPO. Dividing the data into two groups of "hot" and "cold" IPO markets had little impact on the size and significance of the insider ownership variable.

These results, arguing from both the signaling and agency theory perspectives, show that high insider ownership results in significantly higher IPO earnings multiples. Rather than viewing an IPO as a way to bail out and liquidate an investment, the entrepreneurial team and venture capitalists should retain a higher percentage ownership in the firm to help increase its IPO value (Bygrave and Stein, 1989).[16] The available evidence indicates that venture capitalists do use this strategy (Barry et al., 1990; Sahlman, 1990).

Ritter (1987), Beatty and Ritter (1986), and Ibbotson, Sindelar, and Ritter (1988) discuss an investment banker "reputation effect." Public offerings underwritten by an investment banker "certifies" the quality of the issue and issuing firm and lessens risk vis-à-vis a private placement. An investment banker of greater prestige or quality certifies the quality of the underwritten issue, thus increasing the price that investors are willing to pay for the issue.

Whether venture capitalists "add value" to an IPO has been the subject of some debate. Focusing solely on financial variables and analysis, mixed results have occurred.[17]

Baron (1982) hypothesized that investment bankers have more knowledge than the issuer about investor demand and an appropriate IPO price. To compensate the investment banker for his/her information, the issuing firm allows the investment banker to sell securities at a discount from true market value. Baron's model predicts that IPO underpricing should be larger the greater the level of uncertainty regarding the market clearing price. Empirical research by Muscarella and Vetsuypens (1987) does not support this hypothesis. They found that investment banker IPOs which were self-written were underpriced significantly more than offerings in which the banker was not the lead underwriter. If Baron's hypothesis were true, this difference should not exist.

Barry et al. (1990) look at Baron's hypothesis from another angle. Among pre-IPO investors, venture capitalists are thought to be among the most experienced and knowledgeable. They are similar to the large stockholder or "active investor" who has attracted attention in the corporate control literature. Due diligence, background checks, and gathering information from consultants regarding technologies and market potential for new products certainly give them much information on the portfolio firm. Taking firms public over time also gives VCs experience and insight into the IPO process that other team members may not possess. Additionally, several venture capital firms are affiliates of investment banking firms (e.g., Hambrecht and Quist Inc.). If Baron's hypothesis is true, the underpricing of venture-capital-backed IPOs should be less than those of non-venture-backed IPOs. Barry et al. found that this was the case. Barry et al. also discovered that underpricing is lower the larger the venture capital firm; the longer venture capitalists have served on the firm's board; the older the VC firm; the larger the number of IPOs done by the lead VC; and the greater the VC percentage ownership of the firm.

In research examining both IPO and aftermarket performance, Brophy (1988) studied 1,246 IPOs from 1978 to 1985; of these, 210 were backed by venture capital. He found that IPO prices were higher for venture-backed firms than for non-venture-backed firms. He also concluded that the aftermarket performance of the venture-backed firms was superior to that of the non-venture-backed firms. However, Cherin and Hergert (1988), in an analysis of computer industry IPOs, found no difference in the aftermarket performance of venture and non-venture-backed IPOs.

Research by Stein and Bygrave (1990) indicates that prestigious venture capital firms and prestigious venture capital market investment bankers do have a positive impact on venture-backed IPOs. Stein and Bygrave examine a random sample of 77 venture-backed high technology firms that had IPOs between 1978 and 1988. The high technology industries were biotechnology, communications, computer hardware, and computer software. In their sample, 91 different venture capital firms held a total of 164 seats on the boards of the 77 firms. From this, Stein and Bygrave identified the top 20 venture capital firms in terms of the number of board seats held by the VC firm. For the IPO, 52 of the 77 firms (68%) had one of the top four VC investment banks as the lead underwriter.[18]

Stein and Bygrave categorized the IPOs into two groups: those with at least one of the top 20 venture capital firms on their boards (46 IPOs) and those with no top 20 representation. Measuring performance by "times return" (i.e., price per share at time *t* divided by price per share paid by the venture capitalist at his/her initial investment), Stein and Bygrave found that top-20 backed firms performed significantly better at their IPOs than those firms with no top 20 backing. The aftermarket performance differences also indicate that the top 20-backed firms earned better returns than the non-top 20-backed firms. Whether this superior performance results from the venture capitalist adding value to the firm, a "reputation effect" arising from the use of a top 20 venture capitalist, the ability of superior entrepreneurial firms to attract top VC firms to finance them, or the ability of the venture capitalist to exert market power in early stage investing is a topic requiring further research.[19]

Stein and Bygrave also examined the impact of the lead underwriter on IPO and aftermarket performance. Forty-nine of the firms in their sample had one of the four horsemen as lead underwriter. IPO and aftermarket performance, as measured by times return, was significantly better for the firms underwritten by one of the four leading venture-backed investment banking firms.

Other studies comparing the performance of venture-capital-backed and non-venture-capital-backed firms include Lim and Saunders (1990), Megginson and Weiss (1991), and Megginson and Mull (1991). The innovation of the Megginson and Weiss and Megginson and Mull studies is that they examine VC- and non-VC-backed IPOs using a sample that is matched by industry. Once industry differences are controlled, it appears that VC-backed firms have less underpricing and lower initial returns. The VC-backed firms also have higher growth rates of assets and sales, less debt, and more R&D expenditures.

From this brief review of venture capital and IPOs, empirical evidence supports the view that the higher the percentage of insider ownership retained at IPO, the better the IPO earnings multiple. Evidence regarding "certification" or "reputation" effects leans toward the view that VCs do play an important certification role in the going public process, which allows VC-backed firms to go public with less underpricing than non-VC-backed firms.

An area that has yet to be researched involves a second way for VCs to cash out: having the portfolio firm acquired by or merged with another firm. Little evidence exists on the relative multiples of IPO versus acquisition, or on the advantages of gaining greater liquidity by converting shares in the VC-backed firm into shares of another firm which already has an active secondary market.

## V. CONCLUSION

Kierulff (1986) states: "A theory in any of the functional business disciplines . . . is comprehensive only to the extent that it can explain and predict behavior in extreme cases. Thus, if a theory does not work well in the entrepreneurial arena, it is most important to find out why" (p. 148). Overall, financial theory does a satisfactory job in explaining observed behavior in venture capital. In the "knife-edge" world of entrepreneurs seeking the funding that will help make or break their dream, agency relationships and the implications of agency theory can explain many of the items contained in the venture capitalist–entrepreneur financing agreement. Williamson's (1988) theory of transaction-based financing methods holds promise as well if a rationale for preferred equity can be developed and shown to be superior to debt or common equity. The prevalence of nondiversified venture capital investment portfolios can perhaps be justified in the context of models such as that of Statman (1987), where the benefits of diversification may not outweigh the costs of diversification for the typical venture capital firm. Signaling theory needs to be reexamined in the light of what venture capitalists and entrepreneurs tell us: namely, that equity issues, especially IPOs, are indicators of success. If finance researchers would study the venture capital process more closely, perhaps additional insights would be gleaned that could be applied to the theories of capital structure, capital budgeting, investment analysis, and portfolio construction. As far as mainstream finance is concerned, venture capital is a neglected area of research, both empirically and theoretically. Agency, signaling, transaction costs, portfolio, and networking theory need to be examined in light of the venture capital investment process.

Empirical studies of the venture capital process are hindered by a lack of hard data. Most studies are cross sectional in nature; longitudinal data are difficult to come by. Most venture capital firms are private, so data gathering is difficult. Many empirical studies must rely on survey data or information gleaned from interviews (Fried and Hisrich, 1988). Several researchers have been able to gain access to venture capitalists' private documents (Hoban, 1981; MacMillan and Subba-Narasimha, 1986) but that is the exception rather than the rule. A proprietary data base on venture capital deals is maintained by Venture Economics of Wellesley Hills, MA. Other data bases on small business are maintained by the Small Business Administration and the National Federation of Independent Businesses (NFIB).

However, they are of little use in financial research as they do not contain data on financial variables.

The several empirical findings from proprietary data bases must be interpreted circumspectly until other researchers can access those data bases and verify previous research designs, methods, and results.

The use of surveys in empirical studies of venture capital requires that work be done to address issues such as the reliability and validity of previously used survey instruments. To verify previous findings, survey replication is an area which needs examination. Though surveys are not held in high esteem by many finance researchers, they should and will continue to be used in venture capital research. Given the personal nature of the venture capital decision process, surveys should continue to be used regardless of the existence of an accessible, well-developed data base. Venture capitalists are investing in a person (or team) with an idea. Venture capitalists' judgments of the team and their business plan affect whether the plan is funded; the working relationship between the team and venture capitalist may affect the success of the deal. There are few other subject areas in business that cut across as many disciplines—both business and nonbusiness—as the study of entrepreneurship and venture capital.[20]

To be truly useful, financial research should result in some practical insight or application that can be used by practitioners. Another as of yet unresearched area is the impact academic research has had on venture capital practice. In the areas of investment analysis, portfolio construction, and capital budgeting, corporations do research and analysis in competition with and along side academics. Venture capital firms for the most part do not do their own theoretical or empirical research; they are too busy evaluating deals, conducting due diligence, and overseeing their portfolio firms. Academics may have a unique opportunity in the area of venture capital to see their research findings become common knowledge or everyday practice and truly add value to a field.

## ACKNOWLEDGMENTS

The author acknowledges helpful comments from Bill Bygrave, Bruce Kirchhoff, and Bill Wetzel. All errors and shortcomings are the author's responsibility.

## NOTES

1. The fact that many VC deals result in losses or below-market returns does not indicate that the due diligence process is faulty or unable to separate good and bad investments. All the due diligence process must do is separate out, on average, those deals with higher a priori probabilities of success from those with lower a priori probabilities of success.

2. If all projects are blindly accepted (subject to funds availability) a "lemons" problem will quickly arise (Chan, 1983). These investment pools will need to do—or have entrepreneurial teams think that

they do—some background checking into team characteristics, experiences, planned technology, and planned market.

3. Of course, it is next to impossible to empirically verify the average quality of referred deals versus cold calls. Perhaps the referred deals were so attractive they would have received funding even if they were cold calls. Nonetheless, there is a perception in the venture capital community that referred deals signal more attractive deals than unsolicited deals.

4. Curiously, Cooper and Carleton (1979, p. 528) state, without any empirical references or proof, that "debt is heavily used in venture capital financing."

5. King (1988) also points out a tax advantage to the entrepreneurial team if preferred stock financing is used. In many start-ups, entrepreneurial team members invest equity in the firm at cheap prices. If VCs invest in the firm's common equity at a price greater than the team's self-investing cheap price, the team faces an unfavorable tax situation. The team would have to choose between recognizing the cheap price they paid as a "bargain" (by making an election under Section 83 (b) of the Internal Revenue Code) or face the possibility of an even larger bargain later under delayed vesting. By allowing outside investors to purchase senior securities this tax complication is sidestepped. See also Darrow (1989).

6. These five items were capable of sustained intense effort; thoroughly familiar with market; demonstrated leadership in the past; evaluates and reacts to risk well; and has a track record relevant to the venture. It is straightforward that high ratings in these items for an entrepreneurial team would help the VC to sleep better at night.

7. The "openness," "effectiveness," and "performance" variables used in the study were subjective responses given by venture capitalists and entrepreneurs to a survey instrument.

8. One exception to this rule are small business investment companies (SBICs). Many SBICs issue government-backed debt to finance start-up companies.

9. Leveraged lease arrangements allow the lessor to take advantage of the tax deductibility of interest and accelerated depreciation expenses. The savings to the lessor can be passed along to the lessee in the form of reduced lease payments.

10. Stakeholders include customers, suppliers, distributors, and employees. They hold "implicit claims" on the firm. For example, implicit claims held by customers include a commitment by the firm to supply spare parts or announced (but perhaps not fully developed) product improvements. Implicit claims held by workers include promises about the "work environment, the evaluation process, and the opportunity for advancement" (Cornell and Shapiro, 1987, p. 6).

11. Long and Malitz (1985), discussed above, develop a framework with conclusions similar to Williamson's.

12. Thus the transactions cost view ignores the role of managerial preferences (Barton and Gordon, 1987, 1988) in selecting capital structures. The concept of a weighted average cost of capital to evaluate project net present values also seems to be dismissed in favor of comparing returns and costs on a project-by-project basis.

13. Small business investment companies must meet stringent government regulations and usually invest debt rather than equity.

14. The Venture Economics data base is the industry standard. Work by Venture Economics personnel and Bygrave have helped the data base grow so that it contains information on almost half the new venture capital invested in the United States. Quarterly data from over 200 venture capital partnerships are contained in the data base. This is the first data base that allows longitudinal analysis of venture capital returns.

15. Tinic (1988) reviews studies that show initial returns of unseasoned equity issues are greater than 17%. Ibbotson, Sindelar, and Ritter (1988) review studies reporting IPO to aftermarket returns of 11.4 and 18.8%.

16. Both the Downes and Heinkel and McBain and Krause studies included venture capitalists as insiders in their calculations of insider stock ownership.

17. Management-oriented research has also examined this question. Studies by Sapienza and Timmons (1989) and Rosenstein et al. (1989, 1990) seek to determine if venture capitalists' managerial inputs, advice, and oversight add value to venture-capital-backed firms.

18. The top four investment banking firms bringing venture-backed firms to IPO are the so-called four horsemen: Alex, Brown & Sons; Robertson, Colman, and Stephens; Hambrecht and Quist Inc.; and L.F. Rothschild, Unterberg, Towbin.

19. A possible reason for the superior performance by the top 20-backed firms is that a top 20 venture capital firm can exercise power and influence over its portfolio firms and is thus able to invest in a portfolio firm at a cheap price. If the most respected and reputable venture capital firms can exert market power in their early stage investments, the result will be a larger times return value for them at IPO. Stein and Bygrave (1990) do not mention or test this possibility.

20. Examples of nonbusiness disciplines include psychology, political science, and sociology (to determine individual and cultural traits encouraging entrepreneurial activity) as well as English and communications (studies of business plans have examined the usage of verbs and active versus passive voice).

## REFERENCES


Adler, F. (1987). "The Art of Venturing." In *Pratt's Guide to Venture Capital Sources*, edited by S. Pratt and J. Morris. Wellesley Hill, MA: Venture Economics.

Baron, D. (1982). "A Model of the Demand of Investment Banking Advising and Distribution Services for New Issues." *Journal of Finance* (September): 955–976.

Barry, C., Muscarella, C., Peavy, J., and Vetsuypens, M. (1990). "The Role of Venture Capital in the Creation of Public Companies." *Journal of Financial Economics* (October): 447–471.

Barton, S., and Gordon, P. (1987). "Corporate Strategy: Useful Perspective for the Study of Capital Structure?" *Academy of Management Review* (January): 67–75.

Barton, S., and Gordon, P. (1988). "Corporate Strategy and Capital Structure." *Strategic Management Journal* (November): 623–632.

Beatty, R., and Ritter, J. (1986). "Investment Banking, Reputation, and the Underpricing of Initial Public Offerings." *Journal of Financial Economics* 213–232.

Brennan, M., and Schwartz, E. (1988). "The Case for Convertibles." *Journal of Applied Corporate Finance* 55–64.

Brophy, D. (1986). "Venture Capital Research." In *The Art and Science of Entrepreneurship*, edited by D. Sexton and R. Smilor. Cambridge, MA: Ballinger.

Brophy, D. (1988). "More Than Money? The Performance of Venture Capital Backed Initial Public Offerings." *Frontiers of Entrepreneurial Research, 1988*. Wellesley, MA: Babson College.

Bruno, A., and Tyebjee, T. (1985). "The Entrepreneur's Search for Capital." *Journal of Business Venturing* (Winter): 61–74.

Bygrave, W. (1988). *Venture Capital Investing: A Resource Exchange Model.* D. B. A. dissertation, Boston University Graduate School.

Bygrave, W., Fast, N., Khoylian, R., Vincent, L., and Yue, W. (1989). "Early Rates of Return of 131 Venture Capital Funds Started 1978–1984." *Journal of Business Venturing* (March): 93–105.

Bygrave, W., and Stein, M. (1989). "A Time to Buy and a Time to Sell: A Study of 77 Venture Capital Investments that Went Public." Paper presented at 1989 Babson College Entrepreneurship Research Conference; working paper, Babson College.

Chan, Y. (1983). "On the Positive Role of Financial Intermediation in Allocation of Venture Capital in a Market with Imperfect Information." *Journal of Finance* (December): 1543–1568.

Cherin, A., and Hergert, M. (1988). "Do Venture Capitalists Create Value? A Test from the Computer Industry." *Frontiers of Entrepreneurship Research, 1988* Wellesley, MA: Babson College.

Chiampou, G., and Kallett, J. (1989). "Risk/Return Profile of Venture Capital." *Journal of Business Venturing* (January): 1–10.

Cooper, A., and Bruno, A. (1977). "Success Among High-Technology Firms." *Business Horizons* 16–23.

Cooper, I., and Carleton, W. (1979). "Dynamics of Borrower-Lender Interaction: Partitioning Final Payoff in Venture Capital Finance." *Journal of Finance* (May): 517–533.

Cornell, B., and Shapiro, A. (1987). "Corporate Stakeholders and Corporate Finance." *Financial Management* (Spring): 5–14.

Cornell, B., and Shapiro, A. (1988). "Financing Corporate Growth." *Journal of Applied and Corporate Finance* 6–22.

Darrow, J. (1989). "Tax Considerations—From the Company's Standpoint—in Structuring Venture Capital Investments." *Business Lawyer* (November): 233–260.

DeHudy, T., Fast, N., and Pratt, S. (1981). *The Venture Capital Industry: Opportunities and Considerations for Investors*. Needham, MA: Capital Publishing.

Downes, D., and Heinkel, R. (1982). "Signalling and the Valuation of Unseasoned New Issues." *Journal of Finance* (March): 1–10.

Driscoll, F. (1974). "Venture Capital: The Risk-Reward Business." *IEEE International Convention* (March).

Fried, V., and Hisrich, R. (1988). "Venture Capital Research: Past, Present and Future." *Entrepreneurship: Theory and Practice* (Fall): 15–28.

Giammarino, R., and Lewis, T. (1988). "A Theory of Negotiated Equity Financing." *Review of Financial Studies* (Fall): 265–288.

Grossman, S., and Hart, O. (1982). "Corporate Financial Structure and Managerial Incentives." In *The Economics of Information and Uncertainty*, edited by J. McCall. Chicago: University of Chicago Press.

Hall, J., and Hofer, C. (1989). "A Revised Model of Venture Capitalist Decision Making." Paper presented at 1989 Babson Entrepreneurship Research Conference; working paper, University of Florida.

Hoban, J. (1981). "Characteristics of Venture Capital Investments." *American Journal of Small Business* 3–12.

Ibbotson, R., Sindelar, J., and Ritter, J. (1988). "Initial Public Offerings." *Journal of Applied Corporate Finance* 37–45.

Kane, E. (1989). "Understanding the Venture Capital Market." Pp. 9–14 in *Investing in Venture Capital.* edited by D. Fischer. Charlottesville, VA: Institute of Chartered Financial Analysts.

Kierulff, H. (1986). "Additional Directions for Research in Venture Capital." In *The Art and Science of Entrepreneurship*, edited by D. Sexton and R. Smilor. Cambridge, MA: Ballinger Publishing.

King, D. (1988). *Legal Aspects of Venture Capital Financing*. Philadelphia, PA: Morgan, Lewis, and Bockius.

Kraus, A., and Litzenberger, R. (1973). "A State Preference Model of Optimal Financial Leverage." *Journal of Finance* (September): 911–922.

Landry, C. (1989). "Valuing Potential Investments—Part I." Pp. 32–38 In *Investing in Venture Capital*, edited by D. Fischer. Charlottesville, VA: Institute of Chartered Financial Analysts.

Leland, H., and Pyle, D. (1977). "Informational Asymmetries, Financial Structure, and Financial Intermediation." *Journal of Finance* (May): 371–387.

Lim, J., and Saunders, A. (1990). *Initial Public Offerings: The Role of Venture Capitalists*. Charlottesville, VA: Research Foundations of the Institute of Chartered Financial Analysts.

Long, M., and Malitz, I. (1985). "The Investment-Financing Nexus: Some Empirical Evidence." *Midland Corporate Finance Journal* (Fall): 53–59.

MacMillan, I., Kulow, D., and Khoylian, R. (1989). "Venture Capitalists' Involvement in Their Investments: Extent and Performance." *Journal of Business Venturing* (January): 27–47.

MacMillan, I., Siegel, R., and SubbaNarasimha, P. (1985). "Criteria Used by Venture Capitalists to Evaluate New Venture Proposals." *Journal of Business Venturing* (Winter): 119–128.

MacMillan, I., and SubbaNarasimha, P. (1986). Characteristics Distinguishing Funded from Unfunded Business Plans Evaluated by Venture Capitalists." *Frontiers in Entrepreneurship Research, 1986.* Wellesley, MA: Babson College.

McBain, M., and Krause, D. (1989). "Going Public: The Impact of Insiders' Holdings on the Price of Initial Public Offerings." *Journal of Business Venturing* (November): 419–428.

Megginson, W., and Mull, R. (1991). "Financial Characteristics and Financing Decisions of Venture Capital Backed Firms." Working paper, New Mexico State University.

Megginson , W., and Weiss, K. "Venture Capitalist Certification in Initial Public Offerings." *Journal of Finance* (July): 879–903.

Muscarella, C., and Vetsuypens, M. (1987). "A Simple Test of Baron's Model of IPO Underpricing." Working paper, Southern Methodist University.

Myers, S., and Majluf, N. "Corporate Financing and Investment Decisions When Firms Have Information That Investors Do Not Have." *Journal of Financial Economics* (June): 187–221.

Norton, E. (1989). "Determinants of Capital Structure: A Survey." Pp. 323–350 in *Advances in Financial Planning and Forecasting*, Vol. 3, edited by C. F. Lee. Greenwich, CT: JAI Press.

Norton, E., and Tenenbaum, B. (1992). "The Structure of U.S. Venture Capital Deals." *Journal of Small Business Management* (July): 20–29.

Peterson, R., Shulman, J., and Darroch, J. (1987). "Financing Growing Firms: A Life Cycle Model." Working paper # NC 87–21, National Centre for Management Research and Development, University of Western Ontario.

Pinegar, J., and Wilbricht, L. (1989). "What Managers Think of Capital Structure Theory: A Survey." *Financial Management* (Winter): 82–91.

Plummer, J. (1987). *QED Report on Venture Capital Financial Analysis.* Palo Alto, CA: QED Research.

Rea, R. (1989). "Factors Affecting Success and Failure of Seed Capital/Start-Up Negotiations." *Journal of Business Venturing* (March): 149–158.

Reilly, F. (1989). *Investment Analysis and Portfolio Management*, 3d ed. Hinsdale, IL: Dryden Press.

Ritter, J. (1987). "The Costs of Going Public." *Journal of Financial Economics* (December): 269–281.

Rosenstein, J., Bruno, A., Bygrave, W., and Taylor, N. "Do Venture Capitalists on Boards of Portfolio Companies Add Value Besides Money?" paper presented at 1989 Babson Entrepreneurship Research Conference; working paper, Babson College.

Rosenstein, J., Bruno, A., Bygrave, W., and Taylor, N. "How Much Do CEOs Value the Advice of Venture Capitalists on Their Boards?" Paper presented at 1990 Babson Entrepreneurship Research Conference; working paper, Babson College.

Ross, S. (1977). "The Determination of Financial Structure: The Incentive-Signaling Approach." *Bell Journal of Economics* 23–40.

Roulac, S. (1986). "Games the Stock Market Didn't Teach You." *Real Estate Investing*. Charlottesville, VA: Institute of Chartered Financial Analysts.

Sahlman, W. (1988). "Aspects of Financial Contracting in Venture Capital." *Journal of Applied Corporate Finance* 23–36.

Sahlman, W. (1990). "The Structure and Governance of Venture Capital Organizations." *Journal of Financial Economics* (October): 473–521.

Sahlman, W., and Stevenson, H. (1985). "Capital Market Myopia." *Journal of Business Venturing* (Winter): 7–30.

Sapienza, H., and Timmons, J. (1989). "Launching and Building Entrepreneurial Companies: Do the Venture Capitalists Add Value?" Paper presented at 1989 Babson Entrepreneurship Research Conference; working paper, University of Baltimore.

Scott, J. (1976). "A Theory of Optimal Capital Structure." *Bell Journal of Economics* (Spring): 33–54.

Smith, C. (1986). "Raising Capital: Theory and Evidence." *Midland Corporate Finance Journal* (Spring): 6–22.

Statman, M. (1987). "How Many Stocks Make a Diversified Portfolio?" *Journal of Financial and Quantitative Analysis* (September): 353–363.

Stein, M., and Bygrave, W. (1990). "The Anatomy of High-Tech IPOs: Do Their Venture Capitalists, Underwriters, Accountants, and Lawyers Make a Difference?" Paper presented at 1990 Babson Entrepreneurship Research Conference; working paper, Babson College.

Testa, R. (1987). "The Legal Process of Venture Capital Investment." In *Pratt's Guide to Venture Capital Sources*, 11th ed., edited by S. Pratt and J. Morris. Wellesley Hill, MA: Venture Economics.

Thakor, A. (1989). "Strategic Issues in Financial Contracting: An Overview." *Financial Management* (Summer): 39–58.

Tinic, S. (1988). "Anatomy of Initial Public Offerings of Common Stock." *Journal of Finance* (September): 789–822.

Titman, S. (1984). "The Effect of Capital Structure on a Firm's Liquidation Decision." *Journal of Financial Economics* (March): 137–151.

Titman, S., and Wessels, R. (1988). "The Determinants of Capital Structure Choice." *Journal of Finance* (March): 1–20.

Tyebjee, T., and Bruno, A. (1984a). "Venture Capital: Investor and Investee Perspectives." *Technovation* (January): 185–208.

Tyebjee, T., and Bruno, A. (1984b). "A Model of Venture Capitalist Investment Activity." *Management Science* (September): 1051–1066.

Van der Ven, A., Hudson, R., and Schroeder, D. (1984). "Designing New Business Start-Ups: Entrepreneurial, Organizational, and Ecological Considerations." *Journal of Management* 87–98.

Warner, J. (1977). "Bankruptcy Costs: Some Evidence." *Journal of Finance* (May): 337–347.

Wetzel, W. (1987). "Informal Investors—When and Where to Look." In *Pratt's Guide to Venture Capital Sources*, 11th ed., edited by S. Pratt and J. Morris. Wellesley Hill, MA: Venture Economics.

Williamson, O. (1988). "Corporate Finance and Corporate Governance." *Journal of Finance* (July): 567–591.

Wilson, J. (1985). *The New Venturers*. Reading, MA: Addison-Wesley.

Young, J., and Zaima, J. (1988). "The Aftermarket Performance of Small Firm Initial Public Offerings." *Journal of Business Venturing* 77–87.

# INFORMATION CONTENT OF DIVIDENDS:

## A CAUSALITY ANALYSIS

Seong C. Gweon, Cheng F. Lee, and Tai S. Shin


## ABSTRACT

It is widely noted in the financial literature that dividends might convey information about future earnings. At present, empirical studies have provided mixed results. The empirical methods used in the previous studies were obscured by the lack of an exact specification of the dividend behavioral model. The objective of this study is to test the hypothesis of the information content of dividends using the Granger-causality analysis. The results indicate that there exists a unidirectional causality from earnings to dividends, not vice versa. Consequently, the hypotheses should be rejected.


## I. INTRODUCTION

Since Miller and Modigliani (1961) suggested "the information content of dividends," the concept has been widely recognized in both articles and texts on

**Advances in Quantitative Analysis of Finance and Accounting,**
**Volume 2, Part B, pages 167–179.**

**ISBN: 1-55938-565-0**

financial management. The hypothesis implies that dividends convey information about future earnings. When a firm follows a policy of stable dividends an unexpected increase in the dividend payout will be interpreted by investors as a signal that the firm's management expects a higher level of earnings. Furthermore, this dividend increase leads to an increase in the stock price if the message from management leads to higher expected net cash flows for the firm.

However, empirical evidence is mixed at present. In this study, an alternative testing method is used to evaluate the hypothesis. After briefly summarizing the previous studies in Section II, Section III discusses the new methodology in detail and Section IV offers the empirical findings. Concluding remarks are presented in Section V.

## II. BACKGROUND

Recent studies have relied on three approaches to test whether dividends do convey information. Watts (1973) investigated whether an unexpected change in dividends at time *t* could have any explanatory power for the actual change in earnings at time $t+1$. In order to derive the unexpected change in dividends, he regressed the current dividend change on a current and a lagged earnings as well as a lagged dividend. The residual was supposed to contain the information content of dividends, if any, and thus taken as a regressor in the second-pass regression. The cross-sectional distribution showed that the estimated coefficients of the dividend residuals were positive on average as expected but the relationship was not strong for most firms. Laub (1976) expressed disagreement with Watts's conclusions and presented evidence to support the hypothesis using quarterly data instead of annual data.

The second approach is to investigate the relationship between unexpected dividend changes and stock prices. It is assumed that any forecast of future earnings with dividends should be reflected in stock prices at or prior to the announcement of the dividends if the stock market is efficient. Watts argued that "the true test of the triviality of the potential information is whether it is associated with changes in the stock price" (Watts, 1973, p. 203). He used the market model to construct abnormal performance indexes and the return residual technique similar to the one first used by Fama et al. (1969), for two subsamples. The two subsamples were for unexpected dividend increases or decreases. The abnormal performance index for positive dividend residuals was greater than the overall, and the API for negative dividend residuals was less than the overall. However, the difference between the indexes for positive and negative dividend residuals was only 0.5%, which was apparently not large enough to cover the transaction costs. Using a similar method, Pettit (1972) found that a significant level of new information was conveyed by dividend announcements. This conflicting results seem to center on the issue of adequate identification and control of the information conveyed by dividends, that is, the unexpected dividend change variable (see Pettit, 1972, and Watts, 1976).

Aharony and Swary (1980) tried to separate the dividend announcement effect from the earnings announcement effect. Using a naive expectation model for dividends in which the best forecast of the next dividend was the current dividend, they found that changes in dividends provided useful information beyond that provided by changes in earnings. Woolridge (1982) refined Aharony and Swary's dividend expectation model to use actually available forecasts at the time of the dividend announcement.

The third approach concentrates on the explanation of the time-series behavior of dividends. There are two competing models. The partial adjustment model suggests that the firms are reluctant to change their dividend whenever earnings change and shareholders also prefer a steady progression in dividends. Thus dividends would gradually be adjusted for a change in earnings. In other words, dividends would tend to lag behind earnings. The adaptive expectations model, on the other hand, assumes that dividends would change before an actual change in earnings takes place since dividend payout reflects any change in expected earnings. This is equivalent to saying that dividends convey information regarding future earnings.

Ang (1975) showed that the two hypotheses could take on the same econometric equations except for the constant term and the correlated error term. However, the coefficients should be determined differently based on the underlying assumptions of the hypotheses. He assumed, under the partial adjustment model, that it was more likely for a firm to adjust its dividends fully to a relatively long-run earnings change and only partially to a relatively short-run earnings change. Under the information content hypothesis, it was assumed that dividends lead earnings in the long run and the lead diminishes in the shorter run since the firm attempts to forecast the change in long-run earnings. He found that the information content hypothesis was rejected in the long run while the partial adjustment hypothesis was also rejected in the short run. Lee, Djarraya, and Wu (1985) integrated both the information content and the partial adjustment into a generalized model. The coefficients of these models were tested to distinguish between the two hypotheses. They concluded that neither model alone could fully explain the dividend behavior and, based on the estimated coefficients, their generalized model was the most appropriate specification of dividend behavior.[1]

As noted above, all three approaches depend on the specification of the dividend behavior. In addition, the second approach is complicated with the robustness of the market model and the efficiency of the stock market. In the following section, a direct method drawn on Granger-causality testing will be suggested.

## III. METHODOLOGY

The objective of this study is to test whether dividends convey information about future earnings. Specifically, the objective is to test the hypothesis that knowledge of current and past dividends enables a better prediction of future earnings than with current and past earnings alone. Formally, the "economically rational" investors[2] would utilize dividends to forecast future earnings if the additional information provides less expected mean-square forecast error than its own history:

$$\sigma^2 (x \mid \bar{x}, \bar{y}) < \sigma^2(x \mid \bar{x}), \tag{1}$$

where $\sigma^2(x \mid \bar{x}, \bar{y})$ is the minimum-mean-square forecast error of earnings given both past values of earnings and dividends and $\sigma^2(x \mid \bar{x})$ is the minimum-mean-square forecast error of earnings given past earnings only. However, condition (1) exactly corresponds to the condition first set forth by Granger (1969) under which one can say $y$ "causes" $x$. Granger's definition of causality states that $y$ causes $x$ if past values of $y$ can be used to predict $x$ more accurately than simply using the past history of $x$. This definition is, of course, conditional on the assumption that all variables except $x$ and $y$ may be excluded from consideration without giving rise to spurious causality.

A system of two stochastic processes may take the moving average form of a bivariate vector ARIMA (autoregressive and integrated moving average) model:

$$\begin{bmatrix} x_t \\ y_t \end{bmatrix} = \begin{bmatrix} \Psi_{11}(B) & \Psi_{12}(B) \\ \Psi_{21}(B) & \Psi_{22}(B) \end{bmatrix} \begin{bmatrix} a_t \\ b_t \end{bmatrix}, \tag{2}$$

where $[a_t\ b_t]'$ is a random shock vector which is assumed to be nonautocorrelated. $a_t$ and $b_t$ are also uncorrelated for all $t$ $a$ $d$ $s$. The $\Psi_{ij}(B)$ are polynomials in the lag operator $B$, which satisfies the invertibility condition. Equation (2) may be converted into the autoregressive form:

$$\begin{bmatrix} \pi_{11}(B) & \pi_{12}(B) \\ \pi_{21}(B) & \pi_{22}(B) \end{bmatrix} \begin{bmatrix} x_t \\ y_t \end{bmatrix} = \begin{bmatrix} a_t \\ b_t \end{bmatrix}, \tag{3}$$

where the polynomials $\pi_{ij}(B)$ are assumed to satisfy the stationarity condition. Sims (1972) shows that $y$ does not cause $x$ if and only if $\Psi_{12}(B)$ is zero. The condition for feedback is that $\Psi_{12}(B)$ and $\Psi_{21}(B)$ are both nonzero, and independence requires that both equal zero. This causal relationship can also be stated in terms of autoregressive parameters in Eq. (3). If $\pi_{12}(B)$ are nonzero, $y$ causes $x$. There is a feedback relationship between $y$ and $x$ if both $\pi_{12}(B)$ and $\pi_{21}(B)$ contain nonzero coefficients, and $x$ and $y$ are independent if both are zero.

The quantities $x_t$ and $y_t$ can be written in a univariate form:

$$\begin{bmatrix} x_t \\ y_t \end{bmatrix} = \begin{bmatrix} G_{11}(B) & 0 \\ 0 & G_{22}(B) \end{bmatrix} \begin{bmatrix} u_t \\ v_t \end{bmatrix}, \tag{4}$$

where $u_t$ and $v_t$ are white noises that are nonautocorrelated but may be cross correlated, yielding cross-correlation function $r_{uv}(k)$ at various lags $k$. $G_{ii}(B)$ are assumed to be stable convergent polynomials in the lag operator. Following Feige and Pearce (1979), Eq. (2) can be rewritten as

$$\begin{bmatrix} x_t \\ y_t \end{bmatrix} = \begin{bmatrix} G_{11}(B) & 0 \\ 0 & G_{22}(B) \end{bmatrix} \begin{bmatrix} G_{11}^{-1}(B) & 0 \\ 0 & G_{22}^{-1}(B) \end{bmatrix} \begin{bmatrix} \Psi_{11}(B) & \Psi_{12}(B) \\ \Psi_{21}(B) & \Psi_{22}(B) \end{bmatrix} \begin{bmatrix} a_t \\ b_t \end{bmatrix} \tag{5}$$

or

$$\begin{bmatrix} x_t \\ y_t \end{bmatrix} = \begin{bmatrix} G_{11}(B) & 0 \\ 0 & G_{22}(B) \end{bmatrix} \begin{bmatrix} g_{11}(B) & g_{12}(B) \\ g_{21}(B) & g_{22}(B) \end{bmatrix} \begin{bmatrix} a_t \\ b_t \end{bmatrix}. \tag{6}$$

From Eq. (4) it follows that

$$\begin{bmatrix} u_t \\ v_t \end{bmatrix} = \begin{bmatrix} g_{11}(B) & g_{12}(B) \\ g_{21}(B) & g_{22}(B) \end{bmatrix} \begin{bmatrix} a_t \\ b_t \end{bmatrix}. \tag{7}$$

The following holds, under the assumptions that $\Psi_{12}^0 = \Psi_{21}^0 = 0$ and $\Psi_{11}^0 = \Psi_{22}^0 = 1$:[3]

(1) $y$ does not cause $x$ if $\Psi_{21}(B) = 0$, $g_{21}(B) = 0$, or equivalently, $r_{uv}(k) = 0$, for $k > 0$.
(2) $x$ does not cause $y$ if $\Psi_{12}(B) = 0$, $g_{12}(B) = 0$, or equivalently, $r_{uv}(k) = 0$, for $k < 0$.
(3) $y$ and $x$ are independent if $g_{12}(B) = 0$, $g_{21}(B) = 0$, or equivalently, $r_{uv}(k) = 0$, for all $k$.

There are three alternatives that have been proposed in the literature to detect the existence and direction of Granger causality. First, from Eq. (3), assuming $\pi_{11}^0 = \pi_{22}^0 = 1$, and $\pi_{12}^0 = \pi_{21}^0 = 0$, $x_t$ can be expressed as

$$x_t = \sum_{k=1}^{\infty} -\pi_{11}(k) x_{t-k} + \sum_{k=1}^{\infty} -\pi_{12}(k) y_{t-k} + a_t. \tag{8}$$

Under the null hypothesis that $y$ does not cause $x$, $\pi_{12}(k) = 0$ for all $k$. The test thus involves giving a finitely distributed lag estimation to Eq. (8) and testing that all $\pi_{12}(k)$ are jointly equal to zero. This is called the Granger direct test.

Sims (1972) suggested a two-sided distributed lag method to detect the causal relationship between various money measures and GNP. Under the null hypothesis that $y$ does not cause $x$, Eq. (2) may be written as

$$x_t = \Psi_{11}(B) a_t$$

$$y_t = \Psi_{21}(B) a_t + \Psi_{22}(B) b_t. \tag{9}$$

Substituting the first equation for at in the second equation in (9) yields

$$y_t = \Psi_{21}(B)\,\Psi_{11}^{-1}(B)x_t + \Psi_{22}(B)b_t, \tag{10}$$

which shows that $y_t$ can be expressed as a linear combination of past and current $x$. Sims shows that, under the null hypothesis that $y$ does not cause $x$, all the coefficients on the future values of $x$ should be zero when $y$ is regressed on past, current, and future values of $x$. Thus "the Sims test" is to determine if all the $x_{t-k}$, $j < 0$ are zero in the regression model:

$$y_t = \sum_{k=-n_1}^{n_2} x_{t-k} + e_t. \tag{11}$$

In testing on the relevant coefficients in Eq. (11), it is important that the residuals be serially uncorrelated. Sims (1972) prefiltered all the log-transformed data using the prefilter $(1-0.75B)^2$, where $B$ is a back-shift operator. He argued that this filter would leave the regression residuals nearly white noise in most economic time series.

There is a variant of the Sims test that avoids the need to use a prefilter to deal with serial correlation in residuals. Geweke, Meese, and Dent (1983) suggested the lagged dependent variables version of the original Sims method to avoid the prefiltering problem:

$$y_t = \sum_{k=1}^{r} f_k y_{t-k} + \sum_{K=-n_1}^{n_2} h_k x_{t-k} + n_t, \tag{12}$$

where the disturbance $n_t$ is serially uncorrelated by construction (see Geweke et al., 1983, p. 163). Thus, Eq. (12) can be estimated using the ordinary least squares method. Based on the simulation results, Geweke et al. concluded that the Sims lagged dependent variables test performed better than the Sims test using a prefilter or a generalized least squares estimator.

The third procedure suggested by Pierce (1977) and Pierce and Haugh (1977) was to check the independence of two covariance-stationary time series and was based on the cross-correlation function of the two univariate residual series. Let $r_{\hat{u}\hat{v}}(k)$ be the sample cross correlation between the residuals $\hat{u}$ and $\hat{v}$ from the estimation of Eq. (4). The null hypothesis of independence is subject to two statistical tests. First, each lagged cross correlation may be judged against an approximate mean of zero and variance $N^{-1}$. Second, a "portmanteau" chi-square test can be used for any reasonable choice of lag $k$ since a properly adjusted sum of squared cross-correlation estimates follows a chi-square distribution with degrees of freedom equal to the number of lags considered. The statistic to be computed is

$$S = N \sum_{k=-m}^{m} r_{\hat{u}\hat{v}}^2(k) \tag{13}$$

with $2m + 1$ degrees of freedom and $N$ observations. However, this procedure is not used in this study since it is less powerful than the first two procedures and generates dubious results in many cases due to prefiltering to obtain the sample cross correlations.

Sargent (1976) included four lagged values of the dependent variable and six lagged values of the other variable when he tested the causality between the unemployment rate and various causal candidates using the Granger direct test. He found both money supply and wage rate to be significant causal variables influencing the unemployment rate. Other variables such as government surplus and the GNP deflator did not cause the unemployment rate. When he performed the Sims tests with four lead variables and twelve lagged variables he could not reject the hypothesis that money supply or wage rate did not cause the unemployment, indicating seemingly conflicting conclusions.

Using his original test method, Sims (1972) had found that GNP was purely passive, responding to money supply without influencing it. To put it another way, he confirmed that there existed unidirectional causality from the money supply to GNP, not vice versa. However, when Feige and Pearce (1976, 1979) reestimated Sims's regressions utilizing a series-specific ARIMA filter for each dependent variable they found no causality between money and GNP. They concluded that the "particular prefilter chosen can affect the substantive results of the analysis even when the alternative filters utilized whiten the regression residuals" (1979, p. 530). They had similar results using the Granger direct test. They also applied the cross-correlation procedure to the same money and income data for symmetric lag lengths of 4, 8, and 12 months and found that the 5-statistic given in Eq. (13) was significant in only one case.

In Section IV, the causal relationship among dividends, earnings, and price is tested. The primary interest is in the unidirectional causality from dividends to earnings (information about future earnings) and from dividends to price (information about future price).

## IV. EMPIRICAL RESULTS AND ANALYSIS

### A. Data

Quarterly prices, dividends, and earnings were collected for the Dow Jones industrial averages from 1952 through 1981. Quarterly dividends and earnings appeared to be seasonal. The seasonality in accounting data may come from two sources. First, the firm's operations may be subject to seasonal variation. For example, the greater part of sales volume may be transacted in the closing months of the calendar year. Second, the seasonality may also be caused by accounting methods. Quarterly earnings are, after all, an interim estimation, and the expenses in particular do not accrue proportionally as time passes. Current assets, payables, and accruals may also vary in a seasonal fashion. In fact, several authors have tried to construct a "premier" model for quarterly earnings; (1) Watts (1975) and Griffin (1977), Foster (1977), and Brown and Rozeff (1979) proposed "seasonal differencing" before they applied any Box–Jenkins multiplicative nonseasonal or seasonal filters to earnings series.[4]

In this study, earnings and dividend series were seasonally adjusted using the $X$-11 program. Then, all three series were further log-transformed and first-differenced. Differencing is sometimes not enough to achieve the stationarity for a time series under consideration. If relative changes rather than absolute changes are more homogeneous, a logarithmic transformation of the original series will be appropriate since changes in logs are essentially percentage changes.[5]

The entire 30-year period was divided into two subperiods for comparison purposes. Consistent causal relationships among the variables, if any, were expected over time whether the entire period was examined or the subperiods individually.

## B. Granger Direct Test

For each pair of variables, the tests were run in both directions: first, current dividend was regressed on lagged dividends and lagged earnings to permit testing the null hypothesis that earnings do not cause dividends (i.e., that the coefficients on lagged earnings are jointly zero), and then current earnings were regressed on lagged earnings and lagged dividends to permit testing the hypothesis that dividends do not cause earnings (i.e., that coefficients on lagged dividends are jointly zero). This was done for the other two pairs of variables: dividend and price, and earnings and price.

The length of lag is somewhat arbitrary. Sargent (1976) included in his regression on the relationships between unemployment and various causal candidates such as money supply, government surplus, and others, four lagged values of the dependent variable and six lagged values of the other variable. Feige and Pearce (1979) set the lag lengths at four for the causal variable and four or eight for the dependent variable in their study on money and income. Both lengths in their tests gave the similar results. In his study of money-income causality in the United Kingdom, Cuddington (1981) included four lagged values of dependent and independent variables based on his preliminary tests on the lag lengths which had shown no statistical significance of the lags five through eight. However, the length should be set at least to the extent that regression residuals are not serially correlated. Watts (1973) regressed future earnings on current and past earnings and dividends to do a preliminary test of the information content hypothesis:

$$E_t = b_0 + b_1E_{t-1} + b_2E_{t-2} + b_3D_{t-1} + b_4D_{t-2} + v_t, \tag{14}$$

where the $E$s and $D$s are earnings and dividends, respectively. This may be regarded as a Granger test of causality from dividends to earnings with only two lags. The problem with this model is to ascertain an appropriate length of lag for $E$ since the omission of lagged $E$s of which underlying population coefficients are nonzero is likely to produce serial correlation in the residuals. This may result in the "spurious" regression phenomenon.

In the present study, assuming that the impact of new information contained in a variable would decay over four quarters, we included four lagged values of the dependent variable and four lagged values of the other variable, along with a constant. The first estimation equation is

$$E_t = a_0 + \sum_{k=1}^{4} b_kE_{t-k} + \sum_{k=1}^{4} C_kD_{t-k} + V_t, \tag{15}$$

where $E_t$ = earnings, $D_t$ = dividends.

The null hypothesis that dividends do not cause earnings is

$$H_0\colon C_1 = C_2 = C_3 = C_4 = 0.$$

The next estimation goes on to test the causality from earnings to dividends by switching the two variables. The causality was also estimated between each of these two variables and price to test the conjecture that the real variable which might have any information content for earnings is a share price. In other words, a firm's dividend policy is determined based on the past earnings which investors in the market would consider when they make up their minds about how much they would pay for the shares.

The results are reported in Table 1. $F$ ratios are pertinent for testing each null hypothesis. Taken together these tests indicate that the null hypothesis that dividends do not cause earnings cannot be rejected at the 5% level. Rather, earnings appear to cause dividends although the causality for the second subperiod does not show the desired statistical significance.[6] This rejects the information content hypothesis of dividends and, rather, supports the partial adjustment hypothesis. The results also show that any causal relationship between dividends and price should be rejected. One consistent unidirectional causality exists from price to earnings. Investors bid prices of the stocks based on their expectations about the future earnings.

### C. Sims Lagged Dependent Variables Tests

In this modified two-sided distributed lag model, as in the Granger tests, the problem of truncating lags at an appropriate length must be solved. Sims (1972) used, in his original work on money and income, an asymmetrical truncation that

*Table 1.* Granger Direct Tests

| | $F$ | | |
|---|---|---|---|
| *Null Hypothesis* | *1952–1981* | *1952–1966* | *1967–1981* |
| $D$ does not cause $E$ | 0.43 | 0.32 | 0.80 |
| $E$ does not cause $D$ | 2.74* | 2.69* | 0.57 |
| $D$ does not cause $P$ | 1.07 | 1.24 | 0.77 |
| $F$ does not cause $D$ | 1.22 | 0.31 | 1.95 |
| $E$ does not cause $P$ | 0.71 | 1.80 | 0.40 |
| $P$ does not cause $E$ | 3.05* | 3.47* | 3.25* |

*Notes:* All regressions include four lagged values of the dependent and independent variables and a constant. $D$ = dividend; $E$ = earnings; $P$ = price.
*Significant at the 5% level. $F_{0.05}$ (4, 106) = 2.46 for the entire period. $F_{0.05}$ (4, 49) = 2.56 for the first period, and $F_{0.05}$ (4,48) = 2.57 for the second.

contained eight past and eight future lags in their regressions replicating Sims's study. Sargent (1976) included four future and twelve lagged variables in his study on money, unemployment, and other variables.

In this study, four lagged values of the dependent variable (causal variable), and four lagged and four lead values of the other variable were included, along with a constant. The first estimation equation to test the causality from dividends to earnings is

$$D_t = a_t' + \sum_{k=1}^{4} b_k' D_{t-k} + \sum_{k=-4}^{4} C_k' E_{t-k} + V_t', \tag{16}$$

where $D_t$ = dividends and $E_t$ = earnings. The null hypothesis that dividends do not cause earnings is

$$H_0: C_{-1} = C_{-2} = C_{-3} = C_{-4} = 0.$$

The reversal in unidirectional causality was tested by switching the two variables in Eq. (16). The same kind of relationship was also tested between dividends and share price and earnings and share price. The results as shown in Table 2. The null hypothesis that earnings are not caused by dividends cannot be rejected again at the 5% level, whether for the entire period or for the two subperiods. Two unidirectional causalities were found from earnings to dividends and from price to earnings. The first causality was not found significant at the 5% level in two subperiods, probably owing to the reduced number of degrees of freedom. However, the null hypothesis that price does not cause earnings can be rejected.

*Table 2.* Sims Lagged Dependent Variables Tests

| | F | | |
|---|---|---|---|
| *Null Hypothesis* | *1952–1981* | *1952–1966* | *1967–1981* |
| *D* does not cause *E* | 0.45 | 1.05 | 0.53 |
| *P* does not cause *D* | 2.56* | 1.04* | 1.81 |
| *D* does not cause *P* | 1.57 | 0.90 | 2.25 |
| *P* does not cause *D* | 0.83 | 0.80 | 0.30 |
| *E* does not cause *P* | 0.92 | 0.56 | 1.79 |
| *P* does not cause *E* | 2.86* | 2.78* | 3.26* |

*Notes:* All regressions include four lagged values of the dependent and independent variables and four lead values of independent variable and a constant. $D$ = dividend; $E$ = earnings; $P$ = price.

*Significant at the 5% level. $F_{0.05}(4, 97) = 2.48$ for the entire period. $F_{0.05}(4, 42) = 2.59$ for the first subperiod, and $F_{0.05}(4, 41) = 2.60$ for the second.

## VI. CONCLUSION

The purpose of this study was to test the hypothesis that dividends convey information about the future earnings of the firm. The hypothesis can be further extended to the information content of dividends about stock price assuming that the stock market is efficient and stock prices are determined by expected earnings.

Previous studies tested either different models of dividend behavior based on various underlying assumptions or abnormal returns surrounding dividend announcement. Consequently, they suffered lack of true specification of dividend behavior or at best were complicated with the joint test of the market model and the market efficiency. In this study, the Granger causality among three variables was tested: dividends, earnings, and price. The hypothesis that dividends do not cause earnings or price was not rejected. Instead, unambiguous and unidirectional causal relationships from earnings to dividends and from price to earnings were found. The former relationship is consistent with the partial adjustment model of dividends while the latter is consistent with the general perception that stock prices reflect investors expectation about future earnings. Therefore, the information content hypothesis can be supported by the empirical work of this study.

## NOTES

1. There is still a signaling theory to relate a firm's growth potential to its dividend and investment decisions. For example, a signaling equilibrium model has been recently developed by John and Williams (1985) and empirically tested by Lee, Chang, and Finnerty (1985).

2. A nontrivial problem in making predictions is that investors must be well-informed and know the underlying probability distributions, and then use them together with data on all the conditioning variables. This is possible only when the cost of acquiring and utilizing such information is zero. It is assumed that, if the information costs are not negligible, investors should consider the trade-off between the costs and benefits of additional information and would probably prefer a less expensive forecasting scheme at the expense of a larger forecasting error. This type of investor was called "economically rational" by Feige and Pearce (1976).

3. By the first assumption, instantaneous causality is ruled out, and, by the second, the model is normalized.

4. Cuddington (1981) included seasonal dummies in his causality study working on quarterly income and money data. Huang and Kracaw (1984) seasonally adjusted their quarterly data of stock market returns and real activity.

5. Smirlock and Marshall (1983) used the first differences of the natural logs of their annual data. Huang and Kracaw (1984) also took the first differences in logs of the quarterly data.

6. When the entire period is divided into two subperiods, the number of degrees of freedom becomes half smaller, reducing the statistical power of the tests. They will be more prominent in the Sims lagged dependent variables tests, in which more degrees of freedom will be lost due to extra lead values of the independent variable.

## REFERENCES

Aharony, J., and Swary, I. (1986). "Quarterly Dividend and Earnings Announcements and Stockholders Returns: An Empirical Analysis." *Journal of Finance* 35 (March): 1–12.

Ang, J. S. (1975). "Dividend Policy: Informational Content or Partial Adjustment?" *Review of Economics and Statistics* 57 (February): 65–70.

Brown, L. D., and Rozeff, M. S. (1979). "Univariate Time Series Models of Quarterly Accounting Earnings Per Share a Proposed Model." *Journal of Accounting Research* 17 (Spring): 179–189.

Cuddington, J. T. "Money, Income, and Causality in the United Kingdom." *Journal of Money, Credit and Banking* 13 (August): 342–351.

Fama, E., Fisher, L., Jenson, M., and Roll, R. (1969). "The Adjustment of Stock Prices to New Information." *International Economic Review* 10 (February): 1–21.

Feige, E. L., and Pearce, D. K. (1976). "Economically Rational Expectations: Are Innovations in the Rate of Inflation Independent of Innovations in Pleasures of Monetary and Fiscal Policy?" *Journal of Political Economy* 84 (June): 499–522.

Feige, E. L., and Pearce, D. K. (1979). "The Causal Relationship Between Money and Income: Some Caveats for Time Series Analysis." *Review of Economics and Statistics*, (November): 521–533.

Foster, G. (1977). "Quarterly Accounting Data: Time Series Properties and Predictive Ability Results." *Accounting Review* 50 (January): 1–21.

Geweke, J., Meese, R., and Dent, W. (1983). "Comparing Alternative Tests of Causality in Temporal Systems." *Journal of Econometrics* 21 (February): 161–194.

Granger, C. W. J. (1969). "Investigating Causal Relations by Econometric Models and Cross-spectral Methods." *Econmetrica* 37 (July): 424–438.

Granger, C. W. T., and Newbold, P. (1974). "Spurious Regressions in Economics." *Journal of Econometrics* 2 (July): 111–120.

Granger, C. W. T., and Newbold, P. (1977). "Identification of Two-way Causal Systems." Pp. 338–359. In *Frontiers of Quantitative Economics,* edited by M. D. Intriligator. Amsterdam: North-Holland.

Griffin, P. A. (1977). "The Time Series Behavior of Quarterly Earnings: Preliminary Evidence." *Journal of Accounting Research* 15 (Spring): 71–83.

Huang, R. D., and Kracaw, W. A. (1984). "Stock Market Returns and Real Activity—A Note." *Journal of Finance* 39 (March): 267–273.

John, K., and Williams, J. (1985). "Dividends, Dilution, and Taxes: A Signaling Equilibrium." *Journal of Finance* 40 (September): 1053–1070.

Laub, P. M. (1976). "On the Informational Content of Dividends." *Journal of Business* 46 (January): 73–80.

Lee, C. F., Chang, H. S., and Finnerty, J. E. (1985). "Interactions of Dividends and Investment: A Test of the John and Williams Signaling Equilibrium Model." Working paper, University of Illinois at Urbana—Champaign (September).

Lee, C. F., Djarraya, M., and Wu, C C. (1985). "Residual Theory, Partial Adjustment and Adaptive Expectations on Dividend Payment Decisions: An Integration and Extension." Working paper presented at the Western Finance Meetings (November).

Miller, M. H., and Modigliani, F. (1961). "Dividend Policy, Growth and the Valuation of Shares." *Journal of Business* 34 (October): 411–423.

Pettit, R. (1972). "Dividend Announcements, Security Performance, and Capital Market Efficiency." *Journal of Finance* 27 (December): 993–1007.

Pettit, R. (1976). "The Impact of Dividend and Earnings Announcements: A Reconciliation." *Journal of Business* 49 (January): 86–96.

Pierce, D. A. (1977). "Relationships—and the Lack Thereof—Between Economic Time Series, with Special Reference to Money and Interest Rates." *Journal of American Statistical Association* 72 (March): 11–26.

Pierce, D. A., and Haugh, L. D. (1977). "Causality in Temporal Systems: Characterizations and a Survey." *Journal of Econometrics* 5 (May): 265–293.

Sargent, T. J. (1976). "A Classical Macroeconometric Model for the United States." *Journal of Political Economy* 84 (April): 207–237.

Sims, C. A. (1972). "Money, Income, and Causality." *American Economic Review* 62 (September): 540–512.

Smirlock, M., and Marshall, W. (1983). "An Examination of the Empirical Relationship Between the Divide and Investment Decisions: A Note." *Journal of Finance* 38 (December): 1659–1667.

Watts, R. (1973). "The Information Content of Dividends." *Journal of Business* 46 (January): 191–211.

Watts, R. (1975). "The Time Series Behavior of Quarterly Earnings." Working paper, Department of Commerce, University of Newcastle, April.

Watts, R. (1976). "Comments on the Impact of Dividend and Earnings Announcements: A Reconciliation." *Journal of Business* 46 (January): 138–145.

Woolridge, J. (1982). "The Information Content of Dividend Changes." *Journal of Financial Research* 5 (Fall): 237–247.

# THE RISK-SHIFTING PROBLEM AND CONVERTIBLE BONDS

Richard D. MacMinn

## I. INTRODUCTION

The risk-shifting problem is one of several classic conflict-of-interest problems in corporate finance literature. Jensen and Meckling (1976) described the problem as one in which corporate management has the incentive to substitute a risky project for a less risky project and then showed that a risky bond issue would engender an agency cost which would be borne by stockholders. Subsequently, Green (1984) showed that a convertible bond issue could be used to eliminate the risk-shifting problem. In Green's model the corporation could invest in both the more and less risky projects. The purpose of this analysis is to consider the conflict-of-interest problem in the simpler setting in which the projects are mutually exclusive and to focus on both the conditions under which the risk-shifting problem exists and the structure of the convertible contracts which eliminate the problem.[1] In this setting of mutually exclusive projects, the convertible contract which eliminates the risk-shifting problem is not unique. The analysis generates a set of feasible contracts which solves the problem and shows that any convertible contract which allows for

**Advances in Quantitative Analysis of Finance and Accounting,**
**Volume 2, Part B, pages 181–199.**

**ISBN: 1-55938-565-0**

a greater increase in option value than the decrease in straight bond value is in this set.

Corporate management can encounter a conflict-of-interest problem in dealing with bondholders. Since the corporate manager represents the interests of stockholders and bondholders, there is a potential for conflict between the manager and bondholders or, equivalently, between the manager and the bondholders' trustee. This will be the case if it is possible for the manager to take actions that benefit one group and are detrimental to the other. If the bonds represent secured debt then there is no conflict. If not, then an agency problem may exist.

The agency relationship can be thought of as a contract between the principal (i.e., the bondholders' trustee)[2] and an agent (i.e., the corporate manager). The agent acts in behalf of the principal. The contract specifies the bounds on the actions that may be taken by the agent. If the contract covers all possible contingencies then there is no real delegation of authority and so no agency problem. If the contract is incomplete so that the agent has some discretion in the selection of actions, there is at least the potential for a conflict of interests. The conflict occurs because both the principal and the agent behave in accordance with their own self-interests. The principal can limit the divergence of interests by providing provisions in the contract which give the agent the appropriate incentives to act in the principal's interest; in addition, the principal can monitor the activity of the agent. It is not usually possible, however, to specify the contract in such a way as to completely eliminate the conflict-of-interest problem.[3] Hence, it will usually be the case that there is a difference between the action taken by the agent and the action which is in the best interests of the principal. The agency cost is defined, by Jensen and Meckling, as the sum of the monitoring expenditures of the principal, the bonding expenditures of the agent, and the residual loss; this residual loss is the loss in the market value of the corporation.[4]

The agency problem considered here is encountered by the corporate management in selecting among mutually exclusive investment projects. Jensen and Smith (1985, p. 111) noted that

> the value of the stockholders' equity rises and the value of the bondholders' claim is reduced when the firm substitutes high-risk for low-risk projects.[5]

Of course, bondholders are aware of this possibility (this attempt to shift risk), and so it is reflected in a lower value for the corporation's debt issue. The first purpose of this analysis is to demonstrate the conditions under which the risk-shifting problem exists and this is accomplished in Section II. The second purpose is to characterize and construct the convertible bond packages which will reduce or eliminate the risk-shifting incentive. This is accomplished in Section III.

## II. FINANCIAL MARKETS AND THE RISK-SHIFTING PROBLEM

Consider a competitive economy operating between the dates *now* and *then*. Let $\Omega$ denote the set of states of nature and let $\mathfrak{B}$ denote the event space.[6] The set of states of nature is assumed to be finite. It follows that the event space is the set of all subsets of $\Omega$. In a complete financial market system, it is possible to construct stock contracts which payoff one dollar in a particular state $\omega \in \Omega$, and zero otherwise. Call these assets the basis stocks. Let the price of basis stock of type $\omega$ be $p(\omega)$. The corporation which encounters the risk-shifting problem is treated separately. Call it corporation $f$ and let $p_f$ denote the share price of that corporation's stock issue. Let $\Pi_f(I_f, \omega)$ denote the firm's payoff where $I_f$ is the capital value of the input and $\omega \in \Omega$ is the state of nature.

Let $I$ denote the set of agents $i$ in the economy. Let $\Psi$ denote the agent's subjective probability distribution and let $\psi(\omega)$ denote the probability of state $\omega$. Each agent has a utility function $u_i: D \rightarrow \mathbb{R}$, $D \subset \mathbb{R}^2$, which represents preferences for consumption now versus then. Consumption now is determinant but consumption then depends on the agent's decisions and the state of nature which occurs. The agents determine consumption now and then by purchasing/selling basis and corporate stock. The agent's expected utility is

$$\sum_{\Omega} u_i(c_{i0}, c_{i1})\, \psi(\omega),$$

where the pair $c_i = (c_{i0}, c_{i1})$ represents consumption now and then, respectively. Each agent makes decisions now to maximize expected utility.

In the competitive and complete financial market system, the market value of corporation $f$ is

$$V_f = \sum_{\Omega} p(\omega)\, \Pi_f(I_f, \omega).$$

Equivalently, the value of the incorporated firm is the risk-adjusted present value of a portfolio of basis stock which has the same payoff structure as the corporation.

In order to demonstrate the agency problem, suppose the corporation is considering two mutually exclusive investment projects. Call them projects one and two. Let $I_1 = I_2$ denote the dollar cost of the two projects and let $\Pi_1$ and $\Pi_2$ denote the random project earnings.[7] Suppose project earnings are positive for all states. Suppose project two is riskier than project one in the Rothschild–Stiglitz (1970) sense; in particular, let $\Pi_2$ be a mean-preserving spread of $\Pi_1$, as shown in Figure 1, that is, $\Pi_2 = (1 + \delta)\, \Pi_1 - \delta\, E\Pi_1$, $\delta > 0$.[8] Then $\mu_2 = E\Pi_2 = E\Pi_1 = \mu_1$ and $\Pi_2$ has more weight in the tails of its distribution, as may be seen in Figure 1.

In this context, consider the statement by Jensen and Smith. Suppose bondholders believe that the firm will select project one and value the bond issue accordingly.

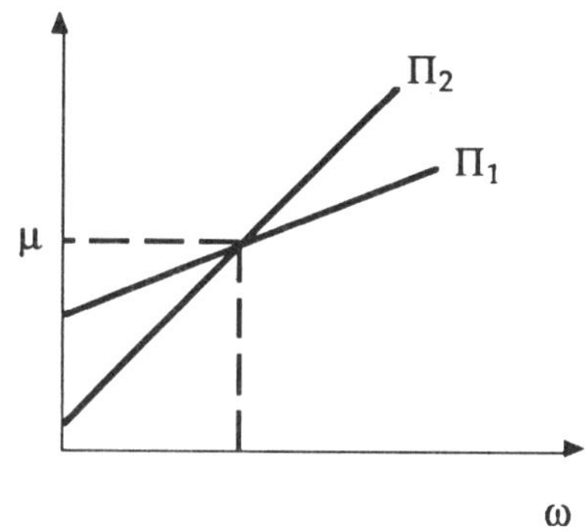


*Figure 1.*

Next, suppose the firm switches to project two. Then the value of the bondholders' claim is reduced by the amount $D_1 - D_2$, as shown in Figure 2. Hence, there are circumstances under which it is not rational for the bondholders to believe any claim made by the firm that project one will be selected. Rational bondholders will protect their interests by considering which project will be selected by a management that acts in the best interests of stockholders.

The first claim to be made here is that there exists a promised payment level $B^*$ such that $S_2{}^L > S_1{}^L$ for $B > B^*$ and $S_2{}^L < S_1{}^L$ for $B < B^*$, where $S_j^L$ is the levered stock value of project $j = 1,2$. This may be done simply by showing that in the unlevered case $S_1{}^U = V_1 > V_2 = S_2{}^U$ and in the sufficiently highly levered case $S_2{}^L > S_1{}^L$. Then the intermediate value theorem yields the existence of a $B^*$, since stock value is a continuous function of $B$.

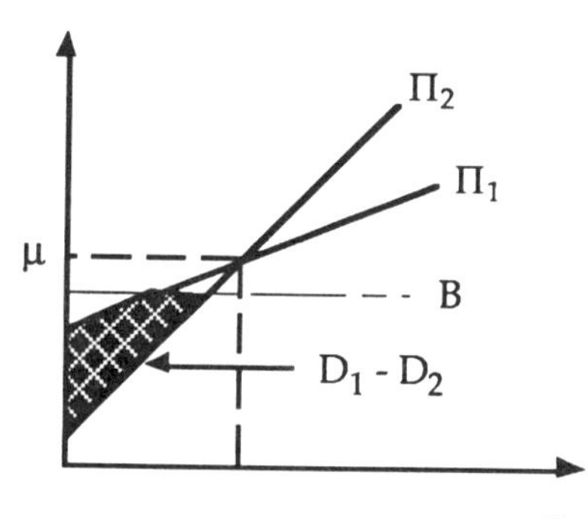


*Figure 2.*

Following the outlined procedure, it must be shown that if the corporation is unlevered and if project two is riskier than project one, then $S_1^U = V_1 > V_2 = S_2^U$. Note that the difference in value is

$$V_1 - V_2 = \sum_{\Omega} p(\omega)\, \Pi_1(\omega) - \sum_{\Omega} p(\omega)\, \Pi_2(\omega)$$

$$= \sum_{\Omega} p(\omega)\, \delta\, (\mu_1 - \Pi_1(\omega))$$

$$= \delta\, (q\, \mu_1 - V_1)$$

$$> 0,$$

since $V_1 < q, \mu_1$, that is, the risk adjusted present value of the project is less than the present value of a safe asset with the same expected payoff.[9] Therefore the value of the unlevered firm which selects project one is greater than the value of the unlevered firm which selects project two, that is, $V_1 - V_2 = S_1^U - S_2^U > 0$. By continuity, it follows that $S_1^L - S_2^L > 0$ for $B$ in a neighborhood of zero.

Second, it must be shown that in the highly levered case the stock market value of the riskier project is greater: $S_2^L > S_1^L$. To do this, simply note that for $B$ sufficiently large, $\max\{0, \Pi_2 - B\} \geq \max\{0, \Pi_1 - B\}$ for all $\omega \in \Omega$ and strictly greater for some $\omega$, as shown in Figure 3. Then it follows trivially that

$$S_2^L = \sum_{\Omega} p(\omega) \max\{0, \Pi_2(\omega) - B\}$$

$$> \sum_{\Omega} p(\omega) \max\{0, \Pi_1(\omega) - B\}$$

$$= S_1^L.$$

Then continuity completes the proof, and a promised payment level $B^*$ exists such that $S_2^L > S_1^L$ for $B > B^*$ and $S_2^L < S_1^L$ for $0 < B < B^*$. Therefore, in the absence of any mechanism to avoid the agency problem, the corporation with a promised payment $B > B^*$ has an incentive to accept the riskier project. The agency cost of debt in this case is

$$V_1 - V_2 = \sum_{\Omega} p(\omega)\, [\Pi_1(\omega) - \Pi_2(\omega)] > 0.$$

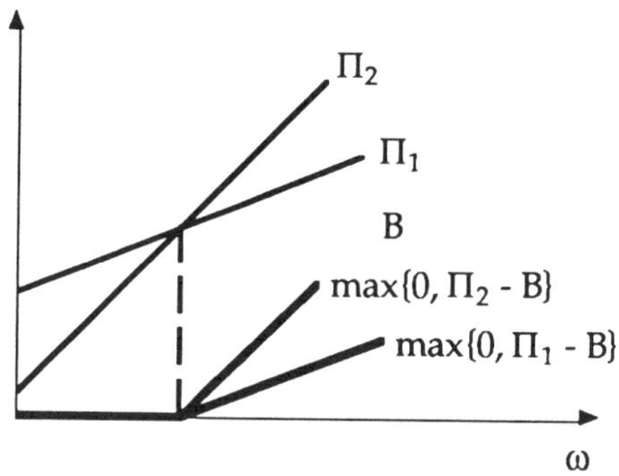


*Figure 3.*

Actually, claiming that the corporation has an incentive to accept the riskier project is deceptive. Suppose the corporation must make a promised payment of $B_1$ dollars in order to finance project one, that is, $D_1(B_1) = I$, given that bondholders believe that project one will be selected. However, if $B_1 > B^*$, then the corporate management has a moral hazard problem since $S_2^L(B_1) > S_1^L(B_1)$. Rational bondholders understand this conflict-of-interest problem and will value the bond issue as if project two will be selected. Since $D_2(B_1) < I$, it follows that the promised repayment must be increased to $B_2 > B_1$ so that $D_2(B_2) = I$. The equity is appropriately priced as $S_2^L(B_2)$ but the agency cost is not directly reflected in this expression. It is possible to rewrite the stock market value $S_2^L(B_2)$ to reflect the agency cost. To do this, note that the promised payment $B_2$ must be selected so that

$$S_2^L(B_1) - S_2^L(B_2) = D_1(B_1) - D_2(B_1).$$ [10]

These differences in value are shown in Figure 4. Note that $S_2^L(B_2)$ may be equivalently expressed as

$$S_2^L(B_2) = S_2^L(B_1) - [D_1(B_1) - D_2(B_1)].$$

Also note that

$$V_1 - V_2 = D_1(B_1) - D_2(B_1) + S_1^L(B_1) - S_2^L(B_1)$$ [11]

$$\Leftrightarrow S_2^L(B_1) = S_1^L(B_1) + [D_1(B_1) - D_2(B_1)] - [V_1 - V_2].$$

Then

$$S_2^L(B_2) = S_1^L(B_1) - [V_1 - V_2].$$

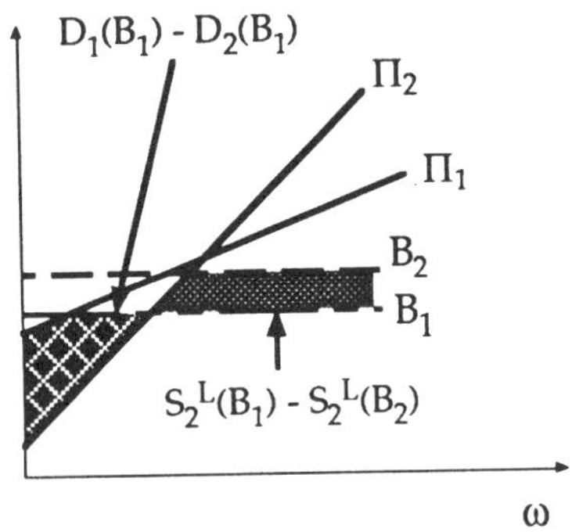


*Figure 4.*

Hence, the stock market value of project two equals that of project one minus the agency cost of the bond issue. Observe that $S_2^L(B_2) < S_1^L(B_1)$. This makes it clear that it would be in the best interests of management to convince bondholders that project one will be selected. Because of the moral hazard problem, however, the straight bond contract cannot be used to convince them. With a straight bond contract, the bondholders must expect the devaluation. What is more, at $B_2$, $S_2^L(B_2) > S_1^L(B_2)$, and the higher promised repayment locks management into the choice of project two.

## III. CONVERTIBLE BONDS AND THE RESOLUTION OF THE RISK-SHIFTING PROBLEM

Next, consider the value of convertible bonds. Suppose that each bond is issued with a call option which gives its owner the right to exchange a bond for $\theta = \gamma(N + n)/B$ shares of stock, where $n$ is the number of new shares which must be issued if the bonds are converted (see MacMinn, 1989). Note that a convertible bond is simply a bond with an attached call option. Also note that $\gamma$ is the fraction of the firm's equity payoff that goes to bondholders in the event that the option is exercised. As has been shown, the payoff on the convertible bond issue is

$$\min\{\Pi, B\} + \max\{0, \gamma\Pi - B\},$$

where $B$ is the exercise value of the call option issue. Then it follows easily that the market value of the convertible bond issue is

$$D^C = \sum_{\Omega} p(\omega)\min\{\Pi, B\} + \sum_{\Omega} p(\omega)\max\{0, \gamma\Pi - B\}$$

$$= D + C.$$

Similarly, the value of the stock is

$$S^C = \sum_{\Omega} p(\omega)\max\{0, \Pi - B\} - \sum_{\Omega} p(\omega)\max\{0, \gamma\Pi - B\}$$

$$= \sum_{\Omega\backslash\mathcal{B}} p(\omega)\{\Pi - B\} - \sum_{\mathcal{E}} p(\omega)[\gamma\Pi - B]$$

$$= S^L - C,$$

that is, the stock market value of the firm with convertible debt is equivalent to the stock market value of the firm with the simple debt contract minus the value of the option. In the second expression for $S^C$, $\mathcal{B}$ is the bankruptcy event and $\mathcal{E}$ is the exercise event. Note that the bankruptcy event is $\mathcal{B} = \{\omega \in \Omega \mid \Pi(\omega) < B\}$ and the exercise event is $\{\omega \in \Omega \mid \gamma\Pi(\omega) \geq B\}$, where the events are shown in Figure 5. It may be noted that since the corporate value is not affected by the introduction of an option to convert, it follows that, ceteris paribus, the option reduces the stock market value.

Now consider how management can construct a convertible issue which will convince the bondholders that project one will be selected. In fact, suppose management constructs the package to convince bondholders that project one will be selected and to maximize the stock market value of the corporation by eliminat-

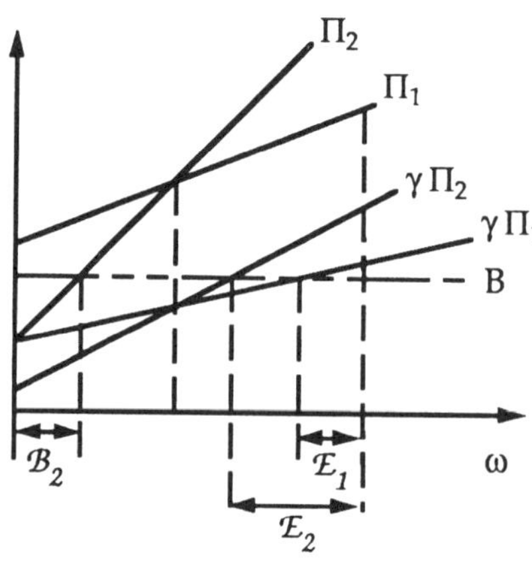


*Figure 5.*

ing the agency cost of the bond issue. Suppose management selects the provisions of the bond issue, $(B, \gamma)$, so that $C_2 - C_1 > D_1 - D_2$; this is simply the condition that the difference in the value of the call options exceeds the difference in the value of the straight bond issues. If bondholders believe that the firm will select project one and so value the bonds accordingly, then by switching to project two the firm can capture the amount $D_1 - D_2$; equivalently, $D_1 - D_2$ represents the devaluation of the debt claim. $D_1 - D_2$ is represented by the lightly shaded area in the following figure. Similarly, if project two is selected, given that bondholders believe project one will be selected, then $C_2 - C_1$ represents the increased value of the bondholders' options. The net transfer of wealth to bondholders is $C_2 - C_1 - (D_1 - D_2)$. Note that

$$C_2 - C_1 > D_1 - D_2$$

$$\Leftrightarrow D_2 + C_2 > D_1 + C_1$$

$$\Leftrightarrow - D_2{}^C < - D_1{}^C$$

$$\Rightarrow V_2 - D_2{}^C < V_2 - D_1{}^C < V_1 - D_1{}^C$$

$$\Leftrightarrow S_2{}^C < S_1{}^C.$$

Hence, any feasible convertible contract which satisfies the condition $C_2 - C_1 > D_1 - D_2$ will convince bondholders that firm management will select project one. Figure 6 represents the trade-off between bond values and option values.

Having shown that it is possible to convince bondholders that project one will be selected, it remains to be shown that management has the incentive to select that project. This, however, is also a simple matter. Since the manager is an initial shareholder, all that must be shown is that a convertible contract $(B, \gamma)$ exists such that the following three conditions are satisfied: (1) $C_2 - C_1 > D_1 - D_2$; (2) $D_1{}^C = I$; (3) $S_1{}^C(B, \gamma) > S_2{}^L(B_2)$. Conditions (1) and (2) ensure the bondholders believe that project one will be selected and that the bond issue covers the investment expenditure. Condition (3) shows that the manager and stockholders prefer project one. To establish condition (3) simply note that

$$S_1{}^C(B, \gamma) = V_1 - D_1{}^C(B, \gamma)$$

$$= V_1 - I$$

$$> V_2 - I$$

$$= V_2 - D_2(B_2)$$

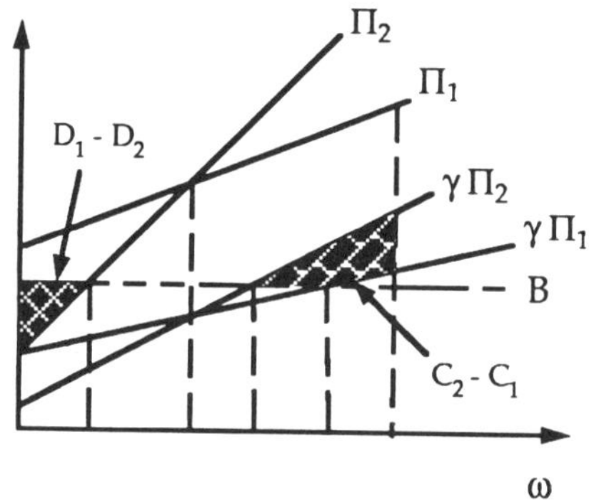


*Figure 6.*

$$= S_2^L(B_2).$$

The second equality follows by condition (2). Thus, managers and stockholders prefer this convertible bond contract. It may also be noted that this convertible contract preserves the stockholders' value since $S_1^C(B, \gamma) - S_2^L(B_2) = V_1 - V_2 > 0$, that is, the contract completely eliminates the agency cost of debt.

Now consider the set of convertible bond contracts which are feasible, finance project one, and solve the risk-shifting problem. Since the pair $(B, \gamma)$ completely specifies the contract, the feasible contract set may be written as $\mathcal{H} = [0, \overline{B}] \times [0, 1]$, where $\overline{B}$ is the smallest promised payment which satisfies $D_1(\overline{B}) = V_1$. Then the convertible bond contract is a function $D^C\colon \mathcal{H} \rightarrow \mathbb{R}$ such that

$$D^C(B, \gamma) = \sum_{\mathcal{B}} p(\omega)\, \Pi(\omega) + \sum_{\Omega \backslash \mathcal{B}} p(\omega)\, B + \sum_{\mathcal{E}} p(\omega)\, [\gamma\Pi(\omega) - B]$$

$$= \sum_{\mathcal{B}} p(\omega)\, \Pi(\omega) + \sum_{\mathcal{D}} p(\omega) B + \sum_{\mathcal{E}} p(\omega)\, \gamma\Pi(\omega),$$

where $\mathcal{D} = \Omega \backslash (\mathcal{B} \cup \mathcal{E})$, that is, the event that the firm is not bankrupt and the bondholders do not exercise their conversion option. Let the function $H\colon \mathcal{H} \rightarrow \mathbb{R}$ be defined as

$$H(B, \gamma) = D^C(B, \gamma) - I.$$

Note that the partial derivatives of $H$ with respect to $B$ and $\gamma$ are

$$D_1 H = \sum_{\mathcal{D}} p(\omega) > 0 \text{ if } \mathcal{D} \neq \phi$$

and

$$D_2H = \sum_{\mathcal{E}} p(\omega)\, \Pi(\omega) \text{ if } \mathcal{E} \neq \phi.$$

Hence, for the contracts $(B, \gamma)$ such that $\mathcal{E} \neq \phi$, it follows by the implicit function theorem that there exists a function $h$ such that

$$H(B, h(B)) = 0$$

and

$$h'(B) = -\frac{D_1H}{D_2H} = -\frac{\sum_{\mathcal{D}} p(\omega)}{\sum_{\mathcal{E}} p(\omega)\, \Pi(\omega)} \leq 0,$$

where it exists. Since both partial derivatives are nonnegative, $h$ is a nonincreasing function. In order to determine the properties of the relation $\gamma = h(B)$, let $\Omega = \{\omega_1, \omega_2, \omega_3\}$ and consider the following partitions of the convertible contract set $\mathcal{H}$. Let

$$\mathcal{A} = \{(B, \gamma) \in \mathcal{H} \mid B < \Pi_1(\omega_1), \gamma \in [0, 1]\}$$

$$\mathcal{B} = \{(B, \gamma) \in \mathcal{H} \mid \Pi_1(\omega_1) \leq B < \Pi_1(\omega_2),\ \gamma \in [0, 1]\}$$

$$\mathcal{C} = \{(B, \gamma) \in \mathcal{H} \mid < \Pi_1(\omega_2) \leq B, \gamma \in [0, 1]\}.$$

Note that the bankruptcy event is empty for contracts in $\mathcal{A}$, while it is $\{\omega_1\}$ and $\{\omega_1, \omega_2\}$ for contracts in $\mathcal{B}$ and $\mathcal{C}$, respectively. These subsets of the contract set $\mathcal{H}$ are shown in Figure 7.

Similarly, let

$$\mathcal{D} = \{(B, \gamma) \in \mathcal{H} \mid \gamma > \frac{B}{\Pi_1(\omega_1)}, \gamma \in [0, 1]\}$$

$$\mathcal{E} = \{(B, \gamma) \in \mathcal{H} \mid \frac{B}{\Pi_1(\omega_1)} \geq \gamma > \frac{B}{\Pi_1(\omega_2)}, \gamma \in [0, 1]\}$$

$$\mathcal{F} = \{(B, \gamma) \in \mathcal{H} \mid \frac{B}{\Pi_1(\omega_2)} \geq \gamma > \frac{B}{\Pi_1(\omega_3)}, \gamma \in [0, 1]\}$$

$$\mathcal{G} = \{(B, \gamma) \in \mathcal{H} \mid \frac{B}{\Pi_1(\omega_3)} \geq \gamma, \gamma \in [0, 1]\}.$$

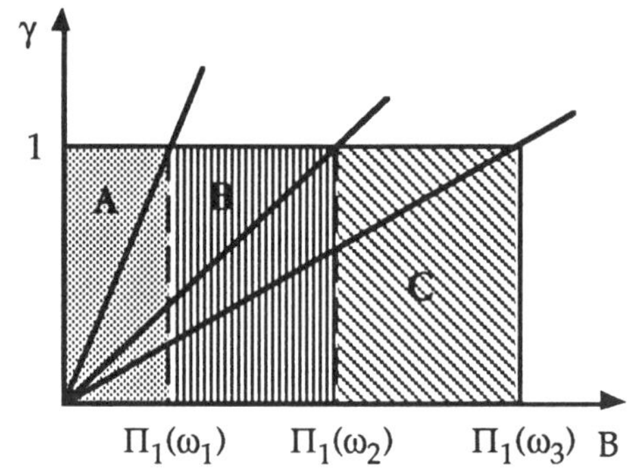


*Figure 7.*

Note that contracts in $\mathcal{D}$, $\mathcal{E}$, $\mathcal{F}$, and $\mathcal{G}$ yield exercise events $\Omega$, $\{\omega_2, \omega_3\}$, $\{\omega_3\}$, and $\phi$, respectively. These subsets of $\mathcal{H}$ are shown in Figure 8. As noted, there is a correspondence between subsets of the feasible contract set $\mathcal{H}$ and the events in $\mathfrak{B}$. For example, contracts in $\mathcal{A} \cap \mathcal{D}$ yield the events $\mathcal{B} = \phi = \mathcal{D}$ and $\mathcal{E} = \Omega = \{\omega_1, \omega_2, \omega_3\}$. The accompanying table specifies the correspondence between the subsets of $\mathcal{H}$ and the events.

| | *Events* | | |
|---|---|---|---|
| *Subsets* | $\mathcal{B}$ | $\mathcal{D}$ | $\mathcal{E}$ |
| $\mathcal{A} \cap \mathcal{D}$ | $\phi$ | $\phi$ | $\Omega$ |
| $\mathcal{A} \cap \mathcal{E}$ | $\phi$ | $\{\omega_1\}$ | $\{\omega_2, \omega_3\}$ |
| $\mathcal{A} \cap \mathcal{F}$ | $\phi$ | $\{\omega_1, \omega_2\}$ | $\{\omega_2, \omega_3\}$ |
| $\mathcal{A} \cap \mathcal{G}$ | $\phi$ | $\Omega$ | $\phi$ |
| $\mathcal{B} \cap \mathcal{E}$ | $\{\omega_1\}$ | $\phi$ | $\{\omega_2, \omega_3\}$ |
| $\mathcal{B} \cap \mathcal{F}$ | $\{\omega_1\}$ | $[\omega_2\}$ | $\{\omega_3\}$ |
| $\mathcal{B} \cap \mathcal{G}$ | $\{\omega_1\}$ | $\{\omega_1, \omega_2\}$ | $\phi$ |
| $\mathcal{C} \cap \mathcal{F}$ | $\{\omega_1, \omega_2\}$ | $\phi$ | $\{\omega_3\}$ |
| $\mathcal{C} \cap \mathcal{G}$ | $\{\omega_1, \omega_2\}$ | $\{\omega_3\}$ | $\phi$ |

Recall that $h$ is not defined for $(B, \gamma) \in \mathcal{G}_1$.[12] Let $\hat{B}$ be the promised repayment on the zero coupon bonds necessary to raise the $I$ dollars given no conversion feature, and let $\hat{B} \in (\Pi_1(\omega_1), \Pi_1(\omega_2))$. Then the path of the function $h$ will either be through $\mathcal{A}_1 \cap \mathcal{F}_1$ or $\mathcal{B}_1 \cap \mathcal{E}_1$. The path will depend on the risk-adjusted present value of the project.[13] For the path through $\mathcal{B}_1 \cap \mathcal{E}_1$, it follows that

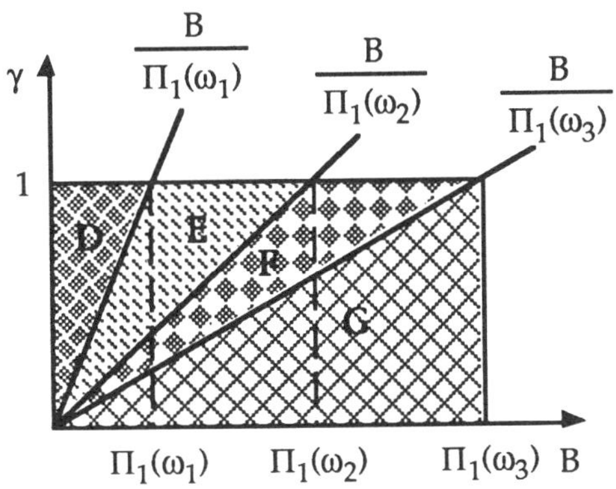


*Figure 8.*

$$h'(B) = \begin{cases} 0 & (B,\gamma) \in \mathcal{A}_1 \cap \mathcal{D}_1 \\ -\dfrac{p(\omega_1)}{p(\omega_2)\Pi_1(\omega_2) + p(\omega_3)\,\Pi_1(\omega_3)} & (B,\gamma) \in \mathcal{A}_1 \cap \mathcal{E}_1 \\ 0 & (B,\gamma) \in \mathcal{B}_1 \cap \mathcal{E}_1 \\ -\dfrac{p(\omega_2)}{p(\omega_3)\,\Pi_1(\omega_3)} & (B,\gamma) \in \mathcal{B}_1 \cap \mathcal{F}_1. \end{cases}$$

This contract line is shown in Figure 9. Note that it is piecewise linear, that is, $h'' = 0$ where it exists. For contracts in $\mathcal{A}_1 \cap \mathcal{D}_1$, investors know that call option will be exercised, and so increasing the promised payment on the bonds will not add

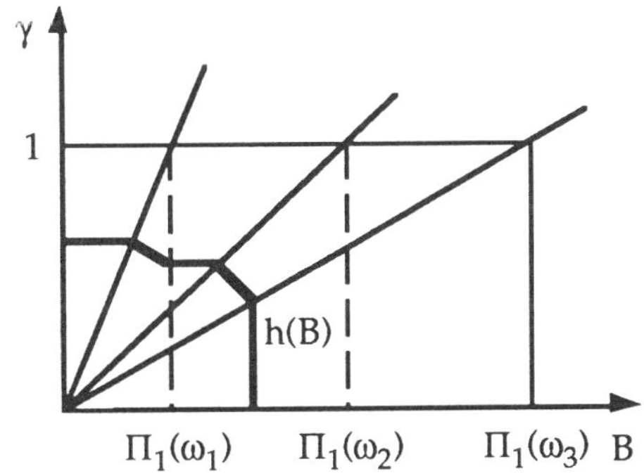


*Figure 9.*

value, that is, $h' = 0$. For contracts in $(\mathcal{A}_1 \cap \mathcal{F}_1) \cup (\mathcal{B}_1 \cap \mathcal{F}_1)$, increasing the promised payment on the bonds will, other things being equal, increase the value of the straight debt component because there is one state in which the bonds will not be converted into stock and the bondholders will receive the increased payment; it follows that an increased payment must be associated with a decreased conversion proportion in order to maintain the same bond value. For contracts in $\mathcal{B}_1 \cap \mathcal{E}_1$, an increased promised payment does not add value because there is no state in which the increased payment would be received. For contracts in $\mathcal{B}_1 \cap \mathcal{G}_1$, increasing the conversion proportion will not add value because there is no state in which the bonds will be called.[14]

Next, consider the set of contracts in $\mathcal{H}$ such that value is independent of project selection, that is, $D_1{}^C(B, \gamma) = D_2{}^C(B, \gamma)$. Recall that

$$D_j{}^C(B, \gamma) = \sum_{\mathcal{B}_j} p(\omega)\Pi_j(\omega) + \sum_{\mathcal{D}_j} p(\omega)\, B + \sum_{\mathcal{E}_j} p(\omega)\, \gamma\, \Pi_j(\omega),$$

for $j = 1, 2$. Let the function $G$: $\mathcal{H} \to \mathbb{R}$ be defined as

$$G(B, \gamma) = D_2{}^C(B, \gamma) - D_1{}^C(B, \gamma).$$

Then

$$D_1 G = \sum_{\mathcal{D}_2} p(\omega) - \sum_{\mathcal{D}_1} p(\omega)$$

and

$$D_2 G = \sum_{\mathcal{E}_2} p(\omega)\, \Pi_2(\omega) - \sum_{\mathcal{E}_1} p(\omega)\, \Pi_1(\omega).$$

For $(B, \gamma)$ such that $\mathcal{E}_1 \cup E_2 \neq \phi$, it follows by the implicit function theorem that there exists a function $g$ such that $G[B, g(B)] = 0$ and

$$g' = -\frac{D_1 G}{D_2 G} = \frac{\sum_{\mathcal{D}_1} -p(\omega) - \sum_{\mathcal{D}_2} p(\omega)}{\sum_{\mathcal{E}_2} p(\omega)\, \Pi_2(\omega) - \sum_{\mathcal{E}_1} p(\omega)\, \Pi_1(\omega)},$$

where it exists. Then, using the table of correspondences, it follows that

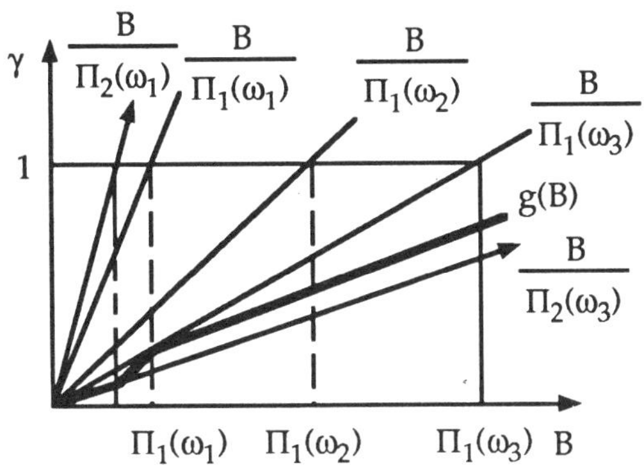


*Figure 10.*

$$g'(B) = \begin{cases} \dfrac{1}{\Pi_2(\omega_3)} & (B, \gamma) \in (\mathcal{A}_1 \cap \mathcal{G}_1) \cap (\mathcal{A}_2 \cap \mathcal{F}_2) \\ \dfrac{p(\omega_1) + p(\omega_3)}{p(\omega_3)\,\Pi_2(\omega_3)} & (B, \gamma) \in (\mathcal{A}_1 \cap \mathcal{G}_1) \cap (\mathcal{B}_2 \cap \mathcal{F}_2) \\ \dfrac{1}{\Pi_2(\omega_3)} & (B, \gamma) \in (\mathcal{B}_1 \cap \mathcal{G}_1) \cap (\mathcal{B}_2 \cap \mathcal{F}_2) \\ \dfrac{1}{\Pi_2(\omega_3)} & (B, \gamma) \in (\mathcal{C}_1 \cap \mathcal{G}_1) \cap (\mathcal{C}_2 \cap \mathcal{F}_2). \end{cases}$$

The function $g$ is shown in Figure 10. For simplicity, it is assumed that $\mu = \Pi_1(\omega_2) = \Pi_2(\omega_2)$. As expected, $g$ is an increasing function.

Notice that all contracts $(B, \gamma)$ above $g$ yield $D_2^C(B, \gamma) > D_1^C(B, \gamma)$. Hence, it follows that all contracts on $h$ and above $g$ solve the risk-shifting problem. Equivalently, the set of convertible contracts which solves the risk-shifting problem is the subset of $\mathcal{H}$ such that

$$\mathcal{K} = \{(B, h(B)) \in \mathcal{H} \mid h(B) \geq g(B)\}.$$

It should be noted that the contract set $\mathcal{K}$ includes the equity contract $(0, \hat{\gamma})$ as a special case but it also includes risky bond instruments. In the absence of other conflict-of- interest problems, the manager and stockholders are indifferent between any pair of contracts in $\mathcal{K}$. More important, however, all contract in $\mathcal{K}$ make management and stockholders better off without making the bondholders any worse off, and this yields the result that the capital structure of the firm is not entirely a matter of irrelevance.

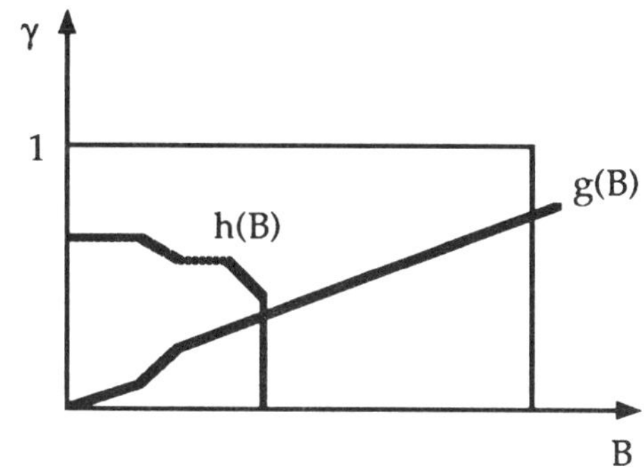


*Figure 11.*

## APPENDIX

*Claim 1:* If the quotient kernel $k(\omega) = p(\omega)/\psi(\omega)$ is decreasing in $\omega$, then $q\,\mu \geq V$.[15]

*Proof.*

$$q\,\mu - V = q \sum_{\Omega} \Pi(\omega)\,\psi(\omega) - \sum_{\Omega} p(\omega)\,\Pi(\omega)$$

$$= \sum_{\Omega} (q\,\psi(\omega) - p(\omega))\,\Pi(\omega).$$

Note that q $\psi(\omega)$ is greater than $p(\omega)$ for some $\omega$ and less than $p(\omega)$ for other $\omega$. In addition, note that

$$\sum_{\Omega} (q\,\psi(\omega) - p(\omega)) = 0.$$

It follows trivially that if $\Pi(\omega)$ is a constant, then $q\,\mu = V$, as expected. Also note that

$$q\,\mu - V = \sum_{\Omega} (q\,\psi\,(\omega) - p(\omega))\,\Pi(\omega)$$

$$= \sum_{\Omega} (q - \frac{p(\omega)}{\psi(\omega)})\,\Pi(\omega)\,\psi(\omega)$$

$$= q\,\mu - \sum_{\Omega} k(\omega)\,\Pi(\omega)\,\psi(\omega)$$

$$= q\,\mu - Ek\,E\Pi - \operatorname{cov}(k, \Pi)$$

$$= q\,\mu - Ek\,\mu - \operatorname{cov}(k, \Pi)$$

$$= -\operatorname{cov}(k, \Pi)^{16}$$

$$> 0,$$

since $k$ is decreasing and $\Pi$ is increasing in $\omega$. Q.E.D.

*Claim 2:* $k$ is a decreasing function.
*Proof.* The first-order conditions for a maximum are

$$\sum_{\Omega} D_1 u\,\psi(\omega) - \lambda = 0$$

$$D_2 u\,\psi(\omega) - \lambda\,p(\omega) = 0$$

These first-order conditions imply that

$$\frac{D_2 u}{\lambda} = \frac{p(\omega)}{\psi(\omega)} = k(\omega).$$

Let the function $F$ be defined as

$$F(c_1, k) \equiv \frac{D_2 u}{\lambda} - k.$$

By the implicit function theorem, there exists a differentiable function $f$ such that $F(f(k), k) = 0$ and

$$f' = -\frac{D_2 F}{D_1 F} = -\frac{-1}{\frac{D_{22} u}{\lambda}} = \frac{1}{\frac{D_{22} u}{\lambda}} < 0.$$

This holds for each investor $i \in I$. Now, let

$$c_1(\omega) = \sum_{I} c_{i1}(\omega) = \sum_{I} f_i(k(\omega)) = f(k(\omega)).$$

The RHS is a decreasing function since $f_i' < 0$ for all $i \in I$. This implies that there exists a function $h = f^{-1}$, or equivalently, that $k = h(c_1)$. Since $\Pi(\omega)$ increases with $\omega$ for all corporations, it follows that in equilibrium, $c_1$ must increase in $\omega$. Actually, all that seems necessary is that the sum of the corporate payoffs be increasing in $\omega$. Then, since

$$h' = \frac{1}{f'} < 0,$$

it follows that $k$ is a decreasing function of $\omega$. Q.E.D.[17]

## NOTES

1. Green also assumed that one project's returns were not only a mean-preserving spread of the others but also a value-preserving spread. The analysis here does not employ the value-preserving-spread notion.
2. The legal trustee for the bondholders may be treated as the single principal. It should be added that the trustee acts on behalf of the bondholders. The trustee's problem is the selection of bond covenants which limit the divergence of interests between corporate management and the bondholders. In general, the trustee may have a problem in selecting covenants which provide a solution to the conflict because of the different risk aversion measures of the bondholders. In the case considered here, however, the bondholders will unanimously support a covenant which provides management with the incentive to maximize the risk-adjusted net present value of the corporation. It should also be noted that in general there may be an agency problem between the trustee and bondholders (i.e., between the agent and the principals). In the case considered here that problem does not arise because of the unanimity.
3. In a complete market setting it is possible to take a normative approach by showing that a contract can be constructed which resolves a conflict-of-interest problem. Alternatively, it is possible to take a positive approach by showing that existing contractual forms can be used to resolve a conflict. The positive approach is taken here. The complete markets assumption simplifies the process of valuing the contracts.
4. Jensen and Meckling (1976) also define the residual loss as the dollar equivalent of the loss in expected utility experienced by the principal. Although this notion of residual loss is measurable for a particular principal, this definition poses problems when a trustee represents many principals because the residual loss of any bondholder will depend on the bondholder's measure of risk aversion and on the proportion of the contract owned.
5. See Jensen and Smith (1985). Also see Green (1984) and Smith and Warner (1979) for similar statements.
6. The events of interest here are the bankruptcy and exercise events: $\mathcal{B}, \mathcal{E} \in \mathbb{B}$.
7. For notational simplicity, we drop the subscript indicating the corporation and replace it with a subscript indicating the project.
8. The state space is still assumed to be finite but it is easier to see the mean-preserving spread when $\Pi$ is drawn as a continuous function of $\omega$.
9. No matter how intuitive this may seem, it is just a claim and needs to be demonstrated. A proof of this claim is contained in the Appendix.
10. This is equivalent to $S_2^L(B_1) = S_2^L(B_2) + D_1(B_1) - D_2(B_1)$, which simply says that if the bondholders believe that the firm will select project one and the firm selects project two, then the stock market value of project two is its true value plus the devaluation of the bond issue.
11. This follows by the MM 58 theorem. See Modigliani and Miller, 1958.
12. This case is considered in the subsequent analysis.

13. Note that $(B, \gamma) = (0, \hat{\gamma})$ is a convertible bond contract which is equivalent to a straight stock issue. The stock value of the new issue is $S_1{}^n = \hat{\gamma} S_1$, where $S_1$ is the total stock value and $\hat{\gamma}$ is the fraction of the firm's equity issued to new equityholders. Then $\hat{\gamma}$ must be selected so that $S_1{}^n = I$, or equivalently,

$$\hat{\gamma} = \frac{I}{S_1}.$$

Also, note that increasing the corporate payoff increases $S_1$ and, other things being equal, decreases $\hat{\gamma}$.

14. Note that the implicit function theorem does yield a function relationship between $B$ and $\gamma$, since $D_1 H > 0$. It follows that there exists a function $g : [0, 1] \rightarrow \mathcal{G}_1$ such that $H(g(\gamma), \gamma) = 0$ and

$$g'(\gamma) = -\frac{D_2 H}{D_1 H} = -\frac{\sum_{\mathcal{E}_1} p(\omega)\, \Pi_1(\omega)}{\sum_{\mathcal{D}_1} p(\omega)} = 0$$

since $\mathcal{E}_1 = \phi$ for all contracts in $\mathcal{G}_1$.

15. Garman (1979) develops the quotient kernel and shows that it can be used to classify models.

16. This equality follows because

$$Ek = \sum_{\Omega} k(\omega)\, \psi(\omega) = \sum_{\Omega} p(\omega) = q.$$

17. See Varian (1985) for a similar conclusion.

## REFERENCES


DeAngelo, H. (1981). "Competition and Unanimity." *American Economic Review* (March).

Garman, M. (1979). "A Synthesis of the Pure Theory of Arbitrage." Working Paper No. 98, Institute of Business and Economic Research, University of California, Berkeley.

Green, R. (1984). "Investment Incentives, Debt, and Warrants." *Journal of Financial Economics* 13: 115–136.

Jensen, M., and Meckling, W. (1976). "Theory of the Firm: Managerial Behavior Agency Costs and Ownership Structure." *Journal of Financial Economics* 3: 305–360.

Jensen, M., and Smith, C. (1985). "Stockholder, Manager, and Creditor Interests: Applications of Agency Theory." In *Recent Advances in Corporate Finance*, edited by Edward Altman and Marti Subrahmanyam. Richard D. Irwin.

MacMinn, R. (1989). "Lecture Notes on Valuing Financial Instruments." University of Texas, March.

Modigliani, F., and Miller, M. (1958). "The Cost of Capital, Corporation Finance and the Theory of Investment." *American Economic Review* (June).

Rothschild, M., and Stiglitz, J. (1970). "Increasing Risk: I. A Definition." *Journal of Economic Theory* 2: 225–243.

Smith, C., and Warner, J. "On Financial Contracting: An Analysis of Bond Covenants." *Journal of Financial Economics* 7: 117–161.

Varian, H. (1985). "Divergence of Opinion in Complete Markets." *Journal of Finance* 11: 309–317.

# EXTERNAL FINANCING COSTS, UNCERTAIN LIQUIDITY NEEDS, AND CAPITAL BUDGETING DECISIONS

T. Harikumar and P. Kadapakkam

## ABSTRACT

Surveys of investment decision making in corporations have repeatedly revealed that managers frequently use other criteria along with the net present value in evaluating projects. While the internal rate of return enjoys widespread usage, the surveys also reveal the intriguing survival of the payback period as a secondary criterion. This paper provides a rationale for the use of the payback criterion by showing that managers prefer earlier realization of cash in the presence of short-term liquidity needs and costly external financing. We also show that such a preference is more pronounced for riskier firms.

## 1. INTRODUCTION

Surveys of investment decision making in corporations repeatedly report that managers frequently use other criteria along with the net present value (NPV) in

**Advances in Quantitative Analysis of Finance and Accounting,**
**Volume 2, Part B, pages 201–214**

**ISBN: 1-55938-565-0**

evaluating projects. Many firms use the internal rate of return. The surveys also reveal that the payback period is often used as a secondary criterion in conjunction with net present value or the internal rate of return. Such evidence is found among small firms as well as large firms in the United States and other countries (see, e.g., Mills, 1988; Mukherjee, 1988; and Scott and Petty, 1984).

The use of the payback period induces a strong preference for projects with larger cash flows in the short term. Since the drawbacks of the payback period are obvious, why is this criterion popular? While some surveys indicate that with time more firms are relying on the net present value, others contradict this finding.[1] At any rate, it is hard to accept the notion that managers were making vastly inferior decisions a couple of decades ago. Rather, the answer perhaps lies in market imperfections which induce a higher value for short-term cash flows.

Narayanan (1985a) provides a justification for emphasizing short-term cash flows based on the information differences between the manager and the shareholders in assessing his performance. The manager's productivity is not directly observable and therefore his wages are based on the firm's past earnings. In such a setting, Narayanan demonstrates that a manager has incentives to improve his wages and reputation by selecting projects yielding cash flows in the short term. While examining factors that mitigate such a preference, Narayanan (1985b) shows that riskier firms rely less on payback.

In this paper, we focus on how flotation costs of external financing induce a preference for short-term cash flows. The dominance of internally generated cash flows as a source of investment funds attests to the significance of costs associated with raising money through new security issues (see Brealey and Myers, 1988, pp. 312–314). In the presence of uncertain future liquidity needs, our analysis suggests that the manager of a firm prefers quicker payback projects. This preference is less pronounced in the presence of costly internal financing. In contrast to Narayanan (1985b), our analysis suggests a potentially greater reliance on payback by riskier firms.

It is important to emphasize that the value of internally generated liquid funds can be assessed only at the corporate level given the overall capital budgeting plans for the present as well as the future. It is difficult, in practice, to require that divisional (or project) managers suitably account for the value of a particular project's impact on the firm's need for internally generated liquid funds.[2] Consequently, firms may require divisions to present for each project a measure of its liquidity (such as payback period) as well as a measure of its value in the absence of liquidity considerations (NPV). Given this information and the future external financing needs of the corporation as a whole, top management may select projects based on their NPV and liquidity. Such a procedure would result in the selection of projects that generate the maximum value net of expected costs of future external financing. Thus, survey results which indicate the use of the payback period as a secondary criterion do not necessarily indicate that management is not engaging in a value-maximizing strategy. The requirement of reporting the payback period may be useful in conveying to divisional managers that liquidity has value.

The rest of the paper is organized as follows. Section II provides a brief discussion of why internally generated liquid funds are valuable. Section III contains a model, within which the preference for projects yielding short-term cash flows in the presence of costs of external financing is formally analyzed. Section IV shows that riskier firms would prefer quicker payback. Other related issues such as internally generated liquid funds in a multiperiod world and impact of firm size are discussed in Section V. The final section contains our conclusions.

## II. VALUE OF INTERNALLY GENERATED LIQUID FUNDS

Internally generated liquid (IGL) funds help the firm to avoid the costs of external financing. In perfect capital markets, there is no value to internal liquidity. However, it can acquire value in the presence of flotation costs or informational asymmetry between insiders and the financial markets regarding the future prospects of the firm. Under information asymmetry, risky securities may have to be issued at a discount to their true value, thereby diluting the existing shareholders' wealth. Myers and Majluf (1984) argue that some firms may forgo profitable projects rather than be subject to such dilution. The value of the forgone projects represents a cost of not having adequate liquidity from within the firm. Firms may attempt to remove informational differences by signaling. However, such signaling may also impose costs.[3] IGL funds are valuable to the extent that they reduce the need to incur these signaling costs.

Internally generated liquid funds also help avoid flotation costs of external financing. Although financial economists have typically brushed aside the economic significance of flotation costs, more recently researchers have studied carefully the impact of the existence of such costs. For instance, Fischer, Heinkel, and Zechner (1989) discuss the implications of flotation costs for the dynamic management of capital structure. The impact of flotation costs on project selection is formally analyzed in the next section. The analysis shows that in the presence of flotation costs and future funding needs, managers trade-off between NPV and payback. Byrne et al. (1967) in an exploratory study consider the selection of projects under payback and liquidity constraints. They assume exogenously specified constraints on payback. Their focus is on developing an algorithm for the constrained maximization problem rather than analyzing the nature of the optimal solution. Further, in their model the preference for liquidity arises due to a penalty on unpaid balances of previous external financing rather than issue costs.

Huberman's (1984) model is closer in spirit to the current analysis. He studies optimal investment in liquid assets (slack). Huberman argues that slack is valuable because it allows for quick exploitation of fleeting investment opportunities. In his model, the manager has to allocate investments between slack and a risky project.

He shows that managers invest in slack until the marginal benefit of not losing a future investment project equals the marginal cost of holding liquid assets yielding subnormal returns. He notes that income from operations would be a cheaper source of liquidity compared to external financing. However, in the wake of bad news regarding earnings prospects, firms will seek external financing in order to maintain the optimal level of liquidity.

An important restriction in Huberman's analysis is that investment projects cannot be financed by contemporaneous external financing and is restricted to liquid funds within the firm. This assumption provides the basis for the value of slack in his model. We allow for projects to be financed externally, though at a cost. Such an assumption is reasonable if the manager knows the timing of probable financing needs, though he may be uncertain of their magnitude. The focus of the analysis is on the costs of acquiring liquidity internally versus the costs of external financing and the consequent impact on the manager's capital budgeting rules for selecting among mutually exclusive projects.

## III. THE MODEL

The analysis is conducted within the framework of a two-period, three-date model. For simplicity, we assume a risk-neutral world and that the time value of money is zero.[4] At $t = 0$, the manager of a firm has $\$I_0$ in investible funds and access to an investment opportunity set characterized by mutually exclusive projects. Each project, $P(\alpha)$, requires an investment outlay of $\$I_0$ and yields a cash flow $C_t$ at time $t$ where

$$C_1 = \alpha G + \varepsilon_1, \text{ and}$$

$$C_2 = (1 - \alpha)G + \varepsilon_2.$$

The random components, $\varepsilon_t$, denote unanticipated cash flows at time $t$. These are assumed to be independent of one another and follow a uniform distribution with bounds $[-h, h]$. The cash flow for any project is thus assumed to have a fixed component ($G$) and variable components ($\varepsilon_t$). The projects in the current investment opportunity set differ in the value of $\alpha$. A project with $\alpha = 0$ has cash flow of $\varepsilon_1$ at $t = 1$ and a cash flow of $G + \varepsilon_1$ at $t = 2$. If instead $\alpha = 1$, the entire fixed-component cash flow of the project ($G$) occurs at $t = 1$. The magnitude of IGL funds at $t = 1$ is $\alpha$G. As $\alpha$ increases from 0 to 1, projects yield greater cash flow in the short term.[5]

### A. Optimal Project Choice When Projects Have Equal NPV

Under risk neutrality and zero time value of money, each project has the same expected NPV of $G - I_0$ as given in Eq. (1).

$$E(NPV) = \alpha G + (1 - \alpha)G - I_0. \tag{1}$$

In this context, the expected NPV does not depend on $\alpha$, and consequently the timing of the realization of the fixed component cash flow is irrelevant. Moreover, in the absence of any liquidity needs at $t = 1$, the manager is indifferent to the choice of $\alpha$ and does not show any preference for realizing cash in the shorter term.

Suppose, at $t = 0$, the manager also knows about a positive NPV opportunity that requires $\$I_1$ (at $t = 1$) and yields an expected cash flow of $\$Y$ at $t = 2$. The manager now faces a need for $I_1$ at $t = 1$.[6] The manager finances the outlay with the internally available cash and, if necessary, goes for an external equity issue.[7] By assumption, the manager has control over the use of the fixed portion of the cash flow and can generate internal funds by choosing an $\alpha > 0$. An external issue is made when $C_1 < I_1$ where $C_1 = \alpha G + \varepsilon_1$. Under these conditions, the expected external financing is given as[8]

$$X = \int_{-h}^{I_1 - \alpha G} [I_1 - (\alpha G + \varepsilon_1)] \frac{1}{2h} \, d\varepsilon_1. \tag{2}$$

Assuming that the manager faces a marginal flotation cost of $\$F$ at the time of an external issue, the overall shareholder's value is given as

$$V(\alpha) = \alpha G + (1 - \alpha)G - I_0 + Y - I_1 - FX. \tag{3}$$

Proposition 1.0 shows that managers are no longer indifferent to the choice of a project.

> *Proposition 1.0*: In the presence of costly external financing and short-term liquidity needs, the manager of a firm prefers a project with an earlier payback denoted by $\alpha^*$ greater than or equal to $(I_1 + h)/G$.

*Proof.* Given in the Appendix.

In the absence of a short-term liquidity need, the manager is indifferent to the timing of the cash flow realization. For any given level of risk in the cash flow, the above proposition shows that the need for financing short-term liquidity induces the preference for an earlier payback.[9] The optimal solution implies that the choice of $\alpha$ ensures sufficient internally generated funds to finance the outlay $I_1$ even at the worst outcome for $C_1$. Thus, when $I_1 + h < G$, $\alpha^*$ is chosen in such a way that the worst cash flow of $\alpha^* G - h$ is equal to $I_1$. However, if $I_1 + h > G$, the choice of $\alpha^*$ is equal to one.

Extending this model to a multiperiod setting implies a cash flow of $C_t = \alpha_t G + \varepsilon_t$, where the sum of $\alpha_t$ across time adds to one. The expected NPV is still $G - I_0$, and in the absence of costly internal financing, the manager's choice of $\alpha_1^*$ at $t = 1$ remains unchanged. In the next section, we analyze the impact of costly internal funds on the preference for projects with earlier payback ($\alpha$).

### B. Optimal Choice of Project When Projects Have Different NPVs

In this section, we consider a case where the choice of an earlier realization of the fixed-component cash flow is achieved at the cost of future value. This assumption is best described in the following examples. Consider the manager of a timber manufacturing firm. At time $t = 0$, he has to decide on how many trees to cut. The firm's current liquidity is directly proportional to the number of trees cut and sold. This, however, precludes the manager from having more wood and, ceteris paribus, more cash flow in the next period. In this context, the value of additional liquidity in relation to the marginal cost suggests the optimal number of trees to be cut—the "project" choice.

The motivation for such a loss in future value is also provided by considering expenditures such as maintenance, advertising, or research and development. A firm may scale back these expenses to increase short-term cash flows. However, such decisions could cause much lower future profits due to higher maintenance costs, lower sales, or lost new product opportunities. While this is in closest conformity with the structure of our model, the analysis provides insights whenever longer term projects are more valuable than shorter term projects. We incorporate this feature by modifying the cash flow $C_t$ as

$$C_1 = \alpha G + \varepsilon_1,$$

$$C_2 = (1 - \alpha)G(1 + g) + \varepsilon_2.$$

The analysis in the previous section assumes that $g = 0$. In the current structure, the manager can generate more funds internally at time $t = 1$ by selecting a project with a higher $\alpha$. However, this liquidity is obtained at the expense of future value since $g > 0$. The manager's problem at $t = 0$ is to select the project $\alpha$ in a manner that maximizes the overall present value to the current shareholders. This value is the total of the expected NPVs from the investments at $t = 0$ and $t = 1$ less expected flotation costs from an external issue at $t = 1$. This is given as

$$\max_{0<\alpha<1} V(\alpha) = \alpha G + (1 - \alpha)G(1 + g) - I_0 + Y - I_1 - FX, \tag{4}$$

where $X$ is the expected external financing as in Eq. (2) and $FX$ is the expected cost of such financing. Proposition 2.0 shows the impact of the trade-off between the costs of external and internal sources of funds on the choice of $\alpha$.

*Proposition 2.0:* In the presence of costly internal and external financing, the optimal choice of $\alpha^*$ is

$$\alpha^* = \begin{cases} 0 & \text{if } F < g \\ I_1/G + [2h(F/2 - g)]/FG, & \text{if } F > g. \end{cases} \tag{5}$$

*Proof.* Given in the Appendix.

*Corollary:* In the event of an uncertain timing of the future investment, the optimal choice of $\alpha^*$ increases with the probability of the investment being made at $t = 1$.

*Proof.* Given in the Appendix.

Setting $g = 0$ yields the result in proposition 1.0 where $\alpha^* = (I_1 + h)/G$. To gain more insight into the solution given in Eq. (5), rearrange Eq. (5) for $F > g$ to obtain

$$g = F\left(I_1 + h - \frac{\alpha^*}{2h}\right). \tag{6}$$

The expression in parentheses on the right-hand side of Eq. (6) is the probability of seeking external financing. Here, $\alpha^*$ is chosen in a manner that the loss in value of providing a dollar of IGL funds ($g$) is equated at the margin to the expected flotation costs of raising a dollar from an external source. If $F < g$, the loss in value will always exceed the savings in flotation costs, and the manager prefers to seek external financing rather than generate funds internally by selecting projects with a higher $\alpha$. Thus, the manager values IGL funds whenever the costs of external financing are high relative to costs of internal financing.

The value of $\alpha^*$ has intuitively appealing features. An increase in future financing needs ($I_1$) or flotation costs ($F$) increases the external financing costs, thereby inducing $\alpha^*$ to increase. An increase in the size of expected operating cash flows ($G$) or the profitability of longer term investments ($g$) results in a lower value of $\alpha^*$.

A comparative analysis of propositions 1 and 2 above provides further insight into the magnitude of the funds generated by the manager internally. Proposition 1.0 characterizes the choice of $\alpha$ in the context of costless internal financing ($g = 0$) and costly external financing. The manager is shown to optimally choose a value of $\alpha$ that prepares him for the worst outcome at $t = 1$, despite the positive probability of having a favorable outcome of $\varepsilon_1$. In the presence of costly internal financing ($g > 0$), proposition 2.0 shows that the choice of $\alpha^*$ is lower than the value in proposition 1.0. Thus, costly internal financing induces the manager to partially rely on the possibility of a favorable realization of $\varepsilon_1$ to finance the investment outlay at $t = 1$.

## IV. CASH FLOW VARIANCE AND THE VALUE OF IGL FUNDS

In this section, we analyze the impact of risk on the choice of $\alpha$ when internal financing is costly. In the absence of risk, substitute $h = 0$ in Eq. (5) to yield a value of $\alpha^*$ equal to $I_1/G$. The optimum $\alpha$ in the presence of risk as given in Eq. (5) is less (greater) than in the case of certain cash flows, whenever $F/2$ is less (greater) than $g$. This is because, when $F/2 < g$, the manager optimally relies on a favorable random outcome to meet the need for $\$I_1$ at least partially.[10] This minimizes the use of costlier IGL funds. It is better to meet unanticipated operating deficits by external financing than to undertake more liquid but less profitable projects. If $F/2 > g$, the converse is true. Here, IGL funds are used to meet the need for $\$I_1$ and additional funds are generated at $t = 1$ to avoid costly external financing of an unfavorable random outcome (i.e, $\alpha^*G - I_1 > 0$). It is interesting to note that the manager emphasizes short-term cash flow ($\alpha^* > 0$) even if $\$I_1 = 0$. This is a striking result pointing to the value of generating internal funds even in the absence of future investment opportunities.

The magnitude of the excess slack depends on the volatility of operating cash flows. Given that the underlying uncertainty is caused by $\varepsilon_1$, we show that the external financing at $t = 1$ exhibits a "put option" feature where the value of the "put" is equal to the expected external financing requirement. The value of the "put" (expected external financing requirement) increases with an increase in the risk of the underlying cash flow from the asset in place. This in turn induces the manager to optimally increase the value of $\alpha^*$, thereby choosing an earlier payback.

*Proposition 3.0:* An increase in the variance of $\varepsilon_1$ (induced by an increase in $h$) increases the expected level of external financing.

*Proof.* Given in the Appendix.

The intuition behind this result is illustrated in Figure 1. For values of $C_1 < I_1$, the manager goes for an external issue of the magnitude $I_1 - (\alpha^*G + \varepsilon_1)$. For $C_1$ greater than or equal to $I_1$, the liquidity needs are fully met from internal sources. The magnitude of external financing is contingent on the realization of the random cash flow and yields a graph similar to the payoff on a long position in a put option. Thus, at $t = 0$, the expected amount of external financing is the value of the put option described in the figure. From the option pricing literature, we know that the value of a put increases with an increase in the variance of the value of the underlying security. In our context, as the put value is the expected magnitude of external financing, an increase in variance ($h$) increases this magnitude.

The impact of an increase in the variance of $C_1$ on $\alpha^*$ is formally stated in the next result.

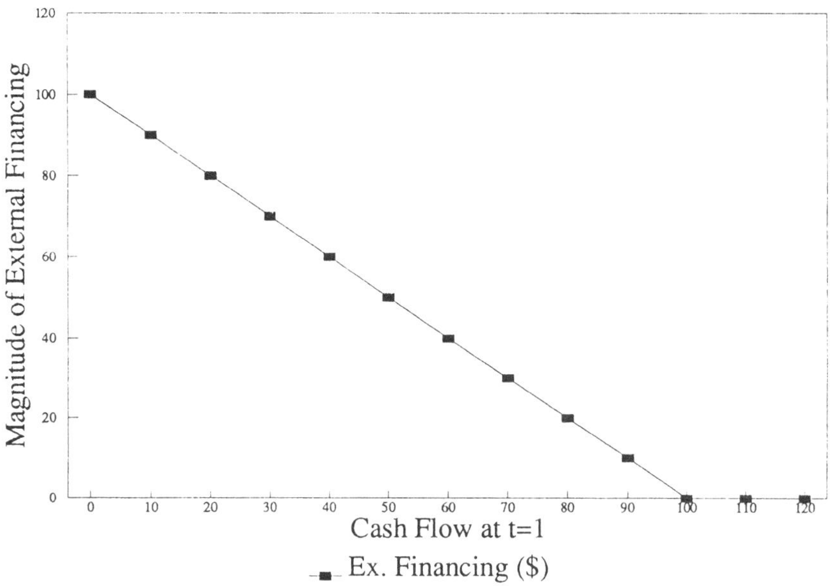


*Figure 1.* Magnitude of external financing required for different values of cash flow at $t = 1$. In this example, $I_1 = \$100$, $\alpha = 0.4$, and $G = 150$. The external financing need is zero when $\varepsilon_1 = \$40$ and $C_1 = \$100$. The external financing need is generally denoted as max $[0, \$100 - C_1]$. This resembles a payoff on a put option.

*Proposition 4.0:* When the flotation cost is significantly high (i.e., $F/2 > g$), the manager of a firm prefers a project with an earlier payback (higher value of $\alpha^*$) whenever the risk of the cash flow at $t = 1$ increases ($h$ increases).

*Proof.* Given in the Appendix.

Note that in the current analysis, riskier firms emphasize the payback period not as an adjustment for the risk of the project but because of costs of external financing.[11] In perfect capital markets, there would be no such motivation for riskier firms to rely on the payback period criterion.

The conclusion that riskier firms place greater emphasis on short-term cash flows is in contrast to Narayanan (1985b), wherein riskier firms place less emphasis on payback. In that paper, if the cash flows are more volatile, a large short-term cash flow is less likely to be attributed to the manager's competence. Therefore, the manager's incentive to prefer quicker payback is reduced.

## V. OTHER ISSUES RELATED TO IGL FUNDS

In this section, we discuss the multi-period case and the potential relationship between firm size and reliance on the payback period.

### A. Financing Needs in a Multiperiod World

The two-period model in Section III allows for a parsimonious depiction of the essential ingredients of the trade-off between liquidity and the value of longer term projects. In a multiperiod world, a firm can be faced with financing needs at different points in time during the life of a project. This aspect requires a broader definition of $\alpha$.

Consider a three-period world in which current investments yielding cash flows at $t = 2$ are more valuable than others yielding cash flows at $t = 1$. Further, profitable investment opportunities exist only at $t = 2$ and not at $t = 1$. In this setting, there would be a liquidity need at $t = 1$ only to cover negative surprises in operations. The critical liquidity need occurs at $t = 2$. Thus, it is likely that projects with cash flows at $t = 2$ might be preferred to those with cash flows at $t = 1$. Additionally, while the marginal cost of carrying internally generated funds from $t = 1$ to $t = 2$ is $g$, the cost of generating excess cash at $t = 2$ is zero. This induces the manager to choose projects that yield cash flows at $t = 2$. Although there is not a strict preference for projects yielding cash at a quicker pace, note that the manager prefers to have IGL funds by $t = 2$. In choosing between projects generating cash by $t = 2$ and those which generate cash only at $t = 3$, the manager will be engaged in a trade-off between liquidity and value similar to the one analyzed earlier.

In this context, liquidity of a project would be defined in terms of cash generated by the time of critical financing needs. This scenario may partially explain the formulation of the decision rule: "Prefer projects whose payback is less than or equal to $T$ years." The specification of the cutoff horizon $T$, would depend on the timing of major financing needs.

### B. Firm Size and Value of IGL Funds

Our analysis suggests that the emphasis on short-term cash flows from operations will increase with the magnitude of flotation costs and the volatility of operating cash flows. While there is no direct evidence in support of these conclusions, it is interesting to note that previous empirical work indicates that smaller firms place greater emphasis on short-term cash flows. Pope (1988) finds that among firms with total assets of less than \$100 million, more than 20% of the managers cited payback as the most useful capital budgeting technique. The corresponding figure for larger firms is 6%.[12] Small firms face significant flotation costs and are riskier than large firms.[13] In addition, they are most liable to suffer from information asymmetries given that large firms attract considerable attention from the media and financial analysts. Any underpricing of the new issue due to information asymmetry represents an additional cost of external financing. The impact of both flotation costs and informational asymmetries is lower for debt than equity securities. To the extent that firms can optimally raise more external funds through debt rather than equity, the value of internal liquidity will be reduced.

## VI. CONCLUSIONS

Managers often use the payback period in making investment decisions. Such an approach emphasizes short-term cash flows. The use of capital budgeting techniques which emphasize short-term cash flows cannot be rationalized under the assumptions of perfect capital markets. Previous researchers have attempted to explain the preference of short-term cash flows on the basis of stockholder–manager conflicts. This paper provides an alternate explanation by focusing on conditions which gives value for internally generated liquid funds.

Raising external funds engenders flotation costs. Furthermore, if information differences exist between managers and financial markets, issuance of new securities can lead to costs in the form of dilution of existing shareholders' claims or additional deadweight signaling costs.

A project with higher cash flows in the near term increases the amount of internally generated liquid funds and reduces the need for external funds over that horizon. Under these circumstances, projects with shorter payback periods would be preferred over other projects that would have the same value in perfect capital markets.

Small firms experiencing considerable growth are more likely to face significant costs of external financing and should be more inclined to a preference for short-term cash flows. As flotation costs and information asymmetries decrease through time due to innovations in regulations and technology, the value of internally generated liquid funds will be reduced. This should lead to a reduction in the use of capital budgeting criteria which emphasize short-term cash flows.

## APPENDIX

*Proof for Proposition 1.0* The overall shareholder's value is

$V(\alpha) = \alpha G + (1 - \alpha)G - I_0 + Y - I_1 - FX$, where $X$ is given as

$$X = \int_{-h}^{I_1 - \alpha G} [I_1 - (\alpha G + \varepsilon_1)] \frac{1}{2h} \, d\varepsilon_1.$$

Differentiating $V(\alpha)$ with respect to $\alpha$ and solving the first-order condition yields an $\alpha^*$ equal to $(I_1 + h)/G$. If $G < I_1 + h$, $\alpha^*$ is equal to one and if $G > I_1 + h$ an $\alpha^*$ equal to $(I_1 + h)/G$ guarantees costless and complete internal financing. The second-order condition suggests that the optimal choice maximizes the shareholder's value.

*Proof for Proposition 2.0* Substituting Eq. (2) for $X$ in Eq. (4) and solving for an optimal $\alpha$ yields the result. An interior optimum occurs when the value of $V(\alpha)$ is maximized at an $\alpha = \alpha^*$ (in Eq. [5]) with $0 < \alpha^* < 1$. Using Eq. (5), we find that $\alpha^* < 1$ when $h_1 < F[G - I_1]/2[(F/2) - g] = h_m$, and $\alpha^* > 0$ when $-FI_1/2[(F/2) - g] < h_1$. Using the condition that $G > I_1$ and $F/2 > g$, we find an interior optimum, when the risk level $h_1 \in (0, h_m)$. Whenever $h_1 > h_m$, $\alpha^* = 1$.

*Corollary* Modify Eq. (2) in the following manner:

$$X = p\int_{-h}^{q_1} [q_1 - \varepsilon_1]\frac{1}{2h}\,d\varepsilon_1 + (1-p)\int_{-h}^{h}\int_{-h}^{q_2} [q_2 - \varepsilon_2]\,\frac{1}{4h^2}\,d\varepsilon_2 d\varepsilon_1,$$

where $p$ is the probability of an investment opportunity occurring at $t = 1$, $q_1 = I_1 - \alpha G$ and $q_2 = I_1 - G(1 + g) + \alpha Gg - \varepsilon_1$. By substituting the above expression for $X$ in Eq. (4) and solving for $\alpha^*$, it is easy to show that $d\alpha^*/dp > 0$.

*Proof for Proposition 3.0* Solving the integral in Eq. (2), we get

$$X = (I_1 - \alpha^*G)^2/4h_1 + (I_1 - \alpha^*G)/2 + h_1/4.$$

$dX/dh_1 = -(I_1 - \alpha^*G)^2/4h_1 + 1/4 > 0$ if and only if $[I_1 - \alpha^*G] < h_1$. By definition, there is at least one state in which external financing is (not needed) needed $(C_1 > I_1)$ $C_1 < I_1$. This implies that $h_1 < [I_1 - \alpha G] < h_1$ for any value of $\alpha$ between 0 and 1. Thus, $[I_1 - \alpha^*G] < h_1$ and $dX/dh_1 > 0$.

*Proof for Proposition 4.0* From Eq. (5), $d\alpha^*/dh_1 = 2[(F/2) - g]/FG > 0$. This implies that an increase in variance induces the manager to optimally increase the amount of internal funds generated earlier by giving up some of the initial project's value.

# NOTES

1. See Canada and Miller (1985) and Pike (1988) for opposing views on this issue.

2. The subsequent analysis reveals that the value of internal liquidity depends on *aggregate* future financing needs as well as on the volatility of *aggregate* future cash flows.

3. Some researchers have proposed the existence of signaling equilibria, wherein no dissipative costs are incurred. (For example, see Brennan and Kraus [1987]). If firms can reveal the true value of their securities without incurring costs, the need to have internal liquidity would be diminished.

4. Equivalently, all variables in the analysis can be considered to be expressed in terms of their present value.

5. If $\alpha$ is negative, the firm invests additional funds in the project at time 1. The constraint that $\alpha$ is nonnegative avoids such a possibility.

6. The project is assumed to be extremely profitable, so that it is worthwhile to undertake it even considering additional financing costs.

7. Cash for the investment outlay can also be raised by spinning off the old project. However, such a sale would also be subject to transaction costs and potentially information asymmetry. The analysis in the text focuses solely on the costs of issuing new securities.

8. An underlying assumption is that the most favorable outcome of the random cash flow ($h$) exceeds the investment needs ($I_1$). Thus, there is a positive probability of avoiding external financing. If, however, $I_1 > (G + h)$, then the firm will always seek external financing and $E(X) = I_1 - \alpha G$. The choice of $\alpha$ will be identical to that under certainty.

9. We induce the preference for earlier payback by assuming short-term liquidity needs. This is similar to the assumption in Narayanan (1985a) that managers are compensated based on short-term earnings measures, which, in turn, induces them to prefer earlier payback. Thus, in the absence of such compensation schemes, there is no incentive for the manager to prefer earlier payback.

10. The probability of an unfavorable outcome is the same as the probability $\varepsilon_1 < 0$. Given that $\varepsilon_1$ follows a uniform distribution, this probability is 1/2. Thus, the expected cost is $F(1/2)$.

11. In fact, $\alpha^* = 1$ when $h > F[G - I_1]/2[(F/2) - g]$.

12. Mills (1988) also cites studies finding evidence that small firms rely more on payback.

13. The size of security issues is positively linked to firm size. Small issues have high flotation costs. See evidence cited in chapter 3 of Phillips and Zecher (1981) and Brealey and Myers (1988, p. 335).

# REFERENCES

Brealey, R. A., and Myers, S. C. (1988). *Principles of Corporate Finance*. New York: McGraw-Hill.

Brennan, M. J., and Kraus, A. (1987). "Efficient Financing under Asymmetric Information." *Journal of Finance* 42 (December): 1225–1243.

Byrne, R., Charnes, A., Cooper, W. W., and Kortanek, K. (1967). "A Chance-Constrained Approach to Capital Budgeting with Portfolio Type Payback and Liquidity Constraints and Horizon Posture Controls." *Journal of Financial and Quantitative Analysis* 2: 339–364.

Canada, J. R., and Miller, N. P. (1985). "Review of Surveys on Capital Investment Evaluation Techniques." *Engineering Economist* 30 (Winter): 193–200.

Fischer, E. O., Heinkel, R., and Zechner, J. (1989). "Dynamic Capital Structure Choice: Theory and Tests." *Journal of Finance* 44 (March): 19–40.

Huberman, G. (1984). "External Financing and Liquidity." *Journal of Finance* 39(July): 895–910.

John, K., and Williams, J. (1985). "Dividends, Dilution and Taxes: A Signalling Equilibrium." *Journal of Finance* (September): 1053–1070.

Mills, R. W. (1988). "Capital Budgeting—The State of the Art." *Long Range Planning* 21 (August): 76–81.

Mukherjee, T. K. (1988). "The Capital Budgeting Process of Large U.S. Firms: An Analysis of Capital Budgeting Manuals." *Managerial Finance*, 28–35.

Myers, S. C., and Majluf, N. (1984). "Corporate Financing and Investment Decisions When Firms Have Information That Investors Do Not Have." *Journal of Financial Economics* 13 (March): 187–221.

Narayanan, M. P. (1985a). "Observability and the Payback Criterion." *Journal of Business* 58 (July): 309–323.

Narayanan, M. P. (1985b). "Managerial Incentives for Short Term Results." *Journal of Finance* 42 (December): 1469–1485.

Phillips, S., and Zecher, J. (1981). *The SEC and the Public Interest*. Cambridge, MA: MIT Press.

Pike, R. H. (1988). "The Capital Budgeting Revolution." *Management Accounting (UK)* 66 (October): 28–30.

Pope, R. (1988). "Current Capital Budgeting Practices: A Comparison of Small and Large Firms." *Southwest Journal of Business and Economics* 4: 16–24.

Scott, D. F., Jr., and Petty, J. W. II. "Capital Budgeting Practices in Large American Firms: A Retrospective Analysis and Synthesis." *Financial Review* 19: 111—123.

# THE RESTRUCTURING OF MANAGEMENT ACCOUNTING COURSES

Jiunn C. Huang and David P. Franz

## ABSTRACT

This paper details the results of a survey conducted to determine the best mix of instructional techniques and topic coverage in management accounting courses in order to better prepare undergraduate accounting students for a career in management accounting. Two respondent groups were identified: chapter presidents of the National Association of Accountants and the campus coordinators of the same organization. Results indicate that typical accounting graduates are mostly marginally prepared to perform effectively in their first job. Both practitioners and educators believed two or three management accounting courses should be required. Practitioners recognized the importance of outside materials like cases, articles, and computer projects in each course of the two- or three-course sequences. Educators, on the other hand, are not willing to give outside materials a weight equal to lectures and discussions until the third course is taught. The findings of this survey should be of interest to practitioners, educators, management accounting textbook authors, and publishers. The perceived lack of preparedness of new accounting graduates should

Advances in Quantitative Analysis of Finance and Accounting,
Volume 2, Part B, pages 215–226.

ISBN: 1-55938-565-0

be of concern to all these parties. The survey identified two solutions to this problem: provide three undergraduate management accounting courses for those students wishing to enter the field; and develop and use additional outside materials such as cases and computer projects in the third course. Both educators and practitioners recommended that the third course should have over 30 percent of its class time devoted to outside materials. If institutions move toward requiring a third course, opportunities should exist for authors and publishers to provide additional reading books, casebooks, and spreadsheet analysis materials that are suitable for an advanced management accounting course.

## I. INTRODUCTION

Two forces provide the impetus to reassess various aspects of the current management accounting curriculum. First, the management accounting profession has been criticized by some accounting educators such as Johnson and Kaplan for not meeting the need of the changing business environment (1987). Second, the National Association of Accountants (NAA) has issued *Education for Careers in Management Accounting* (1988), which recommends three to five courses in management accounting without detailing the contents of the courses.

The purpose of this paper is to report on a survey of management accounting educators and practitioners regarding the following issues. How prepared are management accounting graduates for their first jobs? How many management accounting courses are needed to build a solid management accounting background? Is the existing management accounting curriculum adequate? What is the best mix of the teaching mode? Which topics should be covered in a particular management accounting course?

Previous research in this area has focused on developing a common body of knowledge and on identifying general topics to cover in the undergraduate management accounting curriculum. This study provides an update on the same area and is unique in three aspects: more issues are addressed in this study, the respondent groups surveyed are different from previous studies, and the topic coverage in each management accounting course is identified. An attempt is made to restructure the management accounting courses to prepare accounting students for a management accounting career.

## II. LITERATURE REVIEW

The literature has used surveys of practitioners and educators to identify important topics for the undergraduate management accounting curriculum. Deakin and Summers (1975), Van Zante (1980), and Knight and Zook (1982) cited the development of the Certificate in Management Accounting (CMA) in 1972 as evidence that the educational needs differ for management accountants and for financial accountants. Deakin and Summers (1975) asked practitioners to rate the relative importance of 39 topics to their present work experience. They found that general topics were ranked higher than the specific tools needed to accomplish the tasks.

Van Zante (1980) surveyed both industrial accountants and educators and asked them to rate the importance of 28 topics to the curriculum of an undergraduate accounting major who wishes to enter a career in industrial accounting. He found that the two groups had a correlation of 0.93 for the relative rankings of the topics and that none of the topics was rated of little or no importance.

Knight and Zook (1982) surveyed corporate controllers and certified public accountants (CPAs) in an attempt to identify some of the differences in topic coverage of undergraduate education for students seeking careers in public accounting versus management accounting. They asked the respondents to rate the importance of 72 topics and found significant differences between the ratings of the two groups for 44 topics.

Recently, Van Zante (1989) surveyed nonacademic certified management accountants and requested that they rate the importance of 28 topics to their current position. He compared the results with his 1980 study and found only two topics with significantly higher ratings in 1989—computer systems and computer programming.

Deakin and Summers (1975), Van Zante (1980, 1989), and Knight and Zook (1982) did not identify which topics should be taught in individual courses. Harris and Krogstad (1976) and Depasquale (1985) focused on which courses address the topics on the CMA exam. Harris and Krogstad (1976) examined the profile and content of the first four CMA exams. The profile was broken down by subject area, by topic within managerial accounting, and by topic within financial reporting. Depasquale (1985) identified which courses in "the typical accounting curriculum" cover the 32 major topics on the CMA examination and concluded that the current curriculum is adequate to prepare students for the professional examination.

Despite these efforts, there is still no clear guidance on the composition of undergraduate management accounting courses. DeMaris and Copeland (1984a) call for the development of a well-defined educational program for management accounting. Lander and Reinstein (1987) surveyed randomly selected members of the NAA to link 168 specific knowledge items to 13 management accounting objectives. The resulting common body of knowledge assists in identifying which skills are important to management accounting.

The NAA (1988) issued Statement on Management Accounting 1E, "Education for Careers in Management Accounting," which outlines a curriculum for both 120- and 150-semester-hour programs. The 120-semester-hour program proposes 9–12 semester hours devoted to management/cost accounting. It provides a broad outline of the course content but does not provide detailed recommendations.

## III. METHODOLOGY

Questionnaires were generated and pretested to obtain the opinions of practitioners and educators on various managerial accounting education issues. At the beginning, respondents were asked about their rating of the level of preparedness of typical entry-level managerial accountants with an undergraduate degree in accounting. They were subsequently asked about the number of managerial/cost accounting courses they recommended and their preference of mode of teaching in each recommended course. Respondents were also asked to decide the various topics that are to be included in each course they recommended. Fifteen managerial/cost accounting topics were compiled from more than twenty principle and advanced textbooks. Topics were reviewed and evaluated critically by both educators and practitioners known to the authors to assure their clarity and representativeness. A forced-choice format which required respondents to allocate percentage of time to each topic was used in questionnaires to educators, whereas questionnaires to practitioners asked them to check no more than ten topics to be included in a course. Demographic data were obtained at the end of questionnaires.

The initial questionnaires were presented at a workshop at the authors' institution and pilot-tested by sending them for review and criticism to a total of twenty academics and practitioners known to the authors. Slight revisions were incorporated into the final version of the questionnaire. Questionnaires were mailed to each of the 328 chapter presidents and each of the 567 management accounting campus coordinators of the National Association of Accountants. Chapter presidents were considered to represent practitioners, and management accounting coordinators are most knowledgeable about each school's management accounting curriculum. A total of 278 responses were received from 895 mailings. The response rate for the practitioners was 37 percent while the response rate for the educators was 24 percent. The practitioner respondents have the following profile: more than 50 percent are holding management positions, about 40 percent are primarily responsible for financial reporting and 30 percent for managerial accounting, more than 50 percent are certified, about 50 percent have experience greater than 10 years, and more than 40 percent hold graduate degrees. Accounting educators were spread rather evenly among the ranks. They also have substantial practical experience. More than 79 percent have a CPA and/or CMA certificate. To test for nonresponse bias, late respondents choices (the last 30%) were compared with those of early respondents (the first 30%). No significant differences were noted in the comparison, indicating that a larger response rate was unlikely to alter the results.

*Table 1.* Level of Preparedness

| | *Level of Preparedness* | | | |
|---|---|---|---|---|
| *Respondent Group* | *Highly Prepared* | *Prepared* | *Marginally Prepared* | *Not Prepared* |
| Practitioners | 0 | 37.6 | 57.26 | 5.1 |
| Educators | 0 | 46.5 | 50.4 | 3.1 |
| Overall | 0 | 42.3 | 53.7 | 4.0 |

*Notes:* Mean rating by practitioners: 2.434.*
Mean rating by educators: 2.25.*
$t$-test: $t = 2.2384$.
*Highly prepared = 4, prepared = 3, marginally prepared = 2, not prepared = 1.

# IV. RESULTS

## A. Preparedness of Entry-Level Accountants

Respondents were asked to assess the level of preparedness with respect to management accounting of the typical entry-level individual with an undergraduate degree in accounting. The results appear in Table 1. Overall, 53.7 percent of the respondents said the individuals were marginally prepared, while 4 percent said they were not prepared. No one said they were highly prepared. Accounting educators felt the level of preparedness was better than did the practitioners. The difference in mean rankings between the two groups is statistically significant ($p < 0.001$). Thus a gap of assessment exists between the providers of management accounting education and the users of management accountants.

## B. Number of Required Managerial Accounting Courses

Respondents were asked how many courses in managerial accounting should be required of accounting majors for them to perform effectively in entry-level positions. Results are summarized in Table 2. As Table 2 reveals, overall, more than 80 percent of respondents want two or three courses. Few respondents want to require four courses and very few want only one course. More practitioners want three courses and four courses whereas the major choice of accounting educators is two courses. Since the majority of respondents recommended two or three courses, the subsequent discussion on teaching techniques and topic coverage will focus on these courses.

Educators were asked how many courses their institutions currently required. Comparisons were made against the number of courses they recommended and the results are detailed in Table 3.

*Table 2.* Number of Courses Recommended

| *Respondent Group* | *1* | 2 | 3 | 4 |
|---|---|---|---|---|
| Practitioners | 3.3% | 35% | 43.5% | 19.2% |
| Educators | 3.9 | 45 | 39.5 | 11.6 |
| Overall | 3.6 | 40.2 | 41 | 15.2 |

*Notes:* Number of recommended courses is independent of respondent group. $X^2 = 4.0329$, $p = 0.2577$.

Most (51.2%) require one course, while 45.4 percent require two courses. Very few schools require three or more courses. The paired-*t* test between number of courses recommended and number of courses currently required indicated that there is a significant discrepancy between the two ($t = 14.98$, $p < 0.001$). Thus, it appears that educators do not believe that the number of courses currently offered in their institutions is adequate. They think that more courses are needed to prepare the students for a managerial accounting career. A detailed analysis indicates that a student graduating from an accounting program that requires one management accounting course would often be found marginally prepared by a manager who feels that three management accounting courses should be required.

## C. Instructional Techniques

For each recommended required managerial accounting course, respondents were asked the extent to which various instructional techniques should be used in class. Results for respondents recommending two courses are presented in Table 4. For the first course, lecture time should be 45.24 percent of class time followed by discussion, 39.19 percent, and outside material including practice set, cases,

*Table 3.* Number of Courses Recommended Compared with Number of Courses Currently Required

| | *1* | 2 | 3 | 4 |
|---|---|---|---|---|
| Recommended | 3.9% | 45% | 39.5% | 11.6% |
| Required | 51.2% | 45.4% | 3.4% | 0% |

*Notes:* Average number of courses recommended: 2.5891.
Average number of courses currently required: 1.4031.
Paired *t*-test, $t = 14.98$; $p = 0.000$.

*Table 4.* Instructional Techniques: Two Courses

| | *First* | | | | *Second* | | | |
|---|---|---|---|---|---|---|---|---|
| | *Overall* | *E* | *P* | *t* | *Overall* | *E* | *P* | *t* |
| Lectures | 45% | 48% | 42% | –2.09 (0.039) | 34% | 36% | 31% | –1.07 (0.092) |
| Discussion | 39 | 40 | 38 | –0.88 (0.383) | 37 | 39 | 35 | –1.24 (0.220) |
| Outside materials | 15 | 11 | 21 | 3.48 (0.001) | 26 | 22 | 32 | 2.86 (0.005) |
| Others | 0 | 0 | 0 | –0.17 (0.867) | 1 | 1 | 1 | –0.43 (0.665) |

articles, and computer projects, 15.15 percent. Practitioners want more time spent on outside material and less time on lecture while educators want more time on lecture and less time on outside material. No significant difference was detected between the two groups regarding the percent of time on discussion. The percentage breakdown for the second course showed a strong focus on outside material and less emphasis on lecture with discussion time similar to the first course. Practitioners want the class time of the second course divided almost equally among the three techniques. Results for respondents recommending three courses are presented in Table 5. Again, higher level courses emphasize more outside material, cases and computer projects. In fact, for the third course, both groups were consistent in recommending that more than one-third of class time be devoted to outside materials. Different time allocation to discussion and outside material exists

*Table 5.* Instructional Techniques: Three Courses

| | *First* | | | | *Second* | | | | *Third* | | | |
|---|---|---|---|---|---|---|---|---|---|---|---|---|
| | *Overall* | *E* | *P* | *t* | *Overall* | *E* | *P* | *t* | *Overall* | *E* | *P* | *t* |
| Lectures | 49% | 50% | 47% | –0.7 (0.49) | 38% | 41% | 35% | –1.9 (0.06) | 26% | 26% | 27% | 0.14 (0.89) |
| Discussion | 37 | 42 | 33 | –2.4 (0.02) | 37 | 40 | 35 | –2.1 (0.04) | 34 | 35 | 34 | –0.45 (0.63) |
| Outside material | 14 | 8 | 19 | 4.99 (0.00) | 23 | 18 | 29 | 5.2 (0.00) | 37 | 36 | 37 | 0.43 (0.67) |
| Others | 1 | 1 | 1 | 0.14 (0.89) | 1 | 1 | 2 | 1.16 (0.25) | 3 | 3 | 3 | –0.20 (0.84) |

between the two groups, with practitioners consistently demanding more time for outside material and less time for discussion in both the first and the second courses.

## D. Percent of Time for Each Topic

Educators were asked to specify the percent of time to be devoted to various management accounting topics for each required course they recommended. Subtopics within a major topic were provided to encourage respondents to follow similar lines of thinking. The topics and the subtopics were selected on the basis of an extensive review of popular management/cost accounting textbooks.

The results are presented in Table 6. There is substantial agreement in recommended coverage when comparing the number of courses that should be required. For example, when two courses are required, the emphasis of the first course is on product costing, standard cost, budgeting, cost allocation, cost-volume-profit

*Table 6.* Percent of Time for Each Topic: Educators

| | *Number of Courses That Should Be Required* | | | | |
|---|---|---|---|---|---|
| | *Two Courses* | | *Three Courses* | | |
| *Topics* | *1st* | *2d* | *1st* | *2d* | *3d* |
| Product cost systems | 20% | 7.4% | 23% | 11% | 3% |
| Cost allocations | 9 | 6 | 9 | 8 | 3 |
| Cost estimation | 8 | 5 | 8 | 6 | 5 |
| C-V-P analysis | 9 | 4 | 10 | 6 | 3 |
| Differential cost analysis | 7 | 7 | 7 | 8 | 3 |
| Capital budgeting | 5 | 7 | 5 | 8 | 4 |
| Budgeting | 11 | 5 | 11 | 8 | 5 |
| Standard costs | 12 | 9 | 12 | 8 | 3 |
| Responsibility accounting and performance evaluation | 6 | 9 | 4 | 9 | 7 |
| Quantitative techniques | 2 | 10 | 1 | 8 | 15 |
| Economics of Information | 2 | 6 | 1 | 3 | 9 |
| Impact of changing technology on cost accounting | 2 | 6 | 2 | 4 | 10 |
| Service industries | 2 | 4 | 1 | 2 | 7 |
| Behavioral accounting | 2 | 3 | 2 | 3 | 8 |
| International management accounting | 1 | 3 | 1 | 1 | 6 |
| Other | 0 | 2 | 0 | 0 | 3 |
| | 100% | 100% | 100% | 100% | 100% |

*Table 7.* Percent of Votes for Each Topic: Practitioners

| | *Number of Courses That Should Be Required* | | | | |
|---|---|---|---|---|---|
| | *Two Courses* | | *Three Courses* | | |
| *Topics* | *1st* | *2d* | *1st* | *2d* | *3d* |
| Product cost systems | 88% | 29% | 88% | 35% | 22% |
| Cost allocations | 81 | 33 | 75 | 55 | 26 |
| Cost estimation | 55 | 38 | 49 | 55 | 37 |
| C-V-P analysis | 71 | 38 | 59 | 57 | 43 |
| Differential cost analysis | 48 | 41 | 43 | 65 | 39 |
| Capital budgeting | 57 | 57 | 39 | 73 | 43 |
| Budgeting | 62 | 41 | 45 | 63 | 43 |
| Standard costs | 81 | 26 | 76 | 51 | 31 |
| Responsibility accounting and performance evaluation | 24 | 67 | 31 | 41 | 63 |
| Quantitative techniques | 26 | 60 | 19 | 51 | 67 |
| Economics of information | 26 | 50 | 37 | 39 | 49 |
| Impact of changing technology on cost accounting | 29 | 48 | 29 | 29 | 63 |
| Service industries | 26 | 31 | 16 | 33 | 37 |
| Behavioral accounting | 12 | 31 | 18 | 27 | 63 |
| International management accounting | 7 | 33 | 8 | 16 | 51 |
| Other | 0 | 0 | 0 | 0 | 0 |

(CVP) analysis, cost estimation, and differential cost analysis, which are very similar to those emphasized in the first course when three courses are required. Most of these topics were assigned less time except differential cost analysis in the second course, where two courses and three courses are required. The primary focuses of the second course when two courses are required are quantitative techniques, responsibility accounting and performance evaluation, standard cost, differential cost analysis, and capital budgeting. Coverage on the economics of information and on the impact of changing technology was also suggested. Educators recommending three courses felt that the second course should include more extensive coverage of the subjects from the first courses while adding some coverage in quantitative techniques and the just-in-time (JIT) concept. The third course recommended should emphasize quantitative technique (15%), the impact of changing technology on management accounting (10%), the information economics (9%), behavioral accounting (8%), management accounting for service industries (7%), and international management accounting (6%).

### E. Relative Importance of Each Topic

Practitioners were asked to indicate no more than ten topics that they think must be covered in each course they recommend. The results are shown in Table 7. The top three subjects that should be covered in the first course of both the two-course and the three-course sequences are product costing, cost allocation, and standard cost. Following these topics are CVP analysis, budgeting, cost estimation, capital budgeting, and differential cost analysis. Practitioners recommending two courses selected responsibility accounting and performance evaluation, quantitative techniques, and capital budgeting as the top three subjects in the second course followed by the economics of information, impact of changing technology on cost accounting, differential cost analysis, and budgeting. The clear winner in the second course of the three-course sequence is capital budgeting followed by differential cost analysis and budgeting. In the third course, practitioners justified the course content with quantitative techniques, responsibility accounting and performance evaluation, impact of changing technology on cost accounting, behavioral accounting, and international management accounting.

The relative importance of each subject in each course as perceived by practitioners was compared against the list generated by educators. In all cases, the rank correlations between the two are significant, indicating that the respondents are in strong agreement regarding which subjects should be emphasized in a particular course.

In part because of the recent criticisms of management accounting, both the educators' and the practitioners' topic lists included an Other category. Except for a few educators, the Other category received no support, which indicates general acceptance of the topics to be covered in an undergraduate management accounting curriculum.

## V. CONCLUSION

This paper examined various issues pertinent to the enhancement of the management accounting curriculum. The results of the study suggest general consensus between practitioners and educators on a number of issues such as the number of required management accounting courses and the topic coverage in each course. To prepare undergraduate accounting students for a career in management accounting, two or three management accounting courses should be required. The existing management accounting courses in many accounting programs in the nation are simply inadequate. Traditional topics such as product costing, cost allocation, standard cost, cost-volume-profit analysis, and budgeting should be emphasized in the first course while topics like performance evaluation, quantitative techniques, capital budgeting, cost accounting under a new manufacturing environment, behavioral accounting, and international management accounting should be the primary focuses in the second or third course.

Both practitioners and educators felt that new graduates were marginally or not prepared for their entry-level management accounting positions although the educator group is more generous than the practitioner group in its ratings. We believe that practitioners' assessment should be given more weight since they are in a better position to evaluate the accounting graduates. Also, the reported lack of preparedness supports the National Association of Accountants recommendation in SMA No. 1E for 9–12 semester hours of management/cost accounting in an 120-hour program. While it is easy to recommend that accounting majors take more management accounting courses, the typical undergraduate program has little opportunity for adding courses. Fortunately, SMA No. 1E addresses this problem by proposing the distribution of an entire 120-semester-hour program which provides guidance to individual institutions desiring to increase the number of undergraduate management accounting courses.

Significant differences were found regarding the relative mix of instructional techniques to be used in the classroom. In general, practitioners felt that more time should be devoted to outside material such as cases, articles, computer projects, and guest speakers. Educators, on the other hand, still rely on lecture and discussion as the primary teaching mode in the first and second courses. This discrepancy could contribute to the practitioners' low ratings on the level of preparedness of new graduates.

The findings of this survey should be of interest to educators, management accounting textbook authors, and publishers. The perceived lack of preparedness of new accounting graduates should be of concern to all these parties. The survey identified two responses to this problem: provide three undergraduate management accounting courses for those students wishing to enter the field; and develop and use additional outside materials such as cases and computer projects. Both educators and practitioners recommended that the third course should have over 30 percent of its class time devoted to outside materials. If institutions move toward a third course, opportunities should exist for authors and publishers to provide additional readings in books, casebooks, and computer projects that are suitable for an advanced undergraduate management accounting course.

## REFERENCES

Deakin, E. B., and Summers, E. L. (1975). "A Survey of Curriculum Topics Relevant to the Practice of Management Accounting." *Accounting Review* (April): 380–383.

DeMaris, E. J., and Copeland, B. R. (1984a). "Educational Standards for Management Accountants—A Critical Need." *Journal of Accounting Education* (Spring): 39–53.

DeMaris, E. J., and Copeland, B. R. (1984b). "The Critical Need for Educational Standards in Management Accounting." *Corporate Accounting* (Winter): 47–53.

DePasquale, R. J. (1985). "Does the Typical Curriculum Prepare You for the Exam?" *Management Accounting* (November): 44–51.

Johnson, H. T., and Kaplan, R. (1987). *Relevance Lost: The Rise and Fall of Management Accounting*. Cambridge, MA: Harvard Business School Press.

Harris, J. K., and Krogstad, J. L. (1976). "A Profile and Index of the CMA Examination." *Accounting Review* (July): 637–641.

Knight, R. E., and Zook, D. R. (1982). "Controllers and CPAs Evaluate the Relevance of Education Topics." *Management Accounting* (November): 30–34.

National Association of Accountants (1988). *Statement on Management Accounting 1E: Education for Careers in Management Accounting* (Montvale, NJ: National Association of Accountants).

Schwartz, B. N., and Stout, D. E. (1987). "A Comparison of Practitioner and Educator Opinions on Tax Education Requirements for Undergraduate Accounting Majors." *Issues in Accounting Education* (Spring): 112–126.

Van Zante, N. R. (1980). "Educating Management Accountants: What Do CMAs Think?" *Management Accounting* (August): 18–21.

Van Zante, N. R. (1989). "Preparing for a Career in Industrial Accounting." *Management Accounting* (January): 59.

JAI PRESS

# Advances in Investment Analysis and Portfolio Management

Edited by **Son-Nan Chen,** *University of Maryland* and **Cheng-Few Lee,** *School of Business, Rutgers University*

**Volume 1,** 1991, 293 pp. $73.25
ISBN 1-55938-135-3

**CONTENTS:** 

# Advances in Financial Planning and Forecasting

Edited by **Cheng-Few Lee,** *Department of Finance, School of Business, Rutgers University*

**Volume 4,** 1990, 2 Volume Set
Set ISBN 1-55938-001-2 $157.50

Edited by **Cheng-Few Lee,** *Rutgers University* and **Raj Aggarwal,** *John Carroll University*

**Volume 4, Part A - International Dimensions of Securities and Currency Markets**
1990, 256 pp.
ISBN 1-55938-202-3 (A) $78.75

**CONTENTS: International Financial Planning and Forecasting: An Introduction. PART I: THE INTERNATIONAL FINANCIAL ENVIRONMENT. A Test of the Rationality of Forward Exchange Rates,** *James S. Ang and Ali M. Fatemi.* **Risk Premiums in Foreign Exchange Markets: Theory and Evidence,** *T. J. Chen and K. C. John Wei.* **Purchasing Power Parity: A Re-examination of Prediction Errors,** *G. Geoffrey Booth and Peter E. Koveos.* **Trading Strategies in Foreign Exchange Markets,** *Richard J. Sweeney and Edward J. Q. Lee.* **Pricing of Foreign Currency Options: Theory and Evidence,** *Steve B. Wyatt.* **Market Assessment of Eurodollar Default Risk Premium,** *Janice Wickstead Jadlow.* **Fama's Hypotheses of the Relationship Between Inflation and Nominal Interst Rate: An International Comparison,** *Cheng-Few Lee and Edward J. Bubneys.* **Do Commercial Banks Speculate in the Foreign Exchange Market?,** *Jane-yu Li.* **PART II: VALUING RISKS OF FOREIGN OPERATIONS. Financial Asset Substitutablity and International Asset Pricing,** *Roger D. Huang, and Tsong-yue Lai.* **International Multi-Asset Diversification: A Further Analysis,** *Joanne Hill, Thomas Schneeweis and Jot Yau.* **A Direct Test of the Diversification Service Hypothesis of Foreign Direct Investment,** *Ho C. Yang, James W. Wansley and William R. Lane.* **Ownership, Asset Structure, and Political Risk,** *Frederick J. Phillips-Patrick.* **Socio-Political Events and American Foreign Direct Investment in South and Central America,** *K. Fatehi-Sedeh and M. H. Safizadeh.*